HITLER'S
RAF COLLABORATORS

HITLER'S RAF COLLABORATORS

AGENTS OR TRAITORS: RAF PRISONERS OF WAR ALLEGED TO HAVE ASSISTED THE THIRD REICH

M.S. MORGAN

AIR WORLD

AIR WORLD

HITLER'S RAF COLLABORATORS
Agents or Traitors: RAF Prisoners of War Alleged to Have Assisted the Third Reich

First published in Great Britain in 2024 by
Airworld
An imprint of
Pen & Sword Books Ltd
Yorkshire – Philadelphia

ISBN 978 1 39903 952 9

A CIP catalogue entry for this book is available from the British Library.

Typeset by SJmagic DESIGN SERVICES, India.

Printed and bound in the UK by CPI Group (UK) Ltd.

Pen & Sword Books Ltd includes the Imprints of Atlas, Archaeology, Aviation, Discovery, Family History, Fiction, History, Maritime, Military, Military Classics, Politics, Select, Airworld, Frontline Publishing, Leo Cooper, Remember When, Seaforth Publishing, The Praetorian Press, Wharncliffe Local History, Wharncliffe Transport, Wharncliffe True Crime and White Owl.

For a complete list of Pen & Sword titles please contact

PEN & SWORD BOOKS LTD
George House, Units 12 & 13, Beevor Street, Off Pontefract Road,
Barnsley, South Yorkshire, S71 1HN, England
E-mail: enquiries@pen-and-sword.co.uk
Website: www.pen-and-sword.co.uk

or

PEN AND SWORD BOOKS
1950 Lawrence Rd, Havertown, PA 19083, USA
E-mail: uspen-and-sword@casematepublishers.com
Website: www,penandswordbooks.com

FSC www.fsc.org
MIX
Paper | Supporting responsible forestry
FSC® C013604

Contents

Introduction

During the Second World War, over 10,000 British aviators were detained as prisoners of war in Europe and North Africa, most of them belonging to the Royal Air Force, but there were also a good number of Fleet Air Arm and Army Air Corps aircrew.

The statistics for Royal Air Force aircrew for the 1939-1945 war are a reminder of just how dangerous their roles were.

In Bomber Command crews were expected to complete a first tour of up to thirty operational flights. However, due to some long-range targets, there was an additional parameter of a maximum of 200 operational flying hours. After completing the first tour, crews would be rested for up to six months, the time being spent as an instructor on a training or conversion unit.

Many instructors would return to operations with a second and in a few rare cases, a third tour. Sometimes, the crewmen would actually want to return to operations, some considering training with new airmen to be more dangerous than operations!

Despite the apparent bravado from some, the statistics for Bomber Command were horrifying:

> 51% of all Bomber Command aircrew were killed on operations.
> 12% were killed or wounded in flying accidents.
> 13% were shot down and captured, spending the rest of the war as Prisoner of War.
> 24% survived unscathed.

The specific survival rates from the most prominent Bomber Command aircraft were also shocking:

> 25% of airmen would escape a doomed Halifax or Stirling, but only 15% would escape from a Lancaster.

In Fighter Command, a pilot's tour depended more on fatigue than actual operational flights, the Commanding and Medical Officers determining when a man should be rested and sent to a training unit as an instructor pilot.

The chance of surviving your first tour as a single engine fighter pilot in the RAF was 43 per cent, but this fell to just 18 per cent if you undertook a second tour of operations.

A night fighter pilot/radar operator had a slightly lower chance of 39 per cent after one tour and 15 per cent after two tours (almost certainly due to the risk of night-flying).

Transport Command crews had a better chance of survival, but if they did actually encounter an enemy fighter, their time was invariably up.

Those who did survive and were captured in Europe were sent to the Luftwaffe interrogation centre at Oberursel near Frankfurt. Dulag Luft – or to give it its full title, *Durchgangslager der Luftwaffe* – was a transit camp for new aircrew prisoners. Here they would be processed before being sent on to permanent POW camps.

In a number of cases, the aircrew, especially in the latter years of the war, would be unfortunate enough to fall into the hands of the Gestapo. In most cases they would suffer brutality at the hands of the Gestapo and the SS, often being tortured and threatened with a firing squad. The title *Terror Flieger* (terror flier) was *pinned* on the bomber aircrews by Nazi propaganda supremo Josef Goebbels and the title stuck. In a small number of cases, airmen were beaten to death or strung up by irate German civilians.

The Luftwaffe would, in later years, be praised for its handling of allied aircrew – although there were exceptions. In general, it was better to be a guest of the Luftwaffe than the Gestapo and the SS.

While sat in the various camps across Germany and occupied Europe, large numbers of airmen tried to escape and return to Britain. These men have been immortalised in the many books and movies that have portrayed their valiant exploits and escapes, none more so than the Great Escape in 1944.

The camp names of Colditz Castle and Stalag Luft III at Sagan, are well known to the general public and the prisoners are still held in high regard, but there were a small number of RAF POWs who let the proverbial side down.

Pilot Officer Railton Freeman and Sergeants Jack Alcock and Raymond Hughes are three men who betrayed colleagues and their nation. The three men assisted the Nazi regime, making radio broadcasts and even joining the British Free Corps, a unit of the dreaded Waffen SS. One man allegedly gave information about the Monica radar system to the Luftwaffe, while others got fellow prisoners to divulge information to the Luftwaffe on fake Red Cross forms.

Other prisoners, such as Flying Officer Julius Zuromski and Squadron Leader Robert George Carpenter also came under suspicion, when coded reports from other prisoners arrived at MI9 in London.

Even the senior officers came under scrutiny, with Squadron Leader Elliott, Group Captain Wilson RAAF and Group Captain Harry 'Wings' Day coming under the microscope. The list was quite lengthy, with others believed to have assisted the Nazis, including Sergeants Whillock, Slowey, Tipton and Flight Lieutenant Thomas.

The strangest story was that of Pilot Officer Michael Joyce the first cousin of the infamous traitor William Joyce (Lord Haw Haw).

Enquiries were undertaken during and after the war by the RAF Special Investigation Branch of the Provost Marshal's office, as well as MI9 and MI5. The results of these enquiries would ultimately lead to the imprisonment of some airmen and the release of others.

Providing intelligence, whether it be via fake Red Cross forms or happily divulging information about radar systems was one thing, but some of these men would be taken to Berlin, given pseudonyms and civilian clothes. They lived in comfort and ate in fashionable restaurants, even being paid a salary and expenses in Reichsmarks. Their role was to assist with German propaganda radio broadcasts, and they joined a number of other British traitors, many of whom had relocated to Germany, either just before the war or in 1939-1940.

Some of these people were ardent Nazis with links to Sir Oswald Mosley and his infamous Union of Fascists. Not only would they assist with propaganda, writing or broadcasting, they would also join or associate with a number of British and Commonwealth soldiers who had joined the British Free Corps of the Waffen SS.

What these men did and why – after the war some were indicted and others were released without charge – is examined within this book. Why one man in particular, an ardent Nazi and traitor was not sentenced to death, having liaised with the likes of the infamous William Joyce (known as Lord Haw Haw) is a mystery to this day. Others could not be prosecuted because of legal technicalities, while some having been imprisoned or escaped indictment, appear to have disappeared and very little is known of their later lives post-war. The question is why?

Sadly, not all of our Second World War aviators were heroes, but taking into account the histories of these men, the question is whether they were all traitors, or could some have been agents of the British State?

There has long been a debate whether some of them might actually have been working for the British Intelligence Services, but how could this be? These men were shot down on operations, mostly in the company of other men, some of whom died. How could the British Intelligence Services guarantee that an airman/spy would first of all be shot down on a particular raid or in a particular location; and how could they ensure they survived the ensuing crash? It appears unlikely and this would not be the most expedient or dependable means of deploying an agent.

This book aims to detail the story of these men. Using the intelligence files of MI5 that are now held in the United Kingdom's National Archives, along with information from the Royal Air Force, MI9, newspaper archives and various other sources, I can now tell the story of fourteen of Hitler's alleged RAF Collaborators, men who were alleged to have assisted the German authorities in a number of different ways.

Many of the original interrogation reports and statements are reproduced verbatim in this book. It is worth remembering that some were translated from German and do not translate literally, thereby causing some confusion. Others were written by poorly educated men and the grammar was poor. Please bear this in mind when reading this book, it is not the author's grammar!

Chapter 1

Dulag Luft, German Propaganda Radio and the British Free Corps of the Waffen SS

Although this book concerns the alleged activities of a number of RAF airmen while held in captivity from 1940 to 1945, it is necessary to explain the environment in which they found themselves.

Three main elements run throughout this book and the stories contained within it. The first of these elements is the interrogation centre, more commonly known as Dulag Luft at Oberursel near Frankfurt and the prisoner of war camps such as Stalag Luft I at Barth and Stalag Luft III at Sagan. The second element is the German propaganda radio services and the third, the British Free Corps. This latter unit was a group set-up to recruit British prisoners of war who had volunteered to fight the Russian Army and Communism.

In December 1939, the Luftwaffe opened a new camp at Oberursel near Frankfurt. This was to be the first of a series of new collection and interrogation camps spread across Germany specialising in the handling of newly captured British and Commonwealth airmen. Later it would also handle captured American personnel.

Known as Durchgangslager der Luftwaffe or Transit Camp of the Luftwaffe, it would later become known as Auswertestelle West, but it was more commonly known throughout the war and since, as Dulag Luft.

The Luftwaffe chose Oberursel as the site of its first interrogation centre and it was built on the site of an old poultry farm, north of the main road between Frankfurt and Bad Homburg.

The first prisoners were not newly captured men, but a few British and French airmen captured in the early stages of the war. They had initially been held at Oflag IX-A/H, an old castle at Spangenberg in the state of Hesse and their inclusion at Oberursel would, in effect, make it appear like any other prisoner of war camp. New arrivals would be put at ease by the presence of these old-timer prisoners, but in reality they were to be processed by a very efficient Luftwaffe intelligence system.

The new camp centred around an old farm building known as the Stonehouse, but in time other buildings and wooden huts sprang up with the standard barbed wire fences, guard towers, searchlights and check points. The main evaluation centre comprised of about fourteen buildings, the largest being a U-shaped edifice with 150 solitary confinement cells known as the 'Cooler'. Other buildings would house the record offices, the Commandant's office and quarters, the Red Cross office, stores, German Officers Mess, NCOs and other ranks quarters, as well as the interrogation centre itself.

The initial Camp Commander was Oberst Leutnant Peter-Paul von Donat, but he was soon replaced by Major Theodor Rumpel.

Theo Rumpel had been a First World War Albatross pilot, who was badly injured by a British SE5a over the Western Front in March 1918. He retired from the German Air Force and knew Herman Goering well, having served with him in France. Rumpel worked during the post-war years in the Dutch East Indies and in 1937, he rejoined the new Luftwaffe as a Hauptmann Intelligence Officer. With his negotiating skills from the Dutch East Indies and a very good command of the English language, it was inevitable he should end up as the first commandant of Dulag Luft. He was, however, a gentleman and did not enjoy the role of obtaining military intelligence from captives via subterfuge. In fact, he would often attend with a bottle of schnapps, something that was strictly forbidden by the German High Command.

Life under Rumpel was easier than expected and the Luftwaffe also kept a group of prisoners at the camp for the long-term who would '*assist*' with administration and intelligence work. Some of the men who formed this '*permanent staff*' will feature in this book.

The easy life at Dulag Luft was Major Rumpel's way of interrogating the prisoners and obtaining information. Although it was not as successful as later forms of interrogation, it did get some valuable intelligence.

Wing Commander Harry 'Wings' Day had been at Dulag Luft since its inception. He was one of the initial group that arrived from Spangenberg in 1939. He remained at the camp as the Senior British Officer (SBO) until 1941 and communicated well with Rumpel.

In early 1940, a Sergeant Pilot arrived directly at Dulag Luft. He informed Wing Commander Day that a new official code of communications had been taught to aircrew so they could hide messages in letters home. The RAF intelligence team and MI9 could unpick the real coded message from the usual comments about food, weather and other mundane matters. The code was known as 'Amy' and was one of a number of codes provided to MI9 by the Foreign Office's code experts – the forerunners of GCHQ. This code used a pocket edition of Hugo's French dictionary as its key.

Day had the sergeant pilot show some of the permanent Dulag Luft RAF staff the code, so they too, could send messages home. These messages would be vital in alerting MI9 to the activities of collaborators.

In November 1941, a new commandant, Oberleutnant (Lt. Col.) Erich Killinger, took over. He remained in charge until the end of the war and was a much sterner commandant.

Erich Killinger had been a naval officer and aviator during the First World War. He was a hero after he escaped and returned home after being shot down over Russia in 1915. Killinger was recalled to the service and the Luftwaffe in the late 1930s, flying during the invasion of Poland in 1939, before becoming a Staff Officer in Paris.

Erich Killinger's deputy was Major Heinz Junge, another former First World War pilot, while his adjutant was Leutnant Bottner. Major Otto Bohringer, a wealthy former factory owner, was the Executive Officer to Erich Killinger.

Other Luftwaffe officers who will feature in this story include Hauptmann Hans Vollmann, Leutnant Otto Boninghaus the political interrogator, linked to the Berlin Propaganda Ministry and German radio, as well as Hauptman Offerman, the Chief of Camp Security.

Major Horst Barth, often called Ober Inspektor Barth, was a radio surveillance expert who arrived in 1942. He had been based at Wissant in Northern France with a unit monitoring and deciphering RAF radio communications. They passed their intelligence on to Dulag Luft, but in time, he would also join the Interrogation Centre, concentrating on bugging and listening to the prisoners' conversations, before graduating to the main interrogation team.

Leutnant Koch, Oberleutnant Tobler (an engineering expert) and Oberleutnant Gustav Bauer-Schlichtegroll, a man who would be a prime witness in the post-war trials, were also part of this organisation. Gustav Bauer-Schlichtegroll was a member of the Nazi party and as a technical expert, he sought specialist intelligence from the RAF prisoners of war.

Leutnant Henrich Eberhardt would also become a star witness in the post-war prosecutions. In August 1940, this former schoolteacher and mail censor, was elevated to the post of Welfare and Liaison Officer at Dulag Luft, a position he utilised with some aplomb in order to obtain information and recruit collaborators.

Hauptmann Otto Boehringer would arrive at Dulag Luft in January 1943, he was an old associate of Commandant Erich Killinger from before the war. He assisted with interrogations, but his ability with spoken English failed him and he would later become Killinger's Executive Officer.

The camp at Dulag Luft grew in size and was housing a large number of RAF and Commonwealth airmen by the summer of 1941. Some of the most notable prisoners who passed through Dulag Luft included Douglas Bader, Robert Stanford-Tuck and Roger Bushell. Even men who would go on to become famous post-war, such as the *Carry On* film actor Peter Butterworth were held for a time in the camp and even tried to escape.

One night in June 1941, a large group of airmen tried to escape from Dulag Luft via a tunnel. They were soon recaptured, including Squadron Leader Roger Bushell and sent on to other camps. The camp security was deemed to be so poor, Oberleutnant Franz von Werra, more commonly known as '*The one that got away*', was directed to review the camp's security arrangements and its intelligence gathering capabilities.

Von Werra had recently returned to Germany, having escaped from Canada via the still neutral United States. He had been shot down during the Battle of Britain and processed through the RAF interrogation facility at Trent Park. He had made a number of escape attempts from prisons in the United Kingdom, such as Grizedale Hall in the Lake District, before finally being shipped off to Canada. The Luftwaffe High Command deemed his knowledge and experience to be an asset and they were so impressed by the RAF's collection and gathering of information on the Luftwaffe, Dulag Luft was ordered to start a similar process of intelligence collection.

What many of the British and Commonwealth airmen in 1941 did not know was that they were to become part of a system developed and deployed to obtain the maximum amount of human intelligence; in many cases without the subject even being aware they were providing information to the enemy.

By 1943 and 1944, Dulag Luft possessed a refined and extremely efficient intelligence gathering system and it did not need the brutal methods of the Gestapo. In many respects, it employed the good cop, bad cop scenario, in which the Luftwaffe were the good guys and the Gestapo with their brutal methods were the bad guys. Most prisoners had heard the horror stories about the Gestapo and its tactics, so they were only too happy to be held by the Luftwaffe; but what they did not know was that the Luftwaffe's expert interrogators were watching and listening to everything. Not only would they gather technical and structural intelligence but identify weak individuals who could become collaborators.

Dulag Luft not only had interrogators, it also had experts who analysed everything about the new arrivals. Was a new prisoner injured, susceptible to intimidation, what were their fears about captivity, what were their political views about the war, National Socialism and Communism? All of this information could identify a weak link and a possible collaborator.

One of the few post-war accounts of life in Dulag Luft was written by Raymond F. Toliver and was a biographical account of Hanns Joachim Scharff, the so-called Master Interrogator of the Luftwaffe. Scharff was a non-commissioned officer, but to many of the newly arrived prisoners, he appeared to be an officer – an illusion he did not attempt to correct.

Although Hanns Joachim Scharff dealt almost exclusively with American airmen, his commentary on his own activities at Dulag Luft in Toliver's book, gives an excellent insight into the day to day running of the camp and the process of interrogation.

Hanns Joachim Scharff was the complete opposite of the Gestapo and the expectations of most captured airmen. Instead of threats and torture, he disarmed their physical and mental defences through mind games. In time, the rest of the Luftwaffe interrogation organisation would follow his trend. By collecting information about the opposing allied units, the squadrons' personalities, aircraft and tactics, not to mention even what movie was on at the local cinema; Scharff and his colleagues dismantled any mental defence mechanisms.

Behind the scenes, a mass of clerks and interpreters noted everything from Pathe News bulletins, to newspapers and magazines, not only in the allied countries, but also in neutral nations.

Previous interrogations and the information obtained from other prisoners allowed Scharff and the organisation to build an in-depth knowledge of the allied air forces. A detailed card index was created of known squadrons, personnel within those units, victory claims, decorations awarded and the performance of aircraft. Squadron radio call-signs, pilots' nicknames, girlfriends and much more was listed, no detail was too small and could be useful one day.

A record of previous bombing raids was created, including details of the squadrons involved, even how many aircraft were lost and individual details of the crewmen. If a crewman was reported missing on a previous raid, it was very disarming for Scharff and his colleagues to inform a newly arrived friend of the missing airman that he was not dead, but was in fact safe in a prison camp where they would soon meet again.

These tactics were similar to those used by the RAF from 1940 onwards, when German airmen arrived in British captivity. When news arrived that a prisoner was on their way to the Interrogation Centre, the system sprung into life.

Details of the airman's name and, if known, his squadron would kick-start a search of the archives and records within Dulag Luft. If the airman and their unit was known, their files would be retrieved with a multitude of other facts about their unit, aircraft, personnel and the local environment. This package would be passed to the interrogator, a Luftwaffe NCO or officer who was not only an experienced investigator, but fluent in spoken English. By the time the prisoner arrived in front of them, the interrogator was fully briefed and knew enough about the man, his aircraft or squadron, to strike up a conversation – even with the most reluctant of communicators.

The old adage that every man has a breaking point is true, not only to threats and violence, but to kindness and basic manners. Even allowing a prisoner to go for a walk with a guard was effective and even the time honoured chivalrous act of giving one's parole, not to try to escape was often accepted. (This was in fact forbidden, but it did not stop officers and airmen agreeing to be paroled.) These actions would, in Hanns Joachim Scharff's own words, allow the prisoner to forget they were actually being interrogated and talk freely.

Scharff and his colleagues soon appreciated that prisoners arrived with pre-conceived counter-interrogation tactics. These could be broken down into:

1) I will not talk, but give only my rank, name and serial number.
2) I will see what they ask me and not tell them anything.
3) If they tell me things that they already know, there is no point in withholding an agreement of such facts.

An interrogation could start with a prisoner, who will only give his name, rank and serial number. If that was the case, the interrogator would give a resume of what they already knew about the new arrival. He might tell them their squadron, their aircraft type, where they were shot down, their target, their aircraft's code letters (if the wreck had been found and was not too badly damaged). They may tell the airman the names of his crew, possibly stating whether they are alive or deceased.

If this failed, they could move on to discuss recent squadron losses, what was on at the local cinema, even gossip about someone's girlfriend or a particularly good looking WAAF in the parachute store on their home base. Before long, the prisoner usually moved from his name, rank and serial number, to acknowledging some of the stated facts, or if particularly disarmed, correcting them. (Sometimes the interrogator would deliberately make mistakes, giving the prisoner an opportunity to correct him and start to talk.)

The interrogators would even offer prisoners the chance of meeting the pilot or squadron who shot them down. When he was shot down in 1941, Douglas Bader met with Adolph Galland and members of JG26. He was allowed to inspect a new Messerschmitt 109F and was allegedly told he could take it for a test flight – if he gave his word as an officer and a gentleman to return to the airfield, otherwise Galland would have to take off and shoot him down.

This carefully managed environment worked and even seasoned officers like Colonel Hub Zemke of the 8th Air Force gave him credit. After the war he stated in the Scharff biography:

> *'Scharff really knew his subject and his interrogation procedures, enjoyed his work, and no doubt was effective. I had the impression that it might even be dangerous just to talk about the weather with him as he'd probably gain some important or confidential information from it.'*

During the Second World War, the Luftwaffe interrogators grew in proficiency and obtained a vast amount of intelligence from their 'guests'.

Most never knew they had even provided intelligence to the enemy, before eventually leaving for their permanent prison camp.

This, however, was the pink and fluffy side to Oberursel and its associated interrogation units. However, even Scharff had to admit there were elements from the Gestapo based at Oberursel, after all this was still Nazi Germany.

There were also men from the Propaganda Ministry who were constantly on the lookout for information that could be used against the allied war effort. When William Joyce, also known as Lord Haw Haw, spoke on the radio with his infamous 'Germany calling' mantra, he often spoke about air raids and losses of aircraft from specific squadrons. This information invariably came from prisoners at the interrogation camps like Dulag Luft.

The Luftwaffe also used fake Red Cross forms to obtain information from prisoners. Often to be found with the official Red Cross emblem at the top of the questionnaire, prisoners would be asked for personal details, their squadron, aircraft, home base and crew details etc. As we shall see in this book, these forms played an integral part with the RAF collaborators, but the more astute prisoners realised all was not well, when the 'Red Cross' wanted to know military facts, rather than an individual's personal details.

If all else failed, prisoners could be threatened with being handed over to the Gestapo and their torturers. Although this was rarely used or even required, it was a reserve tactic to obtain intelligence.

Medical treatment was said to have been excellent and all prisoners were given access to some of the best medics in Germany, but there were a few occasions when this was not the case.

There were other allegations to go with the use of fake Red Cross forms. This included the allegation that prisoners in solitary cells, were often roasted and had to strip off when the heating was turned too high. Gasping for air, one man said he lay naked on the concrete floor, taking gasps of cooler air from the outside corridor, via the tiny crack under the cell door.

After the war, Oberstleutnant Erich Killinger and a number of his officers would be charged with mistreatment of the prisoners.

There were Gestapo liaison officers attached to Dulag Luft and although Hanns Joachim Scharff gave the impression that all was well at the camp, there were other ways of using the prisoners. These included using them to obtain information from newly arrived prisoners in exchange for better conditions and home comforts.

A good example of how a new arrival was treated at Dulag Luft can be seen from the following statement from Flight Sergeant Walter Layne, a wireless operator air gunner from 97 Squadron. (Reference: wallyswar.wordpress.com and provided with thanks to the websites author.) He was shot down on 23 September 1943 in a Lancaster:

'On arrival at Dulag Luft he was stripped of his clothing. A thorough search was then made of his body and his clothing for compasses, maps, files, money, keys and anything else that could be used to facilitate an escape, he was then locked up in solitary confinement. The Germans had concluded that they would get better results if they isolated newly captured airmen before and during interrogation.

'After a period of time, Wally Layne was visited in his cell by the "Reception Officer." This officer's duty was to assess the prisoner's character from general conversations with them, determine whether they were frightened or belligerent, etc. and how he might react to future interrogation. His findings were then forwarded to the main interrogator, Major Junge, who would then decide which interrogator was best suited to question a particular prisoner.

'The Reception Officer's questioning of Wally consisted of him producing a form that he claimed was a Red Cross document. After asking for and receiving Wally's name rank and serial number, he attempted to gain from him information of a military nature. Allied aircrews had been briefed about this tactic during their time of training and consequently were prepared for it and in Wally's case, no further information was provided. Wally was then left to contemplate his position. For the next two days and nights, Wally was confined to his cell in solitary confinement. During this time he was subjected to the excessive heat treatment after being taken, twice daily, to the office of one of Dulag Luft's interrogation officers. This routine was interrupted each morning and evening, by a guard bringing him a cup of acorn coffee and a piece of black bread.

'The Luftwaffe officers who spoke impeccable English, questioned Wally about his squadron, aircraft, targets, etc.

> *to which Wally duly replied, with his name, rank and service number as per the Geneva Convention.*
>
> *'Due to his uncooperative nature and his refusal to divulge anything but name, rank and service number, coupled with the fact that when captured he was wearing civilian clothing that he had acquired when he was evading, Wally was threatened with being handed over to the Gestapo as a suspected saboteur. Wally was told, "You are to be shot!"*
>
> *'This was a psychological ploy used by his captors to unsettle him and make him talk, although it did not work!'*

This was typical of the system at Dulag Luft. Even with the end of the war less than a year away, the Dulag Luft system was still in full swing, as can be seen from the comments in the book *Night Fighter Ace* by Tony Spooner.

The book is a biography of the RAF's top-scoring night fighter pilot Bob Braham. On 25 June 1944, Braham and his navigator were shot down by Focke-Wulf 190s and captured in Denmark. After a lengthy train journey they arrived at Oberursel where Braham was placed in a solitary confinement cell for about two weeks and '*extremely poorly fed'*. Bob was very weak and nearly blacked-out if he stood up too quickly. He was also interrogated regularly. As a highly decorated Wing Commander and fighter ace, the Luftwaffe thought he held some major secrets.

The main interrogator was a Hauptman Kock and he translated for Braham when the pilot who shot him down attended for tea and biscuits. Koch, as we shall see throughout this book, was a long-time member of the Luftwaffe team at Dulag Luft, initially being a Leutnant in 1941. He was still practising his art in mid-1944, with the allies having already started to cross France.

In the book, Braham recalls being taken for a walk in the woods by Koch, who argued that it was wrong for Britain and Germany to be fighting one another, the real enemy was Russia and world Jewry.

Eventually, with his interrogation period over, Braham was sent to Stalag Luft III at Sagan.

Another account of the interrogation of a prisoner and the softening-up process they endured, as late as September 1944, can be found in the autobiography of his time as a POW by Polish Squadron Leader Arct. In the book '*Prisoner of war – my secret journal*', Arct describes having bailed out over Arnhem and being taken to Dulag Luft. Upon arrival he was strip searched and placed in a cell alone. The cell had a hard slatted bed, with a sack filled with wood-shavings to act as a mattress. It was cold and dark. He was fed brown bread for breakfast and lunch, followed by a watery soup and bread, plus synthetic coffee for his main meal.

Having injured his ribs when he bailed out, he was examined by a German doctor in his cell, who pronounced it was not serious.

In his first interrogation, Arct recalls being taken to a room where a German NCO took front and side photographic images of him with a Leica camera. His service number was written on a board hung around his neck for the pictures. After this, he was returned to his cell.

The days passed until after another four days, he was taken from the cell to a block of offices where he met a German corporal (we know it was not Hanns Joachim Scharff, as Arct does not appear in the logs of prisoners he interrogated, which he held long after the war).

The corporal rose from his seat and shook his hand while smiling pleasantly. He then apologised for the conditions and promised to move Arct on to a proper camp as soon as possible. The corporal had a sheet of paper and asked him for his name, rank, number and the location in which he landed. He was given cigarettes, but no further questions followed. The two men chatted about the war and the Allied offensive, before Arct was promised a shower, a shave and the use of the prisoners' library. (This was clearly all part of the softening-up process after the solitary confinement, poor food and unhygienic conditions.)

Arct was surprised to have the promises fulfilled, but he was once again returned to his cell for another four days. He was interrogated again by the corporal, this time the questions centring upon Arct himself and not the RAF. In the afternoon, he was taken for a walk, having given his parole for the day not to attempt to escape. They stopped at a Gesthaus (where he probably drank beer or wine) and they chatted about the end of the war.

Clearly Arct did not think he had divulged anything of consequence to the corporal, but as we have seen many men also thought this. In the book, Arct added that he later discovered the interrogator already knew a great deal about him, and '*My treatment must have been some strange sort of policy*'.

Eventually he was taken to the transit camp and on to the camp at Barth.

From the three accounts from September 1943 to September 1944, we can see that the system was still in operation and clearly getting results.

The interrogators were always on the lookout for those who had anti-communist, defeatist or national socialist sympathies – hence the chat with Hauptman Koch outlined above. Such prisoners could always be useful to the propaganda services of the Reich and that is the next area we must consider.

The Nazi party under Josef Goebbels were avid producers of propaganda and they soon built an intricate system, just as complex as those of the Luftwaffe and the Gestapo.

In particular, they were keen to convey propaganda to wartime Britain. The main German radio base was Rundfunkhaus in Berlin. Within the establishment was a section purely aimed at the British people – this was the Buro Concordia, a section linked to the England Section of the Rundfunkhaus.

Professor Reinhard Hermann Haferkorn was the head of the England Section, and he was instrumental in recruiting British prisoners of war to work within the propaganda radio services. He was assisted by a man called Peter Adami. Working in close liaison to Haferkorn was Dr Fritz Hesse, the Head of the England Committee. He had worked as Joachim von Ribbontrop's adviser on English affairs. Hesse's assistant was Hillen Ziegfeld from the German Foreign Office.

In Reinhard Haferkorn's statement, dated 13 July 1945, there is a detailed description of this propaganda network.

The head section was the Propaganda Ministry which Haferkorn dealt with directly.

The Ministry had various units including Haferkorn's section – the Englische (English) Redaktion unit and the Irische (Irish) Redaktion unit, which was headed by Dr Hartmann. Both of these sections were part of the Landergruppe Nordwest of the Auslandsfunk (Foreign Broadcast Department), which was controlled by Eduard Roderick Anton Dietze. Dietze had a Scottish father and a German mother, but was an ardent Nazi.

Auslandsfunk, which comprised of the Buro Concordia, was one of the main departments of the Reichsrundfunk-gesellschaft (RRG) and was controlled by Dr Erich Hetzler.

The head of the RRG was Herr Glassmeyer and later Hans Fritsche. The man in charge of the Auslandsfunk was Anton Winkelnkemper.

In the mid to late 1930s, a number of British nationals went to Germany, some to avoid arrest and suspicion. These individuals held far right-wing views and had links to the British Union of Fascists and other right-wing groups. They would, over the next few years, work with Haferkorn and the others to write, produce and present Nazi radio propaganda. This invariably was broadcast via a number of radio stations which pretended to be covert 'patriotic' channels, broadcasting from within the United Kingdom. In reality they were all in occupied Europe and Germany.

One of the first to be involved was (in 1940) a 31-year-old former British Army officer named Norman Baillie-Stewart.

Norman Baillie-Stewart had served on the North West Frontier before leaving the army. He was then arrested for breaching the Official Secrets Act and jailed in 1933, having sold plans for the new Vickers A1E1 Independent tank to the German intelligence service. Baillie-Stewart has the distinction of being one of the last prisoners to be held in the Tower of London, before serving the remainder of his sentence at Maidstone Prison in Kent.

After release in 1937, he ended up in Berlin and started writing and producing radio material for the Nazi propaganda service. In 1939, he presented the *Germany Calling* English language service, but he was soon to be replaced by the most infamous traitor – William Joyce otherwise known as Lord Haw Haw.

William Joyce was a former member of Oswald Mosley's British Union of Fascists and Director of Propaganda until 1937, when he was sacked. In August 1939, with war imminent, William Joyce and his wife went to Germany and became naturalised German citizens.

Joyce was soon recruited to the Rundfunkhaus and with his clear aptitude for propaganda, the American born presenter soon replaced Norman Baillie-Stewart in presenting the *Germany Calling* program for the rest of the war – much to the annoyance, it is said, of Baillie-Stewart.

The Englische Redaktion section included a number of Britons including William Joyce and his wife Margaret, as well as Edward Salvin Bowlby.

The Buro Concordia contained another group of collaborators including Lieutenant Roy Walter Purdy RNVR. He was captured after his ship HMS *Van Dyck*, was sunk in 1940 at Narvik and he assisted with a number of radio broadcasts using the alias of Wallace. He was a close associate of William Joyce.

There were also sections dealing with politics and the press, but these did not include collaborators.

The English Section or the Auslands-Abteilung was another section, this one under Dr Springborn. This section included the likes of Norman Baillie-Stewart, John Amery and Gerald Hewitt to name but a few.

Gerald Percy Hewitt was another pre-war British Union of Fascists member who later lived in France. He was detained after the German blitzkrieg in 1940 and recruited to write scripts, which were presented on German radio from Paris.

John Amery was the son of a British government minister and an ardent anti-communist. He also lived in France when Germany invaded in 1940, and in 1942 he travelled to Berlin, making a number of pro-German radio broadcasts. Later, he was one of the main proponents of the British Free Corps (Frei Korps), a small unit of British volunteers in the Waffen SS.

Those named above were the main British subjects involved in Nazi radio propaganda, there were others, but these were the main protagonists. In time, they would be joined by a number of prisoners of war. These men were recruited through offers of better conditions, while some held far right-wing views and were sympathetic to the Nazi cause. As we shall see, most would be given pseudonyms which were used in their work for the Germans and radio broadcasts.

The Waffen SS unit known as the British Free Corps, supported by John Amery and a former First World War RAF officer named Vivian Stranders; became a dysfunctional band of renegade British prisoners of war. Most were British and Commonwealth soldiers, but one RAF pilot like the other men, would succumb to the attraction of better living standards, brothels and beer on top of the anti-communist and anti-Semitic views.

The exact number of men who joined the British Free Corps has never been officially acknowledged, but it never surpassed twenty-seven men at any one time. They were a rag-tag bunch, who were undisciplined at times and more of a hindrance than a propaganda success for the Nazis. One man was detained for theft of a weapon and others refused to work on preparing a new football pitch for recruits. They never saw any real active service, even against the Soviets – the reason they were allegedly recruited. In time, they were disbanded to await the arrival of the allied armies and their eventual and inevitable arrest.

A number of men who joined the Free Corps also assisted the German radio propaganda services and can be linked, although in some cases this is tenuous, to the RAF collaborators named in this book.

British Free Corps member Sergeant Roy Courlander was a New Zealand soldier and anti-communist who assisted in radio broadcasts to Britain. Sergeant Frank McLardy, a soldier from Formby near Liverpool was another, and two others – Blackman and Leigh were paid 80 Reichsmarks per radio broadcast by Edward Slavin Bowlby, an Irishman who worked for the German propaganda radio services in Berlin.

The crossover between prisoners of war, the radio propaganda services and the British Free Corps was small, but certainly not insignificant. It caused a major headache for the British authorities who would make every effort to identify and prosecute these men after the war. The nightly broadcasts were not just from Lord Haw Haw but included interviews with a good number of British prisoners of war. Others wrote scripts in the background to be used by the likes of William Joyce, while they lived in civilian clothes under false names, with decent food and comfortable accommodation.

The Royal Air Force was not the only service to have its members collaborate with the Nazi regime, but as we shall see in this book, there were a small number of RAF men who betrayed their country…

Chapter 2

Pilot Officer Benson Railton Metcalf FREEMAN No. 77107

Benson Railton Metcalf Freeman, to give him his full name, was born on 6 October 1903, in Newbury, Berkshire.

He attended the Royal Military Academy at Sandhurst in 1922, before gaining a commission with the King's Own Royal Regiment in August 1924. Freeman showed a great deal of enthusiasm for flying and in 1926, he transferred his commission to the Royal Air Force.

Although he initially trained to fly fighters, Freeman joined No. 16 (Army Co-operation) Squadron at Old Sarum, Wiltshire, in August 1926, with the rank of Flying Officer. He then moved on to No. 26 Squadron at RAF Catterick in February 1929.

In 1931, Freeman left the Royal Air Force and went to live in a house called Downfield, in Brockweir, Gloucestershire, near the Welsh border. He spent his time as a country gentleman engaged in farming, but he started to develop a hatred of communism and became anti-Semitic, openly giving his opinion on both subjects to the local community.

In 1937, Freeman joined Sir Oswald Mosley's Union of Fascists, more commonly known as the British Union of Fascists (BUF). The group had been openly brawling in the streets with their more moderate opposition, while wearing their all-black uniforms and becoming known as the *Black Shirts.* Their activities caused such consternation, it ultimately gave rise to the Public Order Act of 1936 and the banning of all political uniforms in Britain. Despite this public image and its perceived association with Hitler's Nazis, Freeman chose to join the BUF.

Like all members of the BUF, Benson Freeman had a numbered membership card, although he obviously kept it locked away.

Just before the start of the war, Freeman decided to rejoin the RAF and take another commission. This was probably due to his fear of enlistment and an unsatisfactory posting. He returned to flying duties and after an assessment, found himself posted to No. 24 Squadron at RAF Hendon. The unit was a communication squadron and possessed a wide variety of transport aircraft, some of which had recently been pressed into service. In his late thirties, he was probably deemed too old for conversion to modern fighters.

Although Freeman had been a Flying Officer when he left the service in 1931, he started his new commission as a Pilot Officer, junior in grade to his previous rank.

On 22 May 1940, with the Wehrmacht forces pouring into France, Freeman, as co-pilot to a Belgian pilot – Captain Albert Lassair (often said to actually be Lassois) – flew a Savoia registration OO-AGZ, from RAF Croydon to Merville in France. Their cargo was food for the hard-pressed British army. They did not return and both men were posted as missing.

What had happened to Freeman was something of a mystery at the time, but his recent past was beginning to catch up with him.

On 26 May, four days after being posted missing, PC 256 Edgar Day, from St. Briavels Police Station in Gloucestershire, sent a report to his Superintendent. The report which was quickly sent on via Special Branch to the RAF Provost Marshal's office, stated that Freeman was a member of the British Union of Fascists. While living in Brockweir, he had been receiving copies of fascist newspapers such as *Action* and *Onward*.

The police constable had made other local enquiries and found that Freeman openly stated Britain would be better if ruled like Germany, while declaring his admiration of Sir Oswald Mosley. In addition, Freeman's wife Muriel was also said to be a member of the Union of Fascists.

The Royal Air Force were soon to receive the above police report and when they cleared out the missing officer's personal effects, they discovered his Union of Fascists membership card. This information was quickly passed to the RAF Provost Marshal's office, who in turn informed the Security Service – MI5 – of their concerns.

The Provost Marshal's office later stated there was nothing extraordinary in the fact Freeman was posted as missing and captured on 23 May 1940; but they had found his BUF membership card amongst his kit.

At this stage of the Second World War, information about captured airmen was scarce and relied upon the Germans and the International Red Cross. Although it was known that Benson Freeman had been captured, very little other information was forthcoming in 1940. However, like most prisoners of war, Freeman started to write home to his family and on

31 August 1940, the British Postal Censor intercepted a letter to his wife Muriel, who was residing in Maybole, near Ayr in Scotland.

Freeman was detained in Dulag Luft near Frankfurt and wrote the letter on 6 June 1940, around the time of the Dunkirk evacuation. The letter (Ref: National Archives file KV2/631) contained a number of defeatist comments which the censor noted:

> *'I hope to heavens that swine Winston can be thrown out and peace made. It will be awful if we are kept apart for years, but I do hope and think that it will soon be settled...*
>
> *'I do hope the fools at home demand an Armistice. The German Air Force here are very decent to us, I think there is no doubt they have won. France was finished without a fight, the Germans hope for a merciful peace, they only want their former colonies from us...'*

MI9, the prisoner of war Intelligence section, and MI5 were duly informed. It turned out this was Freeman's second defeatist letter and the intelligence community started to build a file. In addition, the RAF Provost Marshal's office were also making their own enquiries.

On 13 December 1940, an officer attended RAF Hendon and met with the Station Commander, Group Captain Seward. In turn, he spoke with the Commanding Officer of No. 24 Squadron – Wing Commander Harry King Goode. Further enquiries were made in the following days with the Wing Commander at RAF Hendon and a fuller picture started to emerge of Freeman's final days with the squadron.

The report stated that over two or three days, around 23 May 1940, a number of aircraft were dispatched to RAF Croydon and sent to Merville in France with food for the beleaguered army. The aircraft included a requisitioned Savoia from the Belgian airline Sabena, piloted by Captain Lassair and co-piloted by Pilot Officer Benson Freeman, while other aircraft included one from Imperial Airways.

Wing Commander Goode stated that the Savoia flown by Lassair and Freeman was destroyed on the ground at Merville by enemy forces. The two Savoia pilots and their aircrew then distributed themselves between the other transport aircraft, to head back home to England. It was deemed by the squadron that Freeman had boarded a Douglas aircraft as this was faster and more comfortable. That aircraft was believed to have been brought down over France by anti-aircraft fire.

The RAF and the Intelligence Services clearly had concerns about Freeman and whether he could have played a part in the loss of the aircraft.

On 20 January 1941, Wing Commander Harry King Goode completed a full statement, witnessed by Flight Lieutenant Hixson from the Provost Marshal's office. He explained that Freeman had joined the unit on 15 January 1940, but he needed re-training as he was 'out of practice'.

It had been found during an assessment that Freeman was actually more suited to single engine machines but was working on multi-engine communications aircraft. (This is not surprising considering his history of flying fighters.) Wing Commander Goode proposed sending Freeman to France to fly single engine aircraft on communications duties, but he immediately reported sick to the Station Medical Officer.

The Medical Officer examined Freeman and declared him to be '*temperamentally unsuitable for posting to France*', or for flying as a first pilot on other aeroplanes. He did however give clearance for him to fly as a co-pilot. Unfortunately, the full details were not available at the time of the statement, as the medical file had been lost in a fire caused by bombing of the airfield in 1940. Wing Commander Goode therefore used Benson Freeman as a second pilot but applied for a Full Medical Board and to have him posted to another unit.

Wing Commander Goode confirmed the assertion that Freeman's Savoia had been destroyed at Merville and that he had tried to get home on the Douglas but was then reported missing after encountering heavy anti-aircraft fire.

Goode also stated that Freeman could not have had any influence over the actions of the Douglas pilot, as he would have been sat in the rear fuselage and not the cockpit. He also added that he did not consider it possible for Freeman to have had anything to do with the loss of the Savoia at Merville airfield. The other pilots who were on the ground at Merville who could have been witnesses, had since been killed and therefore they could not be questioned about the events.

Wing Commander Goode added in his statement that upon examining the personal effects of Freeman, a BUF membership card had been discovered, this showed him as belonging to the Maidstone Branch in Kent.

Goode said, Freeman was rather unpopular in the Mess and was being watched because of his conversations with other officers. He stated:

> *'Although one cannot openly accuse him of anything, his tone always seemed to imply that the German organisation was*

> *much superior to the British and that they made far better use of both men and materials than the British. This was thought to be partly the outburst of a disgruntled officer who considered that he should be of a senior rank to a Pilot Officer. He never mentioned Fascism in the Mess or attempted to convert anyone to its principles.'*

As the early years of the war progressed, the Royal Air Force and MI9 trained aircrew who might in due course be shot down and captured, to send messages home via coded letters. The script was hidden in apparently normal letters, sent to family members from the prison camps. The censors in Britain would examine the coded message, 'picking out' the intelligence.

It was through this system that information soon started to filter through about Benson Freeman, his comments and behaviour in German captivity.

Sydney Smith, in his book '*Wings Day*', a biography of Group Captain Harry 'Wings' Day, mentioned a comment from Day about a pilot who is clearly Benson Freeman, although he uses the alias of Flight Lieutenant Daniel Buchan.

Harry Day, who was the Senior British Officer at Dulag Luft, recalled the officer arriving in the camp. The new arrival, he recounted, had been in the army and then the air force. He had known Day in the late 1920s, before he left the RAF in 1931. He then rejoined the RAF in 1939 and was a pilot in a communications squadron. Prior to the war, the pilot was said to have been a member of Sir Oswald Mosley's British Union of Fascists.

It is clear from the description above that the man described by 'Wings' Day was Pilot Officer Benson Freeman.

In the book, Day recalls that he recognised the man immediately when he arrived at Dulag Luft. He was an '*Amusing talker, even though Communism and World-Jewry were his chief bugbears'*.

Harry Day recalled him as having a great admiration of the Nazis and considered them a bulwark against Communism. When not ranting, he was a witty talker.

Day recalled that the Commandant of Dulag Luft at the time – Major Theodor Rumpel – probably knew more about this pilot's BUF activities than he ever did; and it was no surprise when he (Freeman) had regular direct access to the Camp Commandant.

Harry Day also alleged in the book that the pilot later persuaded the camp officers that British Intelligence had sent a man to the camp to kill him. He was eventually moved to Berlin to work at the German Foreign

Office. Later, he was alleged to have joined the SS Flying Branch and became a Lieutenant in the SS Communications Flight.

Messages continued to filter through about Freeman, but in early 1944, a prisoner was repatriated who would give the authorities a lot more detail about Benson Freeman and his activities. That man was Flight Lieutenant Vincent 'Paddy' Byrne, who had convinced the German medical authorities that he was mentally ill, allowing him to be medically repatriated via the Red Cross.

In fact, the Germans at Dulag Luft had tried to recruit the Irishman in 1940-41, believing he might have Republican sympathies and was ripe for collaboration. 'Paddy' Byrne actually did nothing to discourage the Luftwaffe staff and after clearing it with Harry 'Wings' Day (who in turn had cleared it with London via coded messages in his letters), he played along. Over a period of months, his play-acting changed to feigned madness and he was eventually repatriated in 1944.

Byrne was shot down by ground fire and badly wounded in the leg at Clarmarais Wood, on 23 May 1940, while flying a Spitfire of 74 Squadron the same day, Freeman was allegedly captured. Not only did fate decree he would be shot down on the same day as Freeman, but he was also joined that day as a POW by his friend and former colleague Squadron Leader Roger Bushell of 92 Squadron. Bushell, a trained lawyer, had defended Byrne and Johnny Freeborn at a court martial in 1939, after they had mistakenly shot down British aircraft in an incident that would become known as the Battle of Barking Creek.

At Dulag Luft, both Byrne and Bushell would take issue with Benson Freeman in the coming months of captivity.

As a returning prisoner of war, Byrne held a mass of intelligence about how prisoners were detained, interrogated, what the Luftwaffe intelligence system wanted, and how other prisoners interacted with the Germans, including Benson Freeman.

In his report, dated 27 July 1944 (see Nat. Archives file ref: KV2/631 enclosure 124a), Vincent Byrne stated he had arrived at Dulag Luft in June 1940 and remained in the camp until the end of 1942. He gave a detailed description of the camp and the Commandant and his senior officers, before addressing the issue of Benson Freeman and two other suspect prisoners.

He opened his report by stating:

> *'I wish to make it understood that my report on all officers and NCOs, with the exception of Flight Lieutenant Freeman and in*

a minor degree Squadron Leader Elliott and Sergeant Slowey, is entirely my personal opinion and should be treated as such.'

It was clear from his report, that Byrne and other officers and NCO aircrew clearly believed there were a number of men in Dulag Luft who were apparently sympathetic to the Nazi cause and were collaborating. (Squadron Leader Eric Douglas Elliott and Sergeant John Slowey will be discussed later in this book.)

Byrne stated that Freeman had met him upon his arrival in June 1940 and gave the immediate impression of being pro-German and lacking in moral fibre – dangerous from the view of camp security. Byrne therefore decided to get the confidence and friendship of Freeman, this being deemed essential as a new escape tunnel was being dug beneath Byrne's bed.

Freeman openly admitted to Byrne that he had been a member of the British Union of Fascists and held the view that Britain and Germany should not be at war. Byrne said he was anti-Churchill, anti-Jews, anti-Communism, and clearly believed the future should entail a strong friendship between Britain and Nazi Germany.

One of the camp officers – Leutnant Eberhardt regularly visited Freeman's room and by September 1940, Freeman openly boasted that if he could get his wife to Ireland, he would be prepared to go over to the Germans and assist with their propaganda. Freeman had even written to William Joyce (Lord Haw Haw) in Berlin, telling him how much he appreciated his recent book.

Heinrich Eberhardt was in his thirties and wore spectacles. He had been a teacher before the war and studied British History at the University of London. He was given a civilian role at Dulag Luft and expected to censor the prisoners mail, but there was so little post, he ended up interrogating new prisoners.

In November, Benson Freeman had a long interview with the Camp Commandant who agreed to make enquires with the Propaganda Ministry. He would see if Freeman could join the Ministry in Berlin for a few months, his absence would be explained as a period of medical treatment. The German Propaganda Ministry initially declined the offer but said they would let him know as soon as they could make arrangements.

The Camp Commandant (Rumpel) had asked Freeman if he could get his wife to Ireland or Lisbon, as Germany could then transfer her to join him in Germany.

Two men arrived at the camp from the Propaganda Ministry and they asked if Freeman would assist with a programme from a French station. Freeman was keen to accept, but not before his wife was brought to Germany.

Flight Lieutenant Byrne made it clear that the Commandant and his officers had complete confidence in Benson Freeman, but Byrne believed he also had the treacherous officer's confidence. He therefore decided to tell Freeman about the tunnel under his bed. He did this because he thought Freeman would discover this himself in time and inform Leutnant Eberhardt of the tunnel's entrance. At the same time, Byrne told Freeman not to divulge the secret to the Germans as he had many enemies in the camp and it would be very awkward for him if the Germans discovered the entrance. Freeman promised not to divulge the secret tunnel to the Germans, but he did confide in Byrne that it would be difficult for him when the escape was finally made.

Despite this, Freeman kept silent and continued seeing the Camp Commandant and Leutnant Eberhardt to 'discuss political matters'.

Also in the camp at this time was Squadron Leader Roger Bushell. Bushell would become an infamous repeat escaper, better known to most people as 'Big X' in the Great Escape from Stalag Luft III in 1944, portrayed by Richard Attenborough in the movie.

According to Paddy Byrne, an incident took place one night when Roger Bushell told Freeman that when he returned to England, he would have him court martialled. A vicious argument ensued, overheard by Vincent Byrne and two other unnamed RAF officers.

Bushell later made an escape attempt by hiding in a goat pen and Byrne said that it was with the utmost difficulty that he managed to stop Freeman from reporting this escape to a guard. Unfortunately, a goat is said to have attacked Bushell and nearly foiled his attempted escape! He did escape but was later recaptured outside the camp.

Flight Lieutenant Vincent 'Paddy' Byrne left Dulag Luft in late 1941, but he heard that Freeman had asked Wing Commander Eyres for written permission to give his parole and go and work on Eberhardt's farm. The written permission was given and in the summer of 1942 Freeman went to work on the farm. However, Byrne believed he did not actually go to the farm but went and engaged in propaganda for the Nazis.

In the next chapter, we shall see what captured written records revealed about Freeman's letters and requests at Dulag Luft in mid-1942.

Dulag Luft had by this time become something of an issue for the RAF and MI9. Numerous reports were coming back via the coded letter system and the occasional repatriated airman, stating that there was a small group of permanent POWs at the camp, who enjoyed a better lifestyle than those incarcerated elsewhere in the Third Reich. This group were alleged to assist with interrogations and received more Red Cross parcels than other prisoners. Whether it was true or not, the RAF and MI9 now knew they had a traitor in the form of Pilot Officer Benson Freeman at Dulag Luft. However, they had also been receiving coded messages from some of the permanent prisoners such as Harry Day and Roger Bushell.

On 20 October 1944, a further report (enclosure 129a in file KV2/631 in the UK National Archives), detailed the actions of Benson Freeman. Further letters from Freeman had been intercepted and found to contain further treacherous comments. These included on 14 February 1942, Freeman describing the war as '*This ruddy hoax*' and on 18 November 1942 as '*This financier's bloody war*.'

On 26 May 1942, Freeman wrote to his wife Muriel referring to Winston Churchill as '*That horrible Lord Dunkirk of Dardanelles*' (a clear reference to Churchill's involvement with both Gallipoli and Dunkirk).

Freeman also claimed that the British definition of a Fifth Columnist, was someone who wanted this lovely war to come to an end.

The report stated that Freeman's letters were longer than those of other POWs and he even had access to a camera. He told his wife in May 1942, that he was becoming extremely fond of the beautiful German countryside and the vast majority of Germans were very kind and friendly towards the prisoners.

The report continued, stating that through the most secret channels (coded letters), it was known that Freeman had volunteered to help William Joyce and was advising the Germans on propaganda.

It was also learnt that he was living on the farm of a Luftwaffe interpreter at Dulag Luft. This was a man called Eberhardt, an ardent Nazi.

The report repeated the accusations of Flight Lieutenant Byrne, but added that a statement had been obtained from a returning prisoner (Corporal Francis Paul Maton ref: KV2/264). Maton would himself be court martialled for making propaganda broadcasts and joining the British Free Corps, but he claimed that while speaking on German radio, Freeman and others, such as Baillie-Stewart, William Joyce and John Amery were writing the programmes. Pilot Officer Freeman and the others were allegedly paid 1,000 Reichsmarks per month for their 'work'.

It was also identified that Freeman used an alias of Royce and other POWs had met him while he was using this name. Accusations were also being made that he had tried to join the British Free Corps and wanted a commission, but he had failed to obtain one, subsequently attempting to gain a commission in the Waffen SS.

The intelligence report stated that Benson Freeman had written propaganda leaflets for use by the Luftwaffe, these detailed allegations that British air raids on Hamburg had killed women and children and depicted images of the dead lying in the streets.

On 28 November 1944, a British Renegades notice was published. This warned that Pilot Officer Benson Railton Metcalf Freeman, also known as Royston or Royce, was a former member of the BUF and working for the German Propaganda authorities. He was to be detained and SHAEF (Supreme Headquarters Allied Europe Forces) should be informed immediately.

The proverbial noose continued to tighten around Freeman as the allied forces advanced across Europe. The advancing armies were closely followed by intelligence officers who were quick to locate and identify any evidence of collaboration and collusion.

In the MI5 file at the National Archives, there is an Ausweiss – a German pass in the name of SS-Untersturmführer Freeman and two others. The pass was dated 15 February 1945, at Berlin-Grunewald. The translated document states that the three men were authorised to enter M-Camp IIIA, Luckenwalde on that date. The purpose was for assessing the value by cross-examination of British and American POWs for the radio service in collaboration with SS-Hauptsturmführer Lind. The paper bore the official stamp of Stalag IIIA.

The race was now on to locate Benson Railton Metcalf Freeman and return him to Britain for questioning.

On 9 May 1945, Benson Freeman surrendered to American forces at Lenggries in South-Eastern Germany. He was with two other SS men who had tried to persuade him to escape to Switzerland, but he declined their suggestion. Freeman, thanks to the widespread warning system for war criminals and collaborators, was quickly identified by the Americans and conveyed back to Britain, where MI5 and the RAF SIB were awaiting his return.

MI5 had built a considerable dossier on Benson Freeman, and they continued to gather evidence, taking statements from a large number of former prisoners of war and German detainees. The evidence formed a detailed picture of Freeman's behaviour in the Third Reich. Not only had this former member of Mosley's Union of Fascists assisted the German propaganda services, but he had apparently engaged with the British Free Corps.

While the likes of William Joyce and John Amery had been detained and would in time be sentenced to death, it seemed certain with the evidence that had been collected, that Benson Freemen would follow them to the gallows at Wandsworth Prison and an appointment with Albert Pierrepoint.

In the next chapter, we shall examine the evidence and statements collected by the Security Services and the Royal Air Force Provost Services. Why Benson Freeman had not escaped to Switzerland when he had the opportunity, is a question only he could answer, but he had other questions to answer…

Chapter 3

Witness Evidence Against Freeman

As the allied armies drove across Western Europe, their intelligence teams gathered a mass of evidence on war crimes and collaboration. As they moved towards Germany and the final victory, collaborators like Benson Freeman started to leave their paymasters and seek a future for themselves. As we have already seen, Freeman was detained at Lenggries, about forty miles from the Swiss border, by the American army.

On 29 March 1945, the American army liberated Oberursel and Dulag Luft. They liberated a number of allied prisoners, but they also detained a number of Luftwaffe personnel and a mass of documents.

Unknown to Freeman, the British intelligence services now had copies of his letters to senior British and German officers at Dulag Luft in 1942. (These documents can be found in National Archives file: KV2/631.)

One letter dated 5 March 1942 stated:

> The following prisoners of war at Dulag Luft request to go to another camp with the next transport:
>
> B.R.H. Freeman
> E.A. Galloway
> E. Hill.
>
> In view of the above and the existing feeling within the camp itself, the undersigned officers request to be included:
>
> E.D. Elliott, Squadron Leader
> John Cotton, Lt. Commander RN.

This document shows that Benson Freeman and others clearly wanted to get away from Dulag Luft. Galloway was Sergeant Eric Albert Galloway

No. 746962 of 102 Squadron. He had been shot down on 27 July 1940, on a raid to Mannheim and had spent nearly two years at Dulag Luft. Clearly, he wanted to get away from the permanent staff.

The document does not specify the exact reasons for each airmen, but we know Freeman was a fascist and there were 'rumblings' about Elliott. What this document does display, is a clear atmosphere of accusations and prisoners who suspected others of serious indiscretions.

The other names appear to be possibly Sergeant Edward Hill, a soldier captured at Dunkirk in May 1940. Hill remained at Dulag Luft until the Americans arrived in March 1945. I have been unable to date to find anything about Lieutenant Commander John Cotton, but I now believe this was an error and should have read Lieutenant Commander John Casson RN.

Another document, dated 6 April 1942, is a letter from Freeman to the Senior British Officer (SBO) at the camp. By this time Harry 'Wings' Day had moved on and the SBO was Squadron Leader Eric Douglas Elliott, a man suspected by some of being a collaborator or an appeaser. In addition, he had been joined in mid-March by Wing Commander Anthony Eyre DFC. Eyre was the North Weald Wing Commander, shot down on 8 March 1942. He was now technically the SBO, but Elliott was still in charge while the new arrival got his bearings.

In the letter, Freeman was clearly desperate to escape Dulag Luft, he wrote:

> *Sir,*
> *I have been officially informed that certain officers consider that my presence as a prisoner of war in Dulag Luft is definitely detrimental to present day service policy.*
>
> *This attitude is apparently caused by the fact that I am (or have been) a member of the British Union (British National Socialists) and the fact that I am most strongly opposed to Bolshevism and Communism.*
>
> *I have admitted and confirmed the fact that I most resolutely detest this revolting alien creed and particularly deplore its adoption in England.*
>
> *If this personal viewpoint is considered incompatible and detrimental to present day service policy in one RAF prisoner of war camp? It must obviously be equally so in any other RAF prisoner of war camp.*

Therefore, with your approval as Senior British Officer together with that of the other senior ranking British Officer Wing Commander A. Eyre DFC, I request that you ask the Luftwaffe Commandant of Dulag Luft if arrangements can be made to remove me to a separate place of detention, or German Farm and where I can no longer remain the slightest threat to the goodwill and efficiency of the service.

In order to facilitate these arrangements I should (if necessary and with approval) be prepared to give my parole and any reasonable additional pledges of good conduct, and to also (where necessary and practical) come under the jurisdiction of yourself or the nearest Senior British Officer prisoner of war.

I have the honour to be Sir, your obedient servant,

B.R.H. Freeman Pilot Officer.

It contained an amendment, stating that it had also been seen by Wing Commander A. Eyre on 8 September 1942.

This letter not only outlined the antipathy towards Freeman, but also shows his devious and calculating mind. He knew at this time that Leutnant Eberhardt had a farm and he clearly wished to visit and stay at that location. The question is why? This letter was clearly one of those described by Vincent Byrne in his report upon repatriation in 1944.

We can see that the wheels were in motion for Freeman's betrayal and his full collaboration with the Nazis. This is further evidenced with a letter to Oberst Erich Killinger the Camp Commandant, dated 23 June 1942. The question is what was the involvement of Squadron Leader Eric Douglas and R. Hardy, who also signed the letter? (This is believed to have been Pilot Officer Richard Hardy of 234 Squadron, captured after abandoning his Spitfire on 15 August 1940 near Cherbourg).

The letter stated:

Dear Oberst Lt. Killinger,

We send this note to thank you very much indeed for granting us the facility of such a marvellous walk, together with the much appreciated 'Betriebsöl'.

Your countryside is so beautiful that we shall not want to leave it when the war ends.

I hope that you will agree with us, and decide that such walks are also most beneficial for the health and potential energy of Luftwaffe officers!

Yours sincerely,
E.D. Elliott, B.R.H. Freeman and R. Hardy.

The use of the German word *Betriebsöl* is very interesting, this translates as 'Operating Oil' and makes one wonder what this cryptic phrase actually meant? We know from other prisoners and from the Luftwaffe interrogator Hanns Joachim Scharff, that prisoners were often taken for walks to assist in interrogations. We also know that the giving of parole was forbidden by British authorities. If the collaborator Freeman was no longer being interrogated having been 'in the bag' for two years (as had Elliott and Hardy), what was the point of these walks?

In a later chapter on Squadron Leader Elliott, the letters are discussed in more detail, as well as the reasons behind them.

On 28 June 1945 a statement was taken from the recently captured Leutnant Heinrich Eberhardt. (Reference National Archives file KV2/631 enclosure 180b.) His statement was damning for any defence of Benson Freeman:

'I remember Pilot Officer Freeman very well. He was in the transit camp for a long time. He was not a stool-pigeon. He did not do any work until after the escape of eighteen officers when he was one of the few officers left and he then assisted with the canteen and I believe the Benevolent Fund.

'Freeman had got a political mind. He told me he was a member of the British Union of Fascists in England and used to express himself quite freely to both British and German personnel, that he hated the Russians and particularly Churchill.

'He also criticised the broadcasts of Haw-Haw, saying that it was not suitable for the British generally and for the appeasement between Britain and Germany, which at that time according to his views was possible. He proposed that he could do a better job in propaganda himself. Freeman's views were also known to Leutnant Boninghaus.

'On recollection, I don't think Leutnant Boninghaus had anything to do with Freeman before he went to Berlin. I don't

remember now who made the arrangements, but in the late summer or autumn of 1942, I escorted Freeman to Berlin and then to the Reichssportfeld, and there introduced him to a body of men including Dr Hetzler. Freeman was provided with civilian clothes for the trip to Berlin.

'With Dr Hetzler, he discussed his views of what he thought of German propaganda. Dr Hetzler asked him if he would put his views on paper, which he agreed to do. I do not remember that any proposals were put to him beyond this, but I stayed with him for three or four hours until he was fixed up with ration cards, a clothes permit and arrangements were made for the identity card to be provided by the police. By car, with a driver, Freeman accompanied me to the railway station and returned to Dulag Luft.

'Freeman had told me that he would like to do something in connection with German Propaganda, but he definitely stated that he would not broadcast. He also told Dr Hetzler that he was not prepared to broadcast.

'I met Freeman on two occasions in Berlin whilst I was attending a course there. He was then living at the Alhambra Hotel, Eurfastendam. He told me that he had been writing propaganda articles which had been broadcast and also that he had not broadcast himself. He said he was very dissatisfied with the whole procedure of conducting propaganda and he was generally full of criticisms. I visited him once at an office in Saarlandstrasse, but only remained there for a few minutes, when we left together.

'In October 1943, Freeman visited me at my home in Oberursel which is near Dulag Luft. He was on leave at the time, I think for a fortnight. I was ill at the time. Freeman stayed with me for a few nights and I had to ask him to leave as my being ill was too much for my wife. He understood and left quite friendly.

'Freeman stayed on my father's farm at Hoechst on an occasion when he was on leave from Berlin. I remember it was considered as to whether Freeman could go to this farm whilst he was at Dulag Luft owing to some disagreement of other British officers with him. An effort was made, but the matter could not be arranged and I actually took him from the camp

direct to Berlin after fitting him up with civilian clothes in the Interrogation Centre.'

Once again this extract from the statement of Heinrich Eberhardt corroborates the comments of Flight Lieutenant Byrne and the recovered letters from 1942.

Further evidence was soon available with the statement of Reinhard Hermann Haferkorn, a former professor at Greifswald University, Pomerania. (Ref: National archives file KV2/262 enclosure 84b.) In July 1945, he stated:

> *'As of 1 January 1940, an arrangement was made which enabled me to carry on my work in the teaching profession, in addition to my work at the German Foreign Office.*
>
> *'I commenced my work at the German Foreign Office in Berlin upon the out-break of war and was thereafter employed in control of England-Referat of the Rundrunkpolitische (Foreign Broadcast Department – English section).*
>
> *'I am not clear as to dates, but I remember a RAF officer named Freeman being brought to the Foreign Office, Saarlandstrasse 60, Berlin, after he had been interviewed by Dr Hesse, Chairman of the England Committee of the Foreign Office.*
>
> *'I knew Freeman, because I had seen him in Dulag Luft in February 1941. This interview had been arranged by Major Rumpel, the Commandant of Dulag Luft for the purpose of getting the views of an alleged British fascist. It was not decided at the time, definitely, to obtain the collaboration of Freeman in propaganda work, but more to obtain the general views of someone closely associated with the fascist movement in England.*
>
> *'He talked rather freely on political matters and appeared to be a confirmed fascist on anti-Bolshevik and anti-Jewish matters. I did not discuss with him at the time the possibility of his coming to Berlin to assist in propaganda work there, and I do not know through what channels this was arranged, but I should think about eighteen months later that he was sent to my office by Dr Hesse and introduced to me under the name of Royston.* (Author's note: like all British collaborators, the Germans gave the British personnel pseudonyms.)

'Dr Hesse informed me that Freeman was prepared to work in connection with broadcasting, on condition that he should be given a chance to create a new feature.

'I discussed with Freeman what his ideas were and he suggested a quarter of an hour's feature, with 'hot jazz' interspersed with political wisecracks under the title of "Jazz cracks".

'It was a new feature in propaganda broadcasting which I thought might be given a trial and Freeman suggested that he would select the music and prepare the wisecracks himself, which I agreed he could do, the conditions being that I should supervise the wisecracks and another department the music.

'Accommodation for Freeman to work was arranged in the Foreign Office at Saarslandstrasse and he immediately commenced work.

'The wisecracks he wrote were in the nature of Anti-Jewish and Anti-Bolshevik, and criticisms of the British Government, and at the time, introducing friction between the American and English people. I found that he was capable in this direction and quite efficient, although he was inclined to be a slow worker.

'Programmes were prepared and recorded on records and broadcast every Friday night and repeated Sunday night. They were called the Jazz Cracks programme.

'I am not aware that Freeman ever broadcast. His wisecracks were put over by one of the regular broadcasters.

'Freeman continued with this work of preparing broadcast material until I believe, well towards the end of 1943.

'In addition to this, I understood that he used to meet Dr Hesse at fairly regular intervals and discuss the political situation and receive instructions as to the general line of propaganda to take. Towards the latter part of 1943, there was general criticism about the material of his wisecracks, and Freeman resenting this criticism by the Runkfunk ceased work.

'My impression of Freeman regarding his work in preparing wisecracks material was that he was a very willing worker in this direction, but when approached on doing work of a different nature, he was not helpful or agreeable, as he maintained that wisecracks was the work for which he had been brought there and what he was paid for. Other work

which he was at times asked to do, was to prepare talks on Anti-Jewish lines etc.

'After Freeman was upset by reason of the criticism mentioned, he did little or no work, but remained at the Foreign Office, but spent some of the time on a canoe on the lake at Wannsee.

'In about May or June 1944, Dr Hesse's staff, which included Freeman, was moved to Krummhübel (now in western Poland), where Freeman reluctantly went and was supposed to carry on his work there, but owing to difficulties on obtaining material for his work, not having a wireless or any other means for getting ideas, the result of his work was practically nil.

'I saw Freeman once or twice after he went to Krummhübel, this was when he visited Berlin for the purpose of collecting his Red Cross parcels. During the time Freeman worked in Berlin, he resided at the Alhambra Hotel as far as I know.'

(The words above are from the translated statement, hence the grammar is not perfect). Later in his statement, Haferkorn stated that Freeman had been paid a salary of 800 Reichsmarks a month.

The statement of Haferkorn and that of Leutnant Eberhardt were damning on their own, but very soon other alleged collaborators and traitors were also adding to the evidence.

Gerald Percy Hewitt a former member and contributor to British Union of Fascist 'Action' weekly publication, had escaped to Paris and was detained by the Germans in 1940. He too assisted with Nazi propaganda with the alias name of Smith. In his statement upon arrest (National Archives reference KV2/426), he gave details of RAF officers employed in the propaganda services. One of those he named was Royston – one of the alias names of Freeman. He had been in the room next to Norman Baillie-Stewart when he lived in Berlin. He was described as an ex-military man and unmarried. Hewitt also believed this man had taken part in the 'Anzac Tattoo' radio broadcasts.

It was abundantly clear to the British authorities in 1945, that Benson Freeman was a major part of the German propaganda services at the Foreign Office in Berlin. Armed with this information and evidence, he was to be interviewed by two officers from the Intelligence Service (MI5). (Reference: National Archives file KV2/631 enclosure 154a.)

Evidence with regard to the propaganda services in Germany can be found in the statement of Dr Freidrich Wilhelm Schoeberth, in one of the files on William Joyce. (Ref: KV2/246 enclosure 413b.)

In his statement, Schoeberth, who worked at the German Foreign Office from 1939, under the direction of Professor Haferkorn, states that he was a liaison officer between the Foreign Office and the Runkfunk. He would pass on instructions from Dr Hesse, who was the adviser to Joachim von Ribbentrop, the Minister for Foreign Affairs and former Ambassador to Britain.

Two men – Norman Baillie-Stewart and Vernon – wrote scripts for broadcasting. Schoeberth recalled a man called Royston and identified Freeman as the same individual from a photograph shown to him by the investigators. The man had been in the RAF and a prisoner of war camp. He did not do much and contributed mostly to the political department. Schoeberth did not recall Freeman ever doing any actual broadcasting, but he was responsible for the political comments in the 'Jazz-cracks' programme with Baillie-Stewart.

Schoeberth recalled that Freeman was connected with the SS, PK and Kurt Eggers. (Eggers was a pre-war poet and playwright. He was a fanatical Nazi and worked on SS propaganda before serving on the Eastern Front as a member of the Waffen SS. He was killed in action on 12 August 1943 and the SS propaganda unit was renamed in his honour.)

Schoeberth recalled that all propaganda had been the responsibility of the Wehrmacht until the attempt on Hitler's life in July 1944. After that, the SS Kurt Eggers unit took over the work.

Schoeberth named the following people as working under the direction of Hesse and Haferkorn at the Foreign Office: Baillie-Stewart, Hewitt, Amery, Freeman and P.G. Wodehouse (the English writer). William Joyce and others worked at the Reichsrunkfunk.

In the MI5 file reference KV2/2861 concerning Dr Hetzler, there is a statement from Signalman William Alfred Colledge of the North Somerset Yeomanry.

Colledge was a prisoner of war, captured in Crete in 1941. He claimed to have been approached by the Germans with a view to being parachuted back into Egypt with a radio, but eventually this did not materialise. He was taken to a hospital at Dulag Luft and put in a bed next to British parachutists. He was expected to obtain details of who they were, but he claimed to have told them he was sent to get the information and consequently no intelligence was obtained.

Colledge ended up working at the Buro Concordia in Berlin where he knew a number of collaborators and met William Joyce (Lord Haw Haw). He was aware of Benson Freeman, although he was using the alias of Royston at the time:

> *'Royston, an air force officer, had many privileges and good connections. He managed to be transferred at his own request to official German Radio, after which I seldom saw him, but heard he was in the Free Corps.'*

On 16 May 1945, MI5 officers J.M. Davies and P.A. Edwards met with Freeman at the Endsleigh Hotel. They introduced themselves to Freeman and formally cautioned him, before telling him they wished to obtain an account of his movements whilst a prisoner in Germany. Freeman, to the men's surprise, asked to make a full statement as he wanted to explain everything. He also claimed he had never done anything to the detriment of his country. He added that it was essential they should recognise his principles and that he was a member of the British Union of Fascists before war broke out.

He openly admitted that prisoners disliked him for these views and he had written to William Joyce while in Germany, before meeting with him on two occasions. Freeman stated he did not agree with Joyce's wireless talks and knew that he hated him for this. This, he claimed had been confirmed to him personally by Dr Hesse.

Freeman also denied the rumour that he had written an article for the German army newspaper '*Angriff*' (Attack) and had no part in it. He also did not give permission for his name to be used as the author of the article.

Freeman also told them he would explain his reasons for his actions, as well as joining and wearing the uniform of the Waffen SS in August 1944. He claimed the SS were always pro-English and anti-Communist. He added that he would, with his personal convictions, have joined the SS much sooner, if he had known what they were and their purpose in fighting Bolshevism.

The two intelligence officers must have then been astounded, especially when Freeman offered to go back to Germany to locate and contact the SS leaders who had gone underground. He then added that he believed Britain would co-operate in the fight against the Russians, whose aim was to control Europe, including Britain.

Freeman told the officers, that his own conviction was that the war could have ended long ago, if Churchill and certain other leaders and Jewish financiers had been willing to fight 'the Bolshevik menace' along with Germany.

Freeman then suggested something be done quickly, as the Allies would soon lose the support of the Waffen SS because of the treatment being meted out to them.

He was at pains to categorically state that he was not a traitor, but he could not say the same about some British officers with whom he came into contact in Germany. He told the intelligence officers that enquiries should be made concerning Squadron Leader Keast, who gave information to the Germans, as well as Flight Lieutenant Vincent Byrne, who detested Freeman. It appears Freeman was oblivious to the fact that Byrne had already provided a statement when he was repatriated.

Keast is believed to have been Acting Squadron Leader Francis John Baptist Keast of 419 Flight Special Duties. His Whitley had just dropped an agent over Belgium on 18 February 1941, when they were shot down. John Keast and his entire crew were captured, and he probably kept himself to himself, knowing the Gestapo would certainly have prized his scalp and any information he could provide regarding the dropping of agents.

He also claimed that the executed Roger Bushell (shot after the Great Escape in March 1944) be examined as he was a collaborator. Their actions he claimed were anti-British, while his own were entirely anti-Bolshevik.

Freeman repeated the claims that he had never broadcast on behalf of the Germans and denied ever writing anything for broadcast. He admitted to being in Berlin in civilian clothes and using the name Royston, but he claimed he later used his own name.

Finally, Freeman added that he wrote about three non-political plays of about three hundred words for a man called Hanson who used them for a programme called 'Anzac Tattoo'. He said he saw, 'This ramshackle show produced once' and never had any more connection with Hanson. (Hanson was almost certainly Irwin Gunther Hansen another collaborator employed by the Nazis. He initially worked on the *Ubersesender* for American programmes, but he joined the NBBS when the 'Jerry Calling' programmes were broadcast from about 9 June 1944, just after D-Day.)

The following day, Benson Freeman would write his own statement…

Chapter 4

Freeman's Own Evidence

In the first line of his official statement (National archives file KV2/631 enclosure 155a), Benson Freemen got straight to the point…

> *'I have been bitterly opposed to the appalling menace of Soviet Communism for a long time. I have studied Moscow propaganda for about fifteen years and its hideous exploitation by world Jewry and I am more than dismayed at the fearful fate that awaits this country and Western Europe, and eventually the whole world when this menace overpowers them. I came to those conclusions long before I ever heard of Mosley or Hitler, therefore it is inaccurate to describe my views or actions as Nazi propaganda. National Socialism merely provided the one apparently solid barrier in the path of this Asiatic doctrine from which opposition could be made.'*

This opening statement carried on and even exacerbated the comments Freeman had made to the intelligence officers the day before. Were these words the vitriolic ramblings of a mad man or the carefully considered arguments of a staunch Nazi, who not only assisted with anti-British propaganda, but also joined the Waffen SS?

Benson Freeman continued stating that he had joined the British Union of Fascists in 1937, but he never did any work for them as '*Co-operation of views and policy was disappointing*'. He said he had remained a member as there was no other force opposing the danger to the standards of our civilisation.

He added that he did everything he could as an individual to denounce the clamour for war with Germany, as he believed they were an ally not an enemy. War, he believed, would lead to the reduction of Great Britain as a great power. He continued…

> *'When war was declared on September the 3rd, 1939, I was almost stunned by the shock. I considered it the maddest act in British history and I still do. I had not the slightest wish to be engaged in this criminal struggle, but already my age group was under conscription and one merely had to wait.'*

Freeman explained that he discussed his predicament with his wife and decided to rejoin the RAF, as he was a trained pilot with an exceptional rating. He therefore expected to become an instructor and not take any part in the fighting. He was surprised to have passed the flying medical, as he was ill and felt sick with the thought of war. He was, however, selected for instructional duties, but sent to join No. 24 Squadron at RAF Hendon.

The squadron was a communications unit, using a variety of aircraft types and Freeman disliked what he called '*airline work*'. In addition to this, he claimed to be a rotten navigator and totally unsuited to the work. Freeman therefore went to see his Commanding Officer, who agreed to a posting on the next available Central Flying School (CFS) course. (This appears to be in contradiction to the statement of Wing Commander Goode.)

While he waited for a course vacancy, Freeman claimed his health deteriorated and he was sick with worry. He was so sick the Medical Officer took him off flying duties.

In May 1940, the Blitzkrieg began and he had to resume his flying duties, despite his condition. Freeman said he was still ill with worry and had great trouble staying awake in the air, so he was taken off flying duties once again by the doctor.

On 22 or 23 May, Freeman said he was ordered to fly to Croydon and head for Merville aerodrome in Northern France. He claimed no one expected to get to the airfield, let alone return, but he was too unwell to care and if fit, he would have refused the order to go.

They arrived at Merville and landed, but the airfield was immediately attacked by a number of Messerschmitt 109s, and their Hurricane escort disappeared towards England. Freeman's own aircraft was badly shot up and caught fire, as were the other machines. Eventually, they tried to fly home on a Douglas DC3, but they were attacked by another group of Messerschmitt 109s. The DC3's pilot managed to land in a field, their aircraft being riddled with bullet and cannon holes. The DC3 pilot was killed together with another man, and the rest of the crew, including Freeman were detained by the advancing German infantry.

Freeman described being handed over to the Luftwaffe and ended up at Dulag Luft near Frankfurt am Main. The prisoners were very well treated, but as a communications pilot he claimed not to have been interrogated. Instead, he said he had a number of political discussions with the Camp Commandant, a man called Major Rumpel.

> *'I made no secret of the fact that I was a member of the British Union inside or outside the camp and that I hoped to see the war ended with a satisfactory peace. At the time many others thought so too.*
>
> *'After some time, I became the object of discussion among certain officers, because of my friendship with the Commandant and a Leutnant Eberhardt, this was sponsored largely by Squadron Leader Bushell and one or two others and a Captain Griffith and Flying Officer Boardman. The curious feature of the last two was that they were on amazingly friendly terms with an Ober Leutnant Viergood* (Author: actually Hauptmann Fiergutt, Theo Rumpel's adjutant, but mis-pronounced or mis-spelt in reports). *This German Leutnant was quite a fanatical Nazi, a great drinker and when drunk could become abusive about the English and yet he was permanently in their room ... and there was no limit to the number of electrical gadgets this Ober Leutnant produced for these two officers including mini cameras and typewriters.'*

(Author: Flying Officer John Balfour Boardman, service no. 37931 was a pilot with 77 Squadron when his Whitley was shot down on 28 March 1940. He would be one of the eighteen prisoners to escape from Dalag Luft. What Freeman clearly forgot was that a mini camera and a typewriter could be used to make fake identification and *Ausweiss* passes, needed in any escape attempts. It appears therefore that Boardman was using tact and subterfuge to obtain such tools from the German officer. Captain Griffith appears to actually be Royal Marine Lieutenant Guy Griffiths, one of the first Naval aviators captured in 1939.)

Freeman continued, stating that he was never asked by Rumpel or Eberhardt to do anything treacherous or dirty.

Although Freeman may have appeared to be a madman at first, it was clear that he had planned this post-war response, and his mention of men like Roger Bushell and Vincent Byrne was meant to detract from what they may have told the British authorities over the past few years. Making allegations against these men was a clear attempt to cover his own tracks, Freeman continued…

> *'About this time Squadron Leader Bushell was organising escapes and digging tunnels. He and his crowd put out that I was the danger man of the camp and much care was to be taken. At the same time, he would see me and discuss details as he stated he would like to have my opinion. I criticised the direction of the tunnel and the final tunnel that was built was made in exactly the direction I said I would dig a tunnel (the obvious direction). During the time, I was also kept annoyingly well posted with all the latest news, plans about this confounded tunnel by Flight Lieutenant Byrne.'*

Clearly the paragraph above indicates that Byrne's statement in 1944 was correct. However, whether Freeman knew Roger Bushell had been murdered by the Gestapo and could not provide a counter statement is unclear. He may well have known, as this was major news in the camps, as was the post-war RAF Police investigation to find the murderers. Clearly dead men cannot talk.

Freeman added that he took no part in the tunnel construction, was not asked to assist and was not interested in doing so.

> *'At long last the tunnel was finished, by accident it was nearly discovered by a German Leutnant when a Flying Officer Gould was coming out of the tunnel while the former was in the room, and it was I that managed to avert disaster for which Squadron Leader Bushell praised my presence of mind at the time.'*

It is interesting that Byrne never mentioned this in his statement in 1944, and neither did anyone else in subsequent letters, reports, statements or books.

In his book *The Great Escaper: The life and death of Roger Bushell.* Bushell's biographer – Simon Pearson – makes no mention of Freeman or the near discovery of the tunnel. Similarly, the author Sydney Smith, who wrote Harry 'Wings' Day's biography, makes no mention of such an event.

Freeman's own contorted version of events continued in his statement…

> *'The day before they were due to go, Flight Lieutenant Byrne came to me and said that I must tell Major Rumpel of the tunnel. He said that if Bushell got back to England, you and I will be court martialled. I replied that I had nothing to fear as I had done nothing wrong. I certainly would not do that and I hoped the whole damn pack of the Bushell set got out successfully and then one might get some peace. That night, Flight Lieutenant Byrne, hopelessly drunk, had an offensive row with me over the subject…'*

Clearly, Freeman was confused in relation to 'Paddy' Byrne's intentions. Did he believe, like the Germans, that Byrne had Irish republican sympathies?

Freeman stated that Major Rumpel spoke with each remaining officer who had not escaped, including himself and asked why he had not gone, especially as he was so keen to see his wife again. A rumour was then spread around the camp by 'Paddy' Byrne that Freeman had told the guards about the tunnel.

Regardless of whatever accusations Freeman made about fellow prisoners, he still had some explaining to do…

> *'Major Rumpel had a discussion with me on the effect of William Joyce on the English public and I had told him that I considered this man a howling disaster and a hate-maker of the worse kind possible. Major Rumpel told me that many German people thought the same, but unfortunately, Dr Goebbels had given him a free hand. Major Rumpel suggested that if he could invite Joyce down one night, would I agree to join him and give my views to see if I could enlighten Joyce as tactfully as I could… Joyce never came. Later, Major Rumpel said that Joyce had replied that he was by no means interested in a British officer's views on social questions.*
>
> *'I discussed this with Byrne. He was all for it and said, "You might do a lot of good to promote peace if you could*

> *alter Joyce's views." Byrne suggested that I should write a letter to Joyce flattering him and praising his book and then he might come. I detested the book and the author, but it seemed little to do, so I wrote a letter to Joyce. Joyce however, never appeared.'*

Pilot Officer Freeman stated that Byrne had told the Commandant that both he and Freeman were willing to broadcast peace talks. As a result, Freemen was called to an office to meet with Professor Haferkorn and Professor Leeburg. He was asked if he would broadcast or write for the camp, both of which he refused. He said he was extremely annoyed with Byrne for 'engineering' this.

Freeman also recalled Byrne telling him that he was willing to go to Ireland to select aerodromes for the Germans and he was going to see Major Rumpel about this. Freeman said he had told Byrne not to be so mad and he was surprised he would suggest such a treacherous thing. Byrne also suggested that Major Rumpel would be disgusted that a British officer should offer to do such a thing. Byrne however, got an interview with Rumpel, but in Freeman's own words, '*Was shown the door inside five minutes'*.

Freeman stated that Byrne had been drinking a lot and was so drunk that one day he slipped on ice and banged his head. After that he was no longer sane. This comment alone shows Freeman was twisting the circumstances to assist his own defence case. He must have known Byrne was repatriated due to his poor mental health and decided to use this in his defence. With Roger Bushell dead, he could now dismiss anything Byrne said, as a facet of his poor mental health and something that could not be trusted. What Freeman probably didn't know was that the Irish Republican sympathies of Byrne and his 'madness' were all part of a cover story for an escape.

Next, Freeman moved on to another officer whose reputation he was desperate to dismiss…

> *'Round this time, an officer 'Keast'* (Author: Acting Squadron Leader Francis John Baptist Keast) *came into the camp. Leutnant Eberhardt told me that there was a chap over there with very pro-fascist views and that he knew me. When he told me his name, I said, "My God then he's changed, when he was in the squadron he was 100% Communist."'*

Keast was of a similar age to Freeman and served at the same time as him in 1930. He became a reserve officer in 1934 according to the *London Gazette* but returned to the service on the outbreak of war. The likelihood of him actually being a communist would appear to be very low and almost certainly another fabrication by Benson Freeman. In fact, a review of the No. 24 Squadron Operations Record Books gives a possible indication of the antipathy towards Keast.

Keast had joined the squadron on 26 February 1940 and he was promoted to Flight Lieutenant on 15 May 1940, just nine days before Freeman's capture in France. Benson Freeman probably thought he had been unfairly treated, as not only was Keast promoted, but he also became a first pilot and aircraft captain within days of his arrival on the squadron, whereas Freeman had remained a co-pilot throughout his time right up to his capture. Between late February and 22 May, Keast flew forty-two operational flights to France, while Freeman flew eighteen as co-pilot. As we have seen, Freeman had a poor sickness record and his commanding officer was loath to use him as a first pilot, wanting him transferred from the squadron.

Freeman continued with his statement….

> *'Keast knew my views and I his. Immediately Keast came in the camp, he greeted me as "Quisling" and set about working up opposition to me. He told Wing Commander Day that I was a most dangerous Nazi and the worst possible type of man in the camp. He did everything possible to spread rumours and lies about me and he was violent to mad extremes in his hatred of the Germans.*
>
> *'However, he was too violent and repulsive for the old-timer to put up with. One evening Major Rumpel asked me over for a drink on my birthday and to give me a bottle of wine (which he did to all permanent staff), and he mentioned that he was sorry to hear that I had been the victim of a detestable type of officer. He then said, "I am going to tell you something. Nearly all the people who behave like this have dirty waistcoats, but never have I had such an officer as this Squadron Leader Keast. In the first place, he landed his machine intact. Neither he nor his crew made any attempt to destroy their machine* (a Whitley). *They were found sitting under a hedge smoking. All his maps were found in the machine and since he was on*

agent dropping work they were vital and maps of previous trips were also found. When I interrogated him for about five hours, he told me not only everything, but he would volunteer all the information he could think of. Three times I got on to Berlin, so startling was his information and he seemed unending in his capacity for drink and information".

'I managed to get confirmation of this from Lt. Eberhardt (who was a great friend of mine) in a roundabout way.'

In the June 1941 *London Gazette* there is a mention of Keast being awarded the Distinguished Flying Cross but being reported missing. This was approximately four months after he was shot down. Was this delay due to him hiding his squadron from the Dulag Luft personnel?

Theodor Rumpel was eventually replaced in November 1941 by Oberst Leutnant Erich Killinger. Although Rumpel was an associate of Hermann Goering, the authorities deemed him to be too soft on allied airmen and he was replaced. He would regularly supply alcohol to the prisoners, something which was forbidden. These facts went some way towards the belief that those at Dulag Luft were having an easy time and collaborating.

Benson Freeman was now in full-flow, and he was keen to point out that he was told by a South African pilot, Lieutenant Haller, and several other unnamed individuals, that the RAF were briefing aircrew to be wary of Dulag Luft. They had even been briefed to look out for Freeman, who was a suspected fifth columnist who was giving military secrets to the Nazis.

Freeman completely denied this allegation in his statement, saying he had never known a military secret. He had never made any attempt to get one and even if he did, he would never pass it on, no matter what his own political views were. He continued:

'The Germans searched under the floorboards of the huts every week for tunnels, consequently there were idiotic newcomers who had been instructed by a nitwit at home to dig tunnels. We told them what would happen, for that we were fifth columnists and when the Germans most naturally discovered the tunnels, these extraordinary people were convinced that camp fifth columnists had given them away. In this respect, Byrne and Lieutenant Commander Casson were active in focusing this belief on myself and I also suspect Pilot Officer Walker and possibly a Pilot Officer Marcus Marsh as assistants.

> *'Apart from his fall on his head, Byrne and Lieutenant Commander Casson were doing a tremendous amount of drinking, which, plus their confinement, was transforming them into extremely irresponsible people.'*

It was clear that Freeman was throwing accusation after accusation at those he knew would name him as a collaborator. Lieutenant Commander John Casson was born in London in 1909, he served as the CO of 803 Squadron Fleet Air Arm and led them in a raid against the German battleship *Scharnhorst* near Trondheim on 13 June 1940. Unfortunately, he was brought down by a Messerschmitt 109E of JG77 and spent the remainder of the war in a prison camp. Casson was an active member of the inner circle and close to Roger Bushell – hence Freeman's dislike of him and the accusations.

Pilot Officer Marcus Marsh, service no. 77361, was born in Newmarket in February 1902. He was flying a 214 Squadron Wellington on 9 May 1941, when his machine was brought down and he was sent to Dulag Luft. There is no known evidence against him.

Pilot Officer Walker is possibly Peter Fowler Walker, service no. 85280. He was a navigator on a Wellington which was on its way to join 70 Squadron in Malta from Stradishall, when it hit a barrage balloon cable over St Marie in France on 9 December 1940. Once again, there is no evidence against this man.

These newcomers had been well-briefed and everyone now seemed to suspect Benson Freeman…

> *'By now my name was frequently mentioned by newcomers as having been lectured at the bomber units as a dangerous Nazi camp spy. This gave me considerable worry. I had already been a POW for 2 years and had been separated from my wife. Consequently, I became very bitter and kept myself to myself. By now, we had a new Commandant and he was a dull man, I only spoke to him once when he inspected the camp. Major Rumpel had been a personal and very great friend of mine. We both knew in December 1941 that the possibility of Germany being able to stem and survive the Soviet onslaught was very remote and he told me his views on the Soviet war, which would probably have got him into serious trouble with the authorities…*

> *'Round about May-July (1942), we had a most antagonistic and Communistic bunch of Squadron Leaders in (the camp). They caused as much trouble as they possibly could, not only on these matters, but in the welfare of the camp organisation. On top of this, there arrived a certain tall dark-haired Squadron Leader who immediately had some long conferences with Comrade Lieutenant Commander Casson. He then disclosed some official authority to Squadron Leader Elliott and demanded that he, as Senior British Officer and certain officers (of which I was one), should sign a paper document demanding that the German Commandant should have us removed to another camp. I refused to sign this bit of impertinence, but Squadron Leader Elliott asked me to sign as a personal request as he was going to do so, and he would add a protest and declare that he had the utmost confidence in me and the way I discharged my duties in the camp which was perfectly normal, as up till then I had done absolutely nothing and never intended doing any questionable action, no matter what my beliefs.'*

This letter appears to be the one already located by the authorities and translated. It was dated 5 March 1942 and stated that Freeman, Galloway and Hill requested to go to another camp on the next transport. Under the three names, there was a further request that Squadron Leader Elliott and Lieutenant Commander John Cotton (John Casson?) also be included because of the existing feeling within the camp (Dulag Luft).

Freeman continued in his statement…

> *'A Wing Commander, Auxiliary fighter squadron* (Anthony Eyre) *also endorsed this from his many conversations with me. At this, some of these charming gentlemen declared that I had violently anti-British views and had made anti-British statements. I asked them to produce any such statement. Finally, they said they would produce two other officers as witnesses. One officer said I had declared that the Soviets were the biggest menace to Europe and our alliance with them was a betrayal of our Empire; and the other also related how I had denounced the Soviets. Both flatly refused to admit that I had said anything against England. At this, I asked Squadron*

Leader Cox if it was true that in a roomful of about seven other officers, he had declared that, "If in the coming change of government, a government more Fascist than the Churchill government were to get in, he would willingly join the Red Air Force and bomb the hell out of London!" Squadron Leader Cox proudly admitted this to Casson to the astonishment of Squadron Leader Elliott and the Wing Commander (Eyre). *I remarked that most patriotic Englishmen would wish to do their best to keep the Soviets and their system out of Europe and England. At this, the dark-haired Squadron Leader remarked, "And I wish to see the Soviet system brought to England. It would do us a lot of good". Lieutenant Commander Casson immediately replied, "And I too have for long held that belief."'*

This last paragraph needs closer examination. Freeman was quick to mention two officers but did not give their names. Neither did he give the name of the tall, dark-haired Squadron Leader. In addition, I have been unable to identify Squadron Leader Cox.

The tall dark-haired Squadron Leader who disclosed 'some official authority' to Elliott, may have been Donald MacDonell DFC. Although MacDonell was at Dulag Luft in 1941 and not 1942, this may have been another fabrication of Freeman.

MacDonell was a Scottish aristocrat, who had joined the RAF in the early 1930s and was attached to the Fleet Air Arm, where he struck up a long-term friendship with fellow prisoner John Casson. MacDonell was shot down on 13 March 1941 over Calais and ended up at Dulag Luft where he met up with John Casson.

In his autobiography '*From Dogfight to Diplomacy*', MacDonell describes arriving at Dulag Luft, where he was less than impressed. He described the camp atmosphere as being far too free and easy, with ample supplies of cigarettes, French wine, brandy and cigars. The guards spoke fluent English and it had a holiday camp atmosphere. When he met up with John Casson, he told him he did not like what he had seen, and they were being softened up by the Germans for information. (This was the regime Rumpel had set up.)

MacDonell further states in the book that he was warned upon arrival by Casson about Benson Freeman. Although he does not name him in the text, MacDonell states:

> *'Far more serious, I was to discover, was the presence of a Flight Lieutenant who had been a pilot in a Communications Flight from Hendon and had been captured when the Germans overran an airfield in France in 1940. He was a traitor who spoke openly of treating with Nazi Germany, who sneered at the idea that we could win the war and was far too frequently called to the Commandant's office.'*

Although the dates appear to be inconsistent, (MacDonell was at Dulag Luft in spring 1941 and the letters regarding Freeman were dated March-June 1942), the links with John Casson and the fact he states both men made pro-Soviet comments, may indicate the Squadron Leader was Donald MacDonell, who was quite tall, slim and dark-haired. After all, this would not be the first time Freeman appears to confuse or alter events.

Both Casson and MacDonell would have been a complete antithesis of Freeman. Donald MacDonell being aristocratic, was unlikely to have Communist views and later became an Air Commodore, Chairman of the Battle of Britain Fighter Association and Air Attache at the British Embassy, Moscow.

John Casson's family were in the entertainment business, with his parents engaged in the theatre while he was a magician. In fact, his mother, who was also involved with the National Council for Civil Liberties, was on the Nazi Blacklist – *Sonderfahndunsliste GB* – and identified for arrest and probably destined for execution in the event of a Nazi invasion.

Freeman's statement continued…

> *'My good comrade and roommates, Richard Hardy and Squadron Leader Elliott considered such a state of affairs to be particularly mean and that it was extremely detrimental to the state of my health and mind, and we reckoned it was best that I go out of the camp and give my parole to work on a farm. Squadron Leader Elliott signed a letter on this subject and the Wing Commander* (Eyre) *also signed it. Frankly I did not want to go, as I had a clear conscience. I had many good comrades there and I was very comfortable, particularly as I felt far from well. After a period, a surprise search was made and this letter was discovered and placed before the Commandant. I was told he had forwarded it to*

higher authority and had come to the conclusion that I had better be granted the facilities to go out of the camp on a farm on parole. The Luftwaffe Leutnant Eberhardt stated that I could go on his people's farm and with Squadron Leader Elliott's permission I signed my parole not to escape.'

Clearly, Freeman's recollections differed from those of other witnesses, including Leutnant Eberhardt.

Freeman recalled that in about February 1942, a Baron Guyer had visited Dulag Luft and had a discussion with him. Freeman had expressed a belief that it was essential for Germany to come to terms with England in order that Western Europe be saved. The two men discussed the war with the Soviets and a request was made for Freeman to see Guyer once more. This time, Freeman said he was taken to Berlin by Leutnant Eberhardt…

*'I was taken to a place (the old Polish Embassy) near Norlindorf Platz and introduced to a Dr Hesse (head of the England Committee). Baron Guyer was not there, I was told he was expected, but had not arrived. Dr Hesse was head of the England Committee (*Auswurtiges Amt*) and was actively engaged on trying to get a peace with England. He was extremely anxious to know if I would help for the common good of the two countries, in the promotion of peace and the frustration of Bolshevik plans. I agreed. The next day I was driven out to a place in north-west Berlin. The Reichsportfeld. Later I was introduced to Dr Hetzler. I took an intense dislike to this man and was not at all keen at the idea of assisting this gentleman in anything. There I was given a fairly comfortable room in the Reichsportfeld and kept waiting for several days.*

'I became more and more suspicious of this place. It had military guards, there were other Englishmen there and it had the atmosphere of a prison, a sinister one at that. With the exception of two or three, no Englishman was allowed out, after several days, Dr Hetzler asked me to sign a paper that what he was going to tell me was to be kept secret, which I did. He then said that this was the N.B.B.S.

'I was extremely dismayed at the news, because this was in no way what I wanted, I had no desire to be mixed up

in any phoney secret stations as apart from anything else, they do little or no good. I was kept hanging around for several days. Meanwhile, I managed to communicate these facts by letter to Leutnant Eberhardt. He reported these facts to the Commandant and I think to Baron Guyer and a man called Wiser who came to see me and I went outside with him. Wiser I believe, was a confidential P.K. official working for the Luftwaffe and a very decent man. Wiser said he would get me a passport from the Auswurtigs Amt *and get me out and told me that he would certainly have the matter adjusted with Dr Hesse. Meanwhile, Dr Hetzler told me that he greatly desired me as a broadcaster for the N.B.B.S. and an Englishman who was there, who was more or less Hetzler's right-hand man and operator in chief of this outfit, did his best to persuade me. I detested this outfit, particularly Dr Hetzler, but I was in a tight spot, as it did not require much brains to see the programme of this sinister place and I had to use considerable ingenuity to play for time.*

'To my surprise, Wiser proved as good as his word. He produced a Fremder *(*Ausweiss*) passport and made arrangements for me to co-operate with Dr Hesse and he had me removed from this place. This was fortunate, because the day before Dr Hetzler had told me that he considered my voice ideal for his station and that he desired me to start broadcast work immediately. I had pointed out that this was not my task and in no circumstances was I going to broadcast.*

'The next day, Wiser gave me this passport and had me taken out to a quiet hotel in Kurfushdam, – The Alhambra.

'Dr Hetzler was determined to have me as a broadcaster or to get me fixed. I stayed a few more days there in this electric atmosphere, had a short final interview with this man and went to see Dr Hesse again. Dr Hesse apologised very handsomely and said that all that had been settled, and he hoped I would co-operate with him and work for peace with England and the struggle against the Bolsheviks.'

Freeman added that he soon discovered that at the Reichsportfeld, there were several phoney radio stations, all run by Dr Hetzler. Freeman thought the man was a coward and a scoundrel and hated by German and English alike. Although Hesse was the chief, Hetzler was more powerful, and he dared not cross him. However, Freeman stated that during the two to three years he was 'knocking around' this place and criticising certain things, he was untouchable. Someone high-up must have trusted him and was protecting him, but he did not know who. Freeman continued…

> *'This N.B.B.S. had the finest collection of poor Englishmen one could wish to meet, but in passing I should like to record that one, Palmer, was a sincere man. He was deluded and knew it, but had the courage not to say it, he was sincere in his basic beliefs and managed to avoid becoming a hireling in the sense of the other men. Also, there was one Griffiths, an ex-guardsman (Welsh), he was a socialistic minor and was too ignorant to see the programme until too late I suppose. Shortly after I left, he demanded to go back to the camp and Dr Hetzler sent his special Gestapo man to the unfortunate Griffiths and Griffiths was told to think again, he did and that is only natural.*
>
> *'James also tried later. He was stubborn. Hetzler had him put into prison on some false charge. James was kept there until he gave in and he was in a pretty sorry state when he came out. Vernon tried to arrange for James' release at the wish of Dr Hesse, but Dr Hesse was not powerful enough.*
>
> *'I now had a further interview with Dr Hesse, to my surprise he had no definite plans for me and just put me into an office in 60 Saarlandstrasse. Later, I learned that Joyce who was at the time very close with Dr Hetzler had arranged to fix me out of the way in the Reichsportfeld.'*

Griffiths was William Humphrey Griffiths, an ex-Welsh Guardsman. After the war he received seven years penal servitude for assisting and collaborating with the Nazis. James is believed to have been Charles Patrick Gilbert, known within the unit as Kenneth James. He had been a Channel Islander in 1940 and sent to Berlin, he received nine months imprisonment after the war.

The comment about William Joyce wanting to fix Freeman out of the way in the Reichsportfeld, appears to be yet another contortion of the facts. When Joyce was detained post-war, it appears he was never questioned about the British POW collaborators, or if he was, the files have never been released. Assuming he was not questioned about these individuals, it is possible a great deal of evidence was missed by the investigators, especially in relation to Benson Freeman.

Freeman carried on naming names at the radio stations....

> *'60 Saarslandstrasse was a very depressing building and in a very depressing district. I also met Professor Haferkorn and the little editor of the Camp, that was also a depressing factor. Here, I also met the infamous Baillie-Stewart. The latter had all the outward characteristics of an English officer and gentleman, but was about the weakest moral specimen I ever met. I haven't the slightest doubt, he is busy trying to pin everything on everybody else. Nevertheless, I think he did work as far as he was able to make propaganda that would promote peace between England and Germany. He hated William Joyce and vice versa, chiefly because the latter had pushed him out. He was an expert at making money out of the Reich and his downfall was girls. He spent the greatest part of the day trying to get me to commit myself. He took my phoney name – Royston – as an ideal name for a band, he tried to drag me around with him all over the place. He arranged with a cheap French Count called Moudui, to visit the Aldon. I had actually met Leutnant Eberhardt and went with him. Here I was introduced to a man who said, "Haven't I met you before?" I said, "No." Later, Leutnant Eberhardt said, "Don't you know who that man was, he was the International Red Cross man you met at the camp."'*

Benson Freeman recalled that Baillie-Stewart introduced him to a man called Hanson. This man persuaded Freeman to write a non-political play. Later, Freeman found that this man's work appeared in the Anzac tattoo. Freeman claimed that Hanson and Baillie-Stewart ran the entire show with one object, to milk as much money out of the Propaganda Ministry as possible. Freeman claimed to stay away from both men, but explained that he was supposed to co-operate with Baillie-Stewart on a programme at the Rundfunk.

> *'Stewart was the broadcaster and trouble started immediately. I had my anti-Soviet stuff cut out and finally the mass murder of*

Katyn took place. The way the German broadcast put this over, one could imagine the Germans had shot the Poles themselves. I collected the American broadcast from Telephonic which proved conclusively that the Soviets had made mass murder.'

Freeman claimed he had tried to prove this and stop the broadcasts, but he was ignored and told he was not going to come up to the Rundfunk and dictate. He claimed he had disagreements with Dr Hesse and eventually, he spent the summer in a canoe on the Wansee Lakes.

Freeman said he knew it was only a matter of time before the Soviet hordes swept across Western Europe. He argued so vociferously, that he was accused of having an obsession with the Soviets. Despite these alleged arguments, Freeman maintained that he stayed in Berlin and was not returned to a POW camp.

Eventually, in April 1944, Dr Hesse directed him to go to a place called Krumhubel near Huschberg. There was nothing to do there and the only radio transmitter was not to be used for English broadcasts. When asked by Freeman why he had been sent there, Dr Hesse said it was due to the allied bombing raids, but the worst of the bombing, according to Freeman, was over at that time.

Benson Freeman recalled meeting a man called Vernon, who was a confidant of Dr Hesse. He suggested to Freeman that they were being kept for a peace settlement with England and to give advice, but the British airman dismissed this idea…

'After the Hitler bomb affair (in July 1944), Dr Hesse appeared at Krumhubel. He had only appeared once before for about forty-eight hours and had spoken hardly a word to me. This time, he spent about a week, and spent the entire time talking with Mrs Hesse looking extremely worried (like a man who expects to be arrested). I spoke with Herr Siegfeld of the Auswartiges Amt. *He asked me to help him with some new anti-terror bombing leaflets. He had done some written ones. I suggested that the Blockbuster bomb and the V1 were shown up as two vile weapons of scientific destruction, which were destroying the only two races in Europe and paving a communistic chaos for the advance of the Soviet hordes. Seigfeld agreed with this theme, but later told me that Dr Hesse and some bally committee did not, and they did not*

> *wish the V1 to be bracketed with the Blockbuster. This was so ridiculous, that it made sincere denouncement of the whole business impossible.*
>
> *'I told Seigfeld that I had no time to waste, it was too late and I was going to join the Waffen SS, which was about the only sincere fighters against the Soviet menace. He said he was very sorry not to have my help, but he understood my viewpoint.'*

At this stage of his own statement, Freeman in trying to prove himself to be a man who was not a traitor and a collaborator, was now providing evidence that rather than being a prisoner who could be dispensed with and returned to a camp; was in fact an integral part of the Nazi propaganda system who wanted to join the Waffen SS…

> *'For quite a long time, I had known a number of officers and men of the Waffen SS. To those who don't know the Waffen SS and only know it from the intense Jewish pro-Soviet propaganda, it will be hopeless to waste time in explaining. The plain fact is that there are two SSs, the SS SD which works with the Gestapo and the Waffen SS. The former is loathed and detested by the latter and in every way, they are opposite as the poles and neither has power over the other. The Waffen SS is purely a fighting force pledged to fight the Soviet hordes in any and every way possible. It has long ceased to be a German force and is a European force in the desperate struggle to save Western Europe against Bolshevik destruction. There is no such thing as a foreigner in the Waffen SS. I had personally known Standartenführer (Gunter) D'Aelquin and Sturmbannführer (Anton) Kriegebaum for some time. The Waffen SS is the most pro-British of all the elements in Germany. I joined the Waffen SS of my own free will (I think in September 1944). I told Sturmbannführer Kriegebaum that whereas I felt convinced that Germany had collapsed in the struggle against the Soviet menace nearly three years ago, I was afraid that nothing would prevent a total Soviet victory over Europe. He also was of this opinion.*
>
> *'In the Waffen SS, the freest of discussions took place, including the open criticism of certain leaders and their actions.'*

Benson Freeman's comments about the Waffen SS must have shocked the investigation team. Here was a man, holding a commission in the RAF, who had been trying to prove that he was a patriot and only anti-Soviet. Now he was singing the praises of one of Nazi Germany's foremost combat forces – and one that was suspected of a number of war crimes.

Freeman stated that Dr Hesse had tried to stop him joining the Waffen SS and wanted him to go to a prison camp in Leeberg to obtain material for broadcasts and propaganda. Freeman was to obtain information about the political feelings in England. Freeman claimed to have been rude to Dr Hesse and refused to go. He then rambled on about the fact the propaganda machine was engaged with in-fighting and not dealing with the Soviet menace. Finally, Freeman stated he believed the *Auswartiges Amt* was actually trying to link up with the Soviets in preference to England…

> *'Finally, in 1944, when the Soviet's power to strike was critical and I was daily pointing this out, I was all but forcibly removed by Hesse to this Krumhubel isolation spot. The same affair took place with John Amery and he delayed going to Krumhubel, had several rows with Dr Hesse and finally a violent split occurred and Amery refused to go and I believe went to live near Wansee. Amery tried to raise the Frei Korps* (author: British Free Corps of the SS). *Hesse and the* Auswartiges Amt *were in violent opposition from the start, actually at least 5,000 British soldiers would have fought the Soviets under fair and honest conditions and probably five times that number.*
>
> *'Amery got that through by sheer persistence, but the* Auswartiges Amt, *co-operating with the Wehrmacht, most successfully sabotaged his idea and reduced it to a farce, thirty to fifty stool-pigeons and poor types, that formed a nucleus that prevented any decent soldier from associating with them. Actually, about 130 fine types of soldiers who had come out to fight the Soviets, demanded to return to camp the moment they saw this outfit and its members. Also, they made the conditions as unattractive to new recruits as they possibly could.*
>
> *'Having been kept on ice by Hesse, and the Soviet situation being so terribly critical, and my general suspicion of the* Auswartiges Amt, *I was determined to do what I could and join the Waffen SS. I had known many of the officers and men for a long time. However, Dr Hesse and the* Auswartiges Amt *made*

> *the most violent opposition and from Herr Leeberg, I received threats. Actually, the Reich Foreign Ministry got a letter to stop me. However, I joined the Waffen SS, I only wish I had joined before. They were extremely broad-minded, resolutely pro-English and desperately anxious to do anything possible to stop the Soviet conquest of Europe. The comradeship was terrific, the relationship between officer and man the most democratic I have known yet, the discipline was solid as a rock and lastly, the Waffen SS DO NOT commit atrocities. That is a foul lie.'*

The investigators must have been dumbfounded listening to Freeman. Here was a commissioned officer, not only joining the Waffen SS, but extolling the alleged virtues of the organisation.

Freeman explained that by the time he joined the Waffen SS, there was little that could be done to prevent the onslaught. He did however write a book on the Soviet menace, but it was never published due to the '*chaotic conditions in Feb-March 1945'*. Freeman said he had seen evidence of Soviet atrocities in Hungary in 1945. He continued in his statement…

> *'Plans were made to raise an honest and straightforward British SS regiment for fighting the Soviets. A complete free hand was given and I got the Free Corps to be disbanded. However, events were moving faster and in a consultation with Standartenführer D'Aelquin and Kreigebaum, we decided that it was too late now to be of any value and would only involve the patriots who came out. It was surprising that many applications from Army prisoners of war came for requests to fight the Soviets, but all that was too late to be of any practical use now.*
>
> *'Until the last moment, they cherished the hope that England and America would break with the Soviets and at least allow Germany to fight with them, even if under them in order to save Europe. With this hope in mind, plans were laid to go to the south and prepare everything to negotiate this last minute co-operation, and three Feisler Storch aeroplanes were taken over from the Luftwaffe in order to be able to communicate with British Headquarters in an emergency.*
>
> *'I flew one of those machines from an aerodrome by Potsdam on a Sunday, about a week or ten days before the Soviets had*

the place fixed. We had a lot of difficulty in avoiding low-flying fighters, but we got to Pilsen and then Pocking.

'We flew to Lengrien and landed up the valley in the woods at about 4:30pm. I should say it was about May 3rd, but the Americans were at Bad Toltz by then. Next day was bad weather. Hauptsturmführer D'Aelquin came out on a motorcycle and said Kreigebaum wanted to see me at Hendereis. I went there, Kreigebaum was not there. We waited. We went to look for Kreigebaum. We found his car with some SS men. He had overturned it and was killed. He was a reckless driver in an emergency and the roads were awful.

'Next, I saw Hauptsturmführer Akkermann. I learnt that there was an idea to fly an Obergruppenführer to the American lines to offer the full co-operation of the SS in trying to hold Germany together if they would give any indication of their attitude with regards Soviet Russia. The weather was hopeless with heavy snow. Chaos now reigned everywhere. We had a consultation. I was asked if I wished to hide in a mountain stronghold with them. I know where this place is, but that I will keep (secret). I was asked if I wished to go to Switzerland in a German Red Cross unit with a passport and everything. I thanked them, but I preferred not to.

'Hauptsturmführer Wicklemeyer told me peace was made. We waited for the Americans, but they did not come. They persuaded me to put on civil clothes as they said there are people in England who know the Soviet danger and if you are fool enough to surrender in SS uniform, you only complicate matters. Wicklemeyer wished to return to his wife in Landshut, so I persuaded him to come with me and see how things panned out. We were given a lift to a Nolkshaffen. Nobody took any notice, but at one point the car was taken and the four officers interned.

'I told the American I was a British officer, shot down since May 1940. I was very well treated and that was that. Before I left, I collected a magnificent pistol as a souvenir from one of the numerous dumps.'

Freeman concluded his statement by repeating again that the Waffen SS had treated him well. They had tremendous discipline and they had scattered.

They had no desire he said, to fight the western powers, but some would fight if cornered.

He continued his diatribe that the Soviets were a menace and a danger to Britain and Europe, offering to fly to two locations with a British or American officer to provide terms for co-operation between the Allies and the Waffen SS. He final comment was…

> *'I urge and plead that some notice is taken of this chance to at least consult with the leaders of the Waffen SS on this problem, that overshadows Europe.'*

Freeman noted that his treatment at the hands of his interrogators – Davies and Edwards – had been exceptionally fair and straightforward, before he signed the statement.

The fifteen pages of typed statement were astounding. A commissioned RAF officer had gone from being a fascist member of the BUF, to collaborating in Dulag Luft and the German Foreign Office. Finally, he joined the Waffen SS, singing their praises and proudly proclaiming that they did not commit atrocities and were the last bastion against the Communist hordes. With the likes of William Joyce and John Amery likely to be hanged for their treachery, surely Benson Freeman could expect the same punishment?

On 25 May 1945, a report was sent from MI5 to MI5 Liaison Section at SHAEF.

The report repeated the elements from the evidence in Freeman's own statement and that obtained from MI5/RAF SIB enquiries since 1940. The report stated:

> *'Freeman's early days of captivity in Dulag Luft are of lesser importance in the case, but nevertheless, an account of his actions during this period should prove of considerable value, so as to indicate his frame of mind at that time when he was friendly with and suspected of giving information about escapes to the following German officers at the camp: Major Rumpel and Leutnant Eberhardt'.*

Efforts continued to gather evidence and it was noted that this case took a very high place among service renegade cases.

We shall return to the case of Pilot Officer Benson Freeman in due course, but there were other collaborators…

Chapter 5

Flight Sergeant Raymond Davies HUGHES No. 1697212

Pilot Officer Benson Freeman was a devout fascist who sought to support the Nazi war machine and its propaganda. In this respect Freeman was unusual, but there were other RAF aircrew who decided to collaborate, apparently in a bid to improve their own lot while in captivity; and one of those men was Flight Sergeant Raymond Davies Hughes.

Raymond Hughes, Service Number 1697212, came from North Wales. He was linked to the Wavertree district of Liverpool and still had family in the heavily bombed city during the war.

Hughes volunteered for aircrew duties and was selected as an air gunner. By August 1943, he was serving with 467 Squadron on Lancaster bombers, based at Bottesford. On the night of 17-18 August 1943, Hughes and his crew took part in a major raid on the rocket development facility at Peenemunde on the Baltic coast, when he was shot down.

After parachuting to earth, Hughes was soon captured and sent to Dulag Luft where he stayed for some time.

Messages soon started to filter back to Britain that there was a Sergeant at Dulag Luft who was collaborating with the Germans. Full details were hard to obtain, and various efforts were made to positively identify this man. Initially, the RAF and MI9 thought Sergeant Hughes was a member of the Royal Artillery and enquiries were made without success in November 1943.

Further information arrived at MI9 after a Flight Lieutenant Buchanan was repatriated from Stalag Luft III in October 1943. (The exact identity of this man is still unclear.) Buchanan told MI9 that, '*Sgt Hughes was said to be in German uniform and has interrogated prisoners of war. Known to have flown from Frankfurt at various times*.'

In late November 1943, MI9 discovered that Hughes's initials were believed to be R.D. and his service number, which they believed could be corrupted, was 1697212. They also deduced that he was 'employed' in a Dulag and was probably a member of the Royal Air Force. In fact, they now had their man and the service number was correct, but it would be some months before he was positively identified.

Efforts continued to positively identify R.D. Hughes, but other intelligence now identified a Sergeant air gunner Baker as being similarly involved in betraying his colleagues. In May 1944, a search of personnel files had failed to identify Baker without any first names or initials (this is surprising considering the information from November the previous year).

On 17 August 1944, (see reference: KV2/262 enclosure 41a in the UK National Archives) Squadron Leader Shortland-Jones wrote that it was alleged that a Sergeant air gunner named Baker had turned traitor in the same way as Freeman and was indulging in propaganda activities and furnishing information to the Germans. However, he added they still did not know his identity and even identified a Sergeant Baker from 115 Squadron as a suspect who '*fitted the bill*'.

It appears the first positive identification of Hughes as the traitor was in October 1944. As the Allies advanced across France and captured Paris, the Free French Forces detained a fellow collaborator and fascist named Gerald Percy Sandys Hewitt.

In a statement dated 26 October 1944 (enclosure 48 of National Archives file KV2/262), he stated that Baker was a man:

> '*In his early twenties. I met him at Saarlander Strasse office. He said over a glass of beer at a café, that he came from Wales (I think), that he was an aviator and had come down by parachute over Berlin in August 1943. He had joined the Germans because he hated the Jews. He said his real name was Raymond Hughes, but they called him John Baker for radio purposes. He said he had given the Germans all the plans of the English aerodromes that he knew. I said he had done an extremely wrong and stupid thing. I avoided him completely after this. He also said he had told the Germans all he knew about factories, ammunition dumps and the like. He said, he had been the manager of a shoe shop in London before being in the Air Force.*
>
> '*He was boastful. He said that with him at his hotel – the name of which I forget – was a RAF officer or NCO who was*

> *being approached to join the Germans. But Baker thought he would refuse and would be sent back to camp.*
>
> *'I think he broadcasts on air matters or writes scripts on these. He is not very literate and has to be helped.'*

The British intelligence services now had their man and they confirmed, by checked letters intercepted by censors, that he had been at Dulag Luft from the summer of 1943 to the end of November 1943, when he appeared to have been transferred to Stalag IIID. This was described as a known holiday camp near Berlin to which the Germans sent possible recruits for their propaganda services. They also knew that Baker (Hughes) had been interviewed by Freeman and a returning prisoner of war had now identified Hughes from a photographic album.

As the Allied forces continued their advance, they recovered German files which included information about John Baker. (Reference: National Archives file KV2/262 enclosure 47b.) One document found at the DES Radio Station in Luxemburg noted that a John Baker, an employee of the Foreign Office in Berlin, had complained that he had received an engagement sheet for 60 Reichsmarks, for a record, on 17 January 1944. (Records were recorded for later broadcasts), but he had not received the payment.

Further evidence followed to indicate that Hughes, alias Baker, was involved in recent propaganda broadcasts. A review of broadcasts found that on 10 November 1944, at 20:30 hours, a programme called 'Forces Hour' was broadcast in English with a man calling himself Captain Baker. In a 9-minute-long speech, Baker highlighted the importance of the German forces stand in the Moerdijk area between Rotterdam and Breda. He also stated that the Allies were not using airborne troops due to the battles at Arnhem being too hard a lesson for them. It also quoted the recent bombardment of Antwerp by V1 and V2 missiles. Scribbled in pencil on the report (see ref. KV2/262 enclosure 47a in the UK National Archives) is the comment *'?Hughes?'*

Later in the month, MI5 and MI9 were informed of another captured German document in the name of John Charles Baker from Berlin.

The translated document contained a letter, dated 20 March 1944, from Baker to a Dr George Hans Schulze in Rome. Schulze worked for German Propaganda services and the stationery was that of the Ministry of Foreign Affairs. Schulze was identified as being a foreign language war reporter for broadcasts to Allied troops.

The letter was clearly written to a friend and was signed off, '*Your very sincere friend, Ray.*'

Clearly John Baker was Raymond Hughes.

On 26 January 1945, a Major Kimpton at Box No. 55 in Colwyn Bay (MI5) was contacted by letter and advised that a renegade prisoner of war in Germany – Sergeant Raymond Davies Hughes, RAF – was employed by the German Foreign Office and broadcasting on the German Propaganda station in Berlin, under the name of John Baker. He was also suspected of providing the Germans with information about aerodromes, factories, and ammunition dumps. He is said to have done this because of his hatred of the Jews.

The report stated that his mother lived in Mold, North Wales and Hughes had been reported as missing on operations over Germany on the night of 17-18 August 1943.

The enquiry asked if Major Kimpton could ascertain if anything was known locally about Hughes and his family and whether he had ever come to the notice of the police regarding any connection to the British Union of Fascists.

On 5 February 1945, Detective Sergeant Roberts of Mold Police replied after making enquiries: (reference national Archives file KV2/262 enclosure 64a):

> *'I have to report that I have made discreet enquiries and am informed that Raymond Davies Hughes was born in Nerquis, near Mold, on the 11.8.1923, his mother was then a single woman, his father being Edward Roberts, an insurance agent now residing in Denbigh. Soon after the birth of the boy the mother married John Hughes a bricklayer.*
>
> *'During the period that he attended Mold Alun County School, he is described as being very unsatisfactory. He is a talker and will make an impression upon anyone with whom he came in contact. He would always exaggerate things and is very unstable. He was termed a problematical child and considered to be 'slightly mental'. He is cunning and when he was 11 years of age, he appeared before the court at Mold, charged with obtaining the sum of 2/6d by false pretences.*
>
> *'He is the type of fellow who will side with anyone, and it is said that if he landed in Russia he would have sided with them.*
>
> *'During a period that this youth was home on leave from the Royal Air Force, he told my informant that he had been on the shuttle service to Russia and had been in the big air raids on the Skoda Works and the Emsden Dam. He was on these occasions very talkative and boastful. In his letters home from Germany, he has said that the Germans are alright and*

> *he could not understand why we are fighting them; he also claimed to be studying medicine.*
>
> *'He has not, during his residence in Mold, come to my notice in connection with subversive activity and it is not known that he had any connection with the BUF'.*

The comments of the police informant and those from Gerald Hewitt concerning Hughes being boastful, appear to corroborate one another. It was clear that the Intelligence Services were dealing with an odd character, who was open to treachery, deceit and boastful. In short, he could not be trusted.

As the war drew to a close, the Intelligence Services were pulling all their information together, ready for the expected arrest of Hughes.

On 26 February 1945, the Deputy RAF Permit Officer for the Provost Marshal, Royal Air Force, advised in a report that No. 1697212 Sergeant Hughes, Raymond Davies, was an air gunner in the mid-upper turret and was reported missing from an operation to Peenemunde, on17-18 August 1943. The Lancaster bomber was captained by Pilot Officer Dixon. Whether Hughes had taken part in sorties to Hamburg or attended the Pathfinder Force course had yet to be confirmed.

The authorities checked and rechecked their files, identifying snippets of information that had clearly been missed in the vast deluge of information over the past few years.

One report (see archives file KV2/262, enclosure 25a) was dated 23 October 1943 and had been sent to MI9 on 2 February 1944, it read:

> *'In Dulag Luft, a F/O Tully was interrogated on 9 October by Hughes and Trickes. The former asked questions about squadrons and crews and stated that he, himself, was on a Lancaster captained by P/O Dixon, on a raid to Peenemunde. He stated that he was working his way into the Germans' confidence, with a 99 per cent chance of making a successful escape.*
>
> *'A Lt. Colonel Dene talked to Trickes, Hughes and F/Sgt Alcock and advised them to withdraw their paroles.*
>
> *'Note by MI9: Lt. Colonel Dene is probably Lt. Col. John Anthony Dene DCLI, Personal No. 50934, P/W No. 2908, Stalag Luft 3, captured on 20.9.43.'*

At the end of the war, numerous prisoners of war were repatriated and gave statements concerning their treatment and knowledge of any known collaborators. One of those men was Canadian Flying Officer Ralph Wilbert Tully DFC, the man who had managed to get a coded message back in 1943, about his interrogation by Hughes and Trickes. His statement was one of the best insights of the Dulag Luft system and the activities of Hughes:

> *'In September 1943, I was a navigator on 35 Squadron, stationed at Graveley. On 27 September 1943, I was detailed with my crew to take part in a raid on Hanover. After leaving the target, we were shot down by a German night fighter. I bailed out and was captured about dawn on the 28 September by the local German Home Guard.*
>
> *On 1 October, I arrived at Dulag Luft where I was placed in a cell on my own. Either that day or the next day, a German official came into my cell and asked me to fill in a long form with a Red Cross on the top of it. I gave him my rank, name and number and refused to fill in the remaining questions concerning my squadron, aircraft, etc.*
>
> *'One or two days after this, I was taken out of my cell to an office in the Interrogation Centre, where I was again questioned by a German wearing civilian clothes whose name I believe to be Bauer.* (Author's note – this was clearly Lt. Gustav Bauer-Schlichtegroll.) *He asked a number of questions regarding my squadron etc., but the only thing I told him was the address of my next of kin. As I refused to answer his questions, I was returned to my cell.*
>
> *'During this time I was not allowed to wash. I complained to the guard about this. He said he would fetch somebody. He later brought an American dressed in civilian clothes, who told me he had been shot down on the Ploesti raid.* (Author's note – S/Sgt Trickes, often spelt Trix, was possibly S/Sgt Angelo Triches of 334 BS, 95th Bomber Group. He was posted missing on 13 June 1943 and his body never recovered. So, if this was the American POW, he either disappeared before the end of the war or the Luftwaffe had placed an agent in Dulag Luft using the missing and presumably dead man's identity.
>
> *'The American took me to an office in the Interrogation Centre, where I met another man in plain clothes, who told me his name was Hughes and that he represented the Red Cross. He told me he was on a Lancaster squadron before the war.*

(Author – this could not be true as the Lancaster was not in service before the war and Tully probably knew this.)

'He then asked me questions regarding my squadron, station, group etc., which I refused to answer. He then got up and left the room and when he came back, he told me that I was from 8 Group. He again asked me my squadron, which I refused to answer and he told me I was from 35 Squadron and that the squadron letters were TL. After this he told me he had been shot down in the Peenemunde raid and that he was trying to get confidential German documents. I was then allowed to go and have a wash and a shave and then go back to my cell.

'The next day, I was taken up to the first office I had been in where I saw the German Bauer again. He told me that they knew everything about me and asked me about the 'concrete mixer' and H2S, which I refused to answer.

'He then asked me what training I had done and where I had been in England. He told me that unless I answered these questions, I would be kept in the cells. I refused to give him any information and I was taken back to the cells. That evening, I was taken down to the Transit Camp where I remained for a short time and then I was taken with others to Stalag Luft III at Sagan.

'I was eventually released by the Russians on 22 April 1945 at Luchenwalde.'

We shall now look at the statements obtained from other returning prisoners of war, as well as the Dulag Luft Luftwaffe personnel captured at the end of the war.

The evidence of RAF airmen and Luftwaffe prisoners, as well as some later British Free Corps members, was damning for Raymond Davies Hughes. It was clear that he was every bit as much a traitor as Pilot Officer Benson Freeman.

It was now only a matter of time before Hughes was located and arrested.

Chapter 6

Witness Evidence Against Hughes

An extract from an MI9 report dated 5 May 1945, (reference KV2/262 enclosure 69a) states that Hauptman Hans Vollman had first interrogated Sergeant Hughes, who was shot down during the first big raid on Peenemunde in the autumn of 1943. Vollman claimed that Hughes, upon interrogation, had immediately begun to request a position with German Intelligence.

Vollman went away on leave to get married and when he returned to Dulag Luft Hughes was in civilian clothes and working at Oberursel.

Vollman claimed that Hughes's role was to go to the cells and attempt to get the newly arrived prisoners to fill out forms with information on them. He claimed that Hughes had great success and pretended to be a Luftwaffe fighter ace with nineteen victories.

Another German officer, Leutnant Gustav Bauer-Schlichtegroll, when interviewed, said he knew Hughes well and confirmed the information of Vollman.

Hans Vollman added that Leutnant Koch was the man who actually arranged for Hughes to become an SP (Special Prisoner). Both Vollman and Bauer-Schlichtegroll believed that Hughes later went to Berlin and worked in the Propaganda Ministry.

On 4 June 1945, a statement was taken from Flight Lieutenant David William Thomas, Service Number 45050. He was a ground trade officer who had been captured in the Western Desert in February 1942. He would later be considered a possible collaborator and shall be considered in a later chapter, but he gave a statement about his time at Dulag Luft.

Thomas claimed to have arrived at Dulag Luft about 1 March 1942. He stated:

> *'One day a Fiesler Storch aircraft landed in a field about 800 yards away. I saw an air force Sergeant (Hughes) pass by the Camp wire about 20 yards away from it and enter the aircraft on his own, and the pilot then took off.*

'Two or three days later, a Sergeant Hughes came to the Clothing Store which was outside the Camp's barbed wire fence. When I and other men from the camp went to the clothing store, we were always under guard. Hughes came down to the store with someone, I am not sure who. He was wearing RAF battledress and he asked for a pair of boots. I issued him with the boots and asked him what he was doing. He blushed and looked extremely uncomfortable and said that he could not tell me. I later saw him passing by the camp with females.

'I later had complaints made to me by several officers, including an Australian Pilot Officer F.J. Smith, that Hughes was interrogating prisoners and asking them to fill in the false Red Cross forms.'

As Pilot Officer 'Jeff' Smith belonged to 467 Squadron, Hughes's own unit, he knew the Welshman well and there was no doubt about his identity.

On 19 June 1945, a full detailed statement was taken from Hauptmann Hans Vollman (National Archives file reference KV2/262, enclosure 77b):

'I was employed as an interpreter of prisoners of war at Dulag Luft from November 1942 until April 1945, then I was taken prisoner near Nurenburg by the Americans.

'I remember Sergeant Hughes of the RAF. I interrogated him when he first came to Dulag Luft. He had been seen by Hauptmann von Thaiental regarding his particulars, which had been entered on a form. I am not sure whether it had a red cross on it. We used Red Cross forms for a time, but later they were changed. Hughes had given all the particulars required on the form and I was told by Hauptmann von Thaiental that Hughes was a very free talker.

'I later interrogated Hughes when he told me that he had been shot down on a raid on Peenemunde. He told me the number of his squadron and his group, and he gave me particulars of the tactics of the raid. I cannot now remember the exact words he used, but he answered all questions and gave me all the information I required of him. I saw Hughes on three or four occasions during which he told me he would like to work for the German Intelligence Service and I reported the matter to the Commandant, Oberst Leutnant Killinger.

The Commandant did not direct that he be used as such, as such matters were left for us to decide after reporting it to him.

'About that time I was going away on three weeks leave to be married and Hughes was taken over by Oberst Leutnant Koch who had by this time already interrogated him.

'When I returned from my leave, I found Hughes working there in the Reception Office. He used to go into the Reception Office, but he got his orders from Oberst Leutnant Koch. The person in charge of the Reception Office was Hauptmann Schneidewind. He had a number of assistants, mostly German NCOs. The only British prisoner I know who worked for this office was Sergeant Hughes. He carried on with getting forms filled in for several weeks and was very successful. It was only the front of the form that had printed questions, such as required from the prisoner and on the back of the form, the Receptionist would enter the answers of any other questions he had thought fit to put and his observations respecting the prisoner. This was always of assistance to the Interrogator, as it gave them an idea of the kind of person to be interrogated.

'When I returned from my leave after my marriage, I met Hughes who thanked me for getting him the soft job, he was dressed in civilian clothes and dark sunglasses.

'Sometime later, I interrogated three prisoners of the same crew and found that answers had been given to all the questions and that the back of the form had been filled-up, practically completing the whole of the interrogation; I asked this crew who had interrogated them. They replied, "Your Luftwaffe fighter pilot who says he has shot down nineteen aircraft." This was Hughes.

'Hughes had privileges. For when I first interviewed him and realised he was likely to be useful, I arranged for him to be removed from the ordinary cells and placed in the larger and better cells in the Stone House. He also had freedom about the Interrogation Centre and it is possible that he was allowed out of the Camp to go to Frankfurt. I am not aware of this as this would be arranged by Koch.

'After some weeks, Hughes was sent away to a special camp, this was because he had become suspected, as about that time Winant – the son of the American Ambassador (to the

UK), had been taken prisoner and on first interrogation, he was fairly free in his talk; but he was seen by Hughes one afternoon and on the following morning, he was different and did not talk so freely.

'I was informed of all this by Oberst Leutnant Koch and that it was the reason why Hughes was sent away. I was later told that Hughes was in Berlin working in one of the official offices.

'When I was interrogated by Captain Todd US Army, he showed me a report which had been found in Paris, which was written in English (typed) and I decided that it had been prepared by Hughes, as it referred to tactics of the British Air Force and was the same sort of story that he told me.'

(Author's note: John Winant jr. was a 1st Lieutenant and a B-17 pilot. His father was the US Ambassador to the UK when he was posted missing on a raid to Munster, in October 1943. He was captured and taken to Dulag Luft and later on to Colditz. As a notable prisoner, he was one of those selected by SS Reichsführer Himmler as a possible bargaining chip towards the end of the war.)

Leutnant Heinrich Eberhardt also gave a statement after interrogation. In relation to Hughes he stated:

'I remember Sergeant Hughes RAF. I did not interrogate him or handle him at Dulag Luft. I don't know who did. Hughes was very prominent in the Interrogation Centre. He wore plain clothes – a blue suit. I know he was used for the purpose of getting prisoners of war to fill in forms of their particulars. Forms with a Red Cross on them had been formerly used, but by the time I knew Hughes, the Red Cross markings were not on the forms as it was known that these were being used.

'Hughes appeared to be always very busy and eventually I was told by Leutnant (Otto) Boninghaus that he was taken to Berlin. I have not seen him since.

'I have seen Hughes in the office where the forms were dealt with, the office was under the control of Hauptmann Schneidwind who had a number of German NCOs assisting him. Hughes was the only British NCO I knew of who worked in that office. He usually wore a pair of dark sunglasses.'

On 23 June 1945, Major Caroe, an Intelligence Officer, sent a report stating that he had visited and interviewed various members of staff of Inter-radio, the German propaganda station. From talking to the staff, he identified that the collaborator called Baker was identical with Raymond Hughes. He had worked with the radio station from May to July 1944, when he was suddenly sent away.

Dr Kramer, the head of broadcasting, said Hughes had been sent to him by Dr Haferkorn of the *Auswaertiges Amt*. While with Inter-radio, Hughes lived with a German pilot officer, whom he had allegedly known before the war, this was in a suburb of Fronau in Berlin. Both Dr Kramer and Herr Sperling of the Personal Administration Section were also interrogated and both men identified Hughes from a photograph as being Baker.

Another member of the Dulag Luft Luftwaffe staff gave a statement on 28 June 1945. This was Leutnant Gustav Bauer Schlihtegroll. In his statement, part of which can be found in the National Archives file KV2/262 enclosure 77c, he stated:

> *'I knew Sergeant Hughes RAF, at the Dulag Luft Interrogation Centre. He was handled by Oberst Leutnant Koch and did very much the same work as Alcock, he was much more successful, performed the work more skilfully and over a longer period.* (See later chapter about Alcock.) *Mostly, he took the forms and did his interrogation in the cells, but there was an office there that he sometimes used. He was clever at his work.*
>
> *'I do not remember seeing him in the Administration Offices of the centre where records were kept, but it's a fact that some girls and women were employed there. If he went there, it would be by arrangement with Koch. I heard he eventually went to Berlin.'*

On 11 June 1945, Pilot Officer Francis Dixon the captain of Hughes's Lancaster gave a statement to the RAF Special Investigation Branch investigators.

He described being the captain of the Lancaster and being shot down on the night of 17-18 August 1943, while flying off Stralsund, along the coast from Peenemunde. Two of his crew, Sergeants Lowe and Hayward were killed, but the other crewmen, including Sergeant Hughes, bailed out successfully.

Dixon later learned that Hughes and Sergeants Dickson and Garnett had landed on an island, found a boat and rowed to the mainland before being detained. Sergeant Bicknell landed in a different position.

After he was detained, Pilot Officer Dixon was taken to Dulag Luft and interrogated. He gave only his name, rank and date of birth. After about thirty-six hours, he was sent on to a nearby transit camp. In the transit camp he found the other three surviving members of his crew, but not Hughes. The next time he saw Hughes was on 5 February 1945, when he arrived at Luckenwalde and Stalag IIIA. Hughes arrived the same day, apparently from the camp at Sagan. He continued in his statement:

> *'I had heard about Hughes while he was at Dulag Luft from Pilot Officer Smith, an Australian who I met at Sagan and who was formerly in my squadron. Smith told me he was interrogated by Hughes at Dulag.*
>
> *'After I met Hughes at Stalag IIIA, he told me a long story of his experiences while he had been a prisoner. I cannot clearly recollect now exactly what he told me, but he mentioned he had been to Berlin, that he had been asked to broadcast, which was a failure, because he put on a show of nervousness; that he had been engaged in some propaganda building. He mentioned that he had been to a do with the British Free Corps, that he had been to a broadcasting station south of Berlin, where he had prepared a feature broadcast of a religious nature, which was cancelled before he was able to make it. He said, that in the broadcast, which was to be in Welsh, he had hoped to put in some short messages to his home.*
>
> *'Sergeant Hughes had been one of my crew for five and a half months and we had done twenty operations together, being shot down on the twenty-first. He was a very keen airman, but always very talkative and inclined to be individualistic; he was very willing but drifted a bit in the team spirit. He was the opposite to the person generally of this nature, because instead of lagging, he would get his job done on the aircraft, such as daily inspection on his guns; and then clear off to the section to find out what he could do there. He was very enthusiastic in that direction and at the time we were shot down, was being considered for a commission in connection with which I personally recommended him. He was always very good in the air, had plenty of courage and on two occasions volunteered to make up the crew of another aircraft who were short of an air gunner.'*

Pilot Officer Dixon clearly thought highly of his gunner, what he thought about Pilot Officer Jeff Smith's comments and the fact Hughes admitted working in Berlin is not recorded.

There was now a steady stream of repatriated airmen only too willing to give a statement against Hughes, some of them coming from his own squadron.

Flight Sergeant Ronald Gordon Wellington RAAF was also a member of the same unit – 467 Squadron at RAF Bottesford in 1943.

On 4 October 1943, the air gunner had been on a raid to Kassel, when his Lancaster was hit by flak and brought down. Ron Wellington was injured and unconscious, but the aircraft ditched in the Scheldt Estuary and his crew managed to get him into a dinghy. After eight hours adrift in their dinghy, the crew were captured. In his statement, Wellington said:

> *'I was eventually taken to Dulag Luft, arriving there about 8 October. I was placed in solitary confinement for seven days before anyone came to see me. Then a man in civilian clothes, consisting of a brown suit with a distinctive stripe in it and wearing sunglasses came into my cell. I recognised him at once as Sergeant Hughes from my own squadron, whose aircraft had been shot down in August 1943.*
>
> *'I greeted him as Hughes, and he seemed very surprised* (by Wellington using his name). *He told me that he was representing the Red Cross. He was placed there because he could speak a fair amount of German and Russian. I told him that he should be wearing his uniform if he were in an official capacity and he said the clothes had been specially supplied by the Germans.*
>
> *'He asked me to fill in a Red Cross form which I saw to be false, as it asked for details of my squadron. I filled in my rank, name and number and the names of four members of the crew who were dead. He then asked me to fill in the squadron lettering and squadron number. He asked me the target, but I refused the rest of the information. When Hughes came into my cell, he took me out past the guards and into an office where the interrogation took place. After I refused to give any more information, Hughes took me back to my cell.*
>
> *'I was later interrogated by a German in civilian clothing and was moved later to the transit camp and then on to Stalag IVB.'*

Flight Sergeant Wellington's account was corroborated by another member of his crew – Flight Sergeant 1551970 A.T. Proudfoot, a Scot from Glasgow. In his MI9 repatriation debriefing report (reference: KV2/263 enclosure 92A), he stated:

> *'Hughes, an RAF air gunner of the same squadron as me (467 Sqn), posed as a Red Cross representative and filled in information (which I refused to give) and passed it on to the German interrogating officer.*
>
> *'Hughes was a Flight Sergeant, but when I met him, he was wearing civilian clothes, appeared to have lots of money, a radio set and a German girlfriend who was a telephone operator at Dulag. Later, I heard reports that he was acting as a Flight Lieutenant. He asked questions about gliders etc.'*

The surviving members of Hughes's own crew also made statements, claiming that he was at Dulag Luft, but did not transfer with them on to other camps. They all subsequently heard the stories about Hughes extracting information from other prisoners while at Oberursel.

Another example of Hughes and his activities can be found on the website www.wallyswar.wordpress.com. It is repeated here with the kind permission of the website co-ordinator. The account details the capture of Flight Sergeant Walter Henry Layne, a wireless operator and air gunner from 97 Squadron. Walter, or Wally as he was known, recounts his own Lancaster being brought down on a raid to Mannheim, on 23 September 1943. He parachuted to earth and after evading capture for ten days, he was eventually detained and sent to Dulag Luft.

He was stripped of his clothing and placed in solitary confinement. Sometime later, a Reception Officer attended his cell and produced a form which he claimed was a Red Cross document. Wally gave just his name and rank and was left alone for another two days.

Wally had managed to obtain some civilian clothing before his capture and his refusal to answer questions and his attire, led to him being threatened as a suspected saboteur with the Gestapo and execution.

One day, Wally was visited in his solitary cell by a friendly young man in civilian clothing. The man claimed to have been injured flying for the Luftwaffe and he was now an employee of the Red Cross. He claimed that if Wally answered his questions, it would help facilitate the Red Cross in contacting the airman's family at home. Wally suspected this to be a ruse and did not co-operate.

Wally now knows this man to have been Sergeant Raymond Hughes.

Later, one of the Luftwaffe officers came into Wally's cell and threw a brown folder onto his mattress. It had the number '97' written on the cover. The officer opened the folder and proceeded to show Wally 97 Squadron's latest promotions list, the names of the squadron CO and his flight commanders. There were also photographs of his base at Bourn in Cambridgeshire. The officer told Wally that all he needed was his name to know everything about him and his parent unit. Eventually, the interrogation concluded, and Wally was moved to the transit camp.

It was clear that Raymond Hughes was a traitor and had deceived a good number of airmen into giving information to the enemy. The long list of witnesses included repatriated airmen and the Luftwaffe officers from Dulag Luft, but there was still the issue of what he did in Berlin.

Reinhard Hermann Haferkorn, who gave evidence against Pilot Officer Benson Freeman, told the investigators that Hughes came to Berlin, being brought to the unit by Leutnant Otto Boninghaus from Dulag Luft:

> *'Hughes was known to us in the name of John Charles Baker and was a very different type to the others mentioned.* (Author's note: i.e., Freeman, Baillie-Stewart etc.)
>
> *'In my interview with Hughes, I found him very willing to work for us. I explained what would be required for broadcasting, which was in effect to write material for broadcasting on Anti-Jewish lines, and on the basis of his own experience of Jews, as he told me he worked for them in England. He told me he had no experience of work of the kind but was prepared to try his best in this direction. He was allocated a room at my office and commenced writing material, but on inspection of this, I soon realised that he was not sufficiently educated for the kind of work and that his material was most unsuitable for broadcasting.*
>
> *'As he was unsuitable for work in my department, I passed him over to Professor Mahr, who was in contact with the Irish section of the Rundfunk, and Mahr introduced him to that section. Hughes was given a voice test, but owing to the position of his teeth, he was found unsuitable for broadcasting and then he was given some work assisting in the removal of*

furniture from bombed houses belonging to members of staff in my department.

'Sometime later, Hughes was taken in the staff of Radio Metropole, where he was possibly employed writing scripts and broadcasting.

'Whilst working in my office, it is possible that Hughes met Royston (Benson Freeman) and others and was visited there by Carter. (Author's note: Squadron Leader George Robert Carpenter known as Carter– see later chapter.)

'With regard to the salaries paid to these employees, I believe that Freeman got about 800 marks a month, and Hughes in his capacity would be paid 300-400 marks a month.'

From this statement it is clear there was a route directly from Dulag Luft to the Propaganda Ministry's radio network. The likes of Vollman, Koch and Eberhardt would identify prisoners who would work in the camp, assisting in interrogations and other matters, before being transferred to Berlin with Leutnant Otto Boninghaus. In Berlin, the likes of Dr Hetzler, Dr Hesse and Haferkorn, were only too willing to utilise this new source of propaganda.

Others who followed the path to Berlin included Squadron Leader George Robert Carpenter (alias Carter) and Flying Officer Julius Zuromski (alias Kowalski) and they shall be covered in a later chapter. Carpenter gave a statement about Raymond Hughes and this will be covered in that chapter.

The investigators now had a formidable bundle of evidence to put to Raymond Hughes. They asked for checks to be made of the BBC recordings of broadcast German propaganda programmes over the previous few years, in the search for anything that could be attributed to Hughes.

On 20 July 1945, a report from MI5 to the RAF Special Investigation Branch, (see National Archives KV2/262 enclosure 87B), stated that they had tried to trace these broadcasts. No monitoring reports were made for Radio Metropole as that station only played music and entertainment, not propaganda.

There were also no monitoring reports or recordings of any Welsh language programmes. It was possible that programmes in Welsh were occasionally broadcast from Germany, but it was not a regular feature and the BBC kept no record of them – this was because there was no one on the BBC monitoring staff who could speak Welsh!

Squadron Leader William Percy Thomas was the senior investigating officer at the RAF Special Investigation Branch (SIB) and he interviewed Hughes upon his return to the United Kingdom in the Spring of 1945.

Hughes was now based at RAF Cosford but went on leave to his family home in Mold, North Wales. Hughes knew he was under investigation, but clearly did not seem too concerned about this. On 17 June 1945 he wrote to Squadron Leader Thomas stating:

> Dear Sir,
> I consider it my duty to inform you that I am getting married on 28 June 1945, at St. Ann's Church, Worksop, Notts., to Miss Betty Yvonne Brailsford… I trust that Sergeant Kirk informed you that my leave expires on 13 July 1945 and that normally I will return to 106 PRC Cosford.
>
> Sir, have you any objection to me attempting to get in touch with Squadron Leader Boyd-Carpenter? *(Author: George Robert Carpenter.)* I would like to inform him of my wedding. If you have no objection, Sir, can you assist me in any way, as I've completely lost his address.
>
> May I take this opportunity to thank you in anticipation for your kindness and understanding at all times. I find myself often wondering if my skies are darkening or brightening, but, however, I still think I did as well as a soldier could have done under the circumstances. To be truthful, I really don't know whether I should feel proud of myself or ashamed. Still, time will tell.
>
> I must close for now, thanks very much Sir, for everything.
>
> I remain, your obedient servant,
> Raymond D. Hughes.

The letter to the senior investigating officer is astounding. Either he was completely deluded, or he thought he was safe from prosecution. This was despite the fact that he had written to his parents from Halle-Leipzig jail in Germany on 23 May 1945, after he was detained. His letter copied by the investigators and now held within his file, also indicated an air of delusion and some clear deceit:

> *My darling Mum and Pop,*
> *Gosh! It's really grand being able to write to you all once again without it having to go through the Germans. I quite imagine you've been wondering what's been happening to me during these last few months.*

Right now I'm under close arrest and have been charged with having been seen wearing a German uniform at Dulag Luft in 1943. Really Mum and Pop, this is untrue, I have never even handled a German uniform, let alone wear one. Please believe me Mum no matter what happens. For you to think that your son has been a traitor to this country, I'm sure that would finish you. Have no fear Mum, you always taught me, 'The truth always stands'...

Hughes explained to his parents that he had been shot down by anti-aircraft fire after a running fight with German fighters. He parachuted from their blazing Lancaster and landed on a small island with some burns and a sprained ankle.

He explained that he was captured with two of his crew and placed in a filthy cell in a Russian POW camp at Greifswald.

Eventually he was moved to Dulag Luft with the rest of his crew and placed in cells awaiting interrogation.

Hughes went on over the next few pages to say exactly what he would state in his statement to Squadron Leader W.P. Thomas (RAF SIB).

The letter and his later statement (detailed in the next chapter) would display a number of facts that were true, but were clearly twisted to fit his new narrative of events. Sergeant Hughes clearly wanted to give the impression he was an innocent man, who had found himself in an invidious position and only acted under duress to avoid further punishment.

On 5 June 1945, a further statement arrived implicating Hughes. This time Gunner H.J.B. Colomb of the Royal Artillery stated that he was held at Stalag IIIA at Luckenwalde, about thirty-five miles south-west of Berlin in early 1945.

He was in charge of the prisoners' theatre and in late January or early February 1945, about 3,000 RAF aircrew prisoners arrived from the camps at Stalag Luft VII and Bandeau. They had been evacuated due to the Soviet advance. Among the ranks of these prisoners was a Flight Sergeant Hughes, who according to his own comments, was brought down over Germany in 1943. He was leader of a Welsh male voice choir.

Gunner Colomb claimed that towards the end of March 1945, he was warned about Hughes, as he was under suspicion of collaborating with the Germans. Hughes was on very friendly terms with an associate of Colomb, called J.W.P. Kavanagh. As a result, Colomb warned Kavanagh about Hughes and asked him, if possible, to extract information from him.

Colomb claimed that his friend managed to get a written admission from Hughes that he had been in civilian clothes, working under the Germans and paid by them; he believed the figure was 400 Reichsmarks a month. Hughes had also admitted to assisting at a radio station which broadcast anti-British propaganda.

This information was saved by Colomb and allegedly given to Battalion Sergeant Major Henderson (Royal Artillery), the senior NCO in the camp. However, Hughes then made an allegation that Henderson was on friendly terms with a German woman in the camp. Hughes started to panic and Colomb knew that if he went to the Germans, they would search the camp and men could end up being shot.

The camp was liberated on 21 April 1945 and J.W.P. Kavanagh left to make his own way to the American lines according to Colomb. At the start of May 1945, Colomb also made a bid to get to the American lines and ended up back in England. At the time of his statement, the location of Kavanagh and Sergeant Major Henderson was unknown.

A check of the Commonwealth War Graves Commission register can find no trace of Henderson or Kavanagh and it appears they survived, but no statements were taken from them.

Chapter 7

Hughes's Own Evidence

Raymond Hughes was transferred to London and detained in Kensington with the RAF Special Investigation Branch.

On 31 May 1945, he gave a lengthy statement to Squadron Leader Thomas. This can be found in the National Archives UK file reference: KV2/263.

The statement opened with Hughes saying he had been informed by Squadron Leader Thomas that he was making enquiries about POWs returning from Germany, who may have given assistance to the Germans. He was formally cautioned and said he was quite willing to make the statement.

Hughes gave details of being shot down and the names of his crew. When he landed by parachute he sprained his ankle and linked up with colleagues Sergeants Garnett and Dickson. They had landed on an island off the German coast and found a rowing boat which had no oars, so they used two of the boats floorboards and tried to paddle to Sweden across the Baltic Sea.

Unfortunately, they did not succeed and headed back to the German coastline, where they were detained near Greifswald.

The airmen were held in a local camp before being transported to Dulag Luft, but first they had to identify the body of their wireless operator Sergeant Peter Love in a local mortuary. On their way to Oberursel, they were joined by the rest of their crew and taken by lorry to the railway station. Placed in a cattle wagon, the train headed south via Berlin and Nordhausen where they were allowed out of the truck to exercise.

Hughes claimed they had arrived at Dulag Luft on 21 August 1943 and he was placed in a solitary cell. After forty-eight hours, he was given a form to fill in by a German officer. The officer entered Hughes' name, rank, number and next of kin, home address, religion, state of health and place and time of capture on the form; but Hughes claimed he refused to answer questions about his squadron, group, aircraft code letters and crew. He also declined to say what his role was, although clearly his uniform brevet would indicate his trade.

Sergeant Hughes claimed the German officer said he could go and play football with the others if he just answered the questions, before adding that if he did not answer, he would be handed over to the Gestapo. Despite the threat, Hughes claimed he still refused to answer and was put back into his cell alone for another twenty-four hours.

Another German officer attended the cell with an incomplete form. He placed this on the table and Hughes could see the code letters of his Lancaster on the form. This officer then went through the form, filling in the answers to the questions, while telling Hughes that they had all the information, but needed to check it with Hughes. He then asked for the names of his crew, which Hughes provided. Hughes added:

> *'Two or three hours later, a man in a civilian suit came to my cell and in perfect English said, "The quarters are not very good here, would you like to move into better quarters?" I told him I was going out that night and he replied, "No you're not, you are staying here and you may as well get better quarters."*
>
> *'Later that evening a German Corporal came and moved me to another building and a much better and larger cell. I was in this cell for about fourteen days, during which time, through the bars, I saw two men in civvys whom I had previously seen; one in British uniform and the other in American uniform.*
>
> *'I immediately thought of the snoops in German camps we in the squadron had been warned about whilst in England. I did not speak to them through the window, but I spoke to them the following day in the washroom, when they were again in uniform. The American told me he was a Staff Sergeant and a pilot of a Liberator, and that he had done thirty-nine operations before being shot down. I later saw his documents in the camp office and found him to be a Sergeant air-gunner who's correct name I believe was Trix, but also Raymond* (Author: actually Tricks). *The other officer I found to be a Polish Spitfire pilot whose name was Flying Officer Zuromski who had been shot down. He spoke a lot about Biggin Hill. I never saw his documents. His face was badly burned and he had a beard.*

'I asked these officers why they were in civilian clothes and they told me that if I asked the guard, he would let me out. I did so, but I was not allowed out.

'The next thing that happened, I was visited by Lt. Boninghaus who I afterwards found was the political interrogator. He told me he was the welfare officer and was looking after the interests of the fellows in the camp. I told him I was in the boot trade and that I studied in Doctor Scholes School of Chiropody. He told me he had connections with the Scholes people and that he had travelled in England. He mentioned the name of a fruiterer in Mold, North Wales, where I lived, called Londell, he also mentioned the name of the local hairdresser which was correct.

'In his conversation he said, "I'm surprised that you British have the Russians as your allies." I replied that, "I'm surprised that you have the Japs." He asked me my views on communism. I told him I hated communism, but that Russia was our ally and there was nothing I could do about it. There was nothing further of a political nature said and he left.

'I was later twice questioned by different officials about Pathfinders. I told them I knew nothing about Pathfinders. One of them was a long conversation, in which the officer told me a lot I had never heard of about Pathfinders, but I realised in the conversation that certain raids to which he referred had happened. He also discussed the types of attack, but I could only say maybe and yes and no, as I know very little about Pathfinder techniques. He also questioned me about Monica and produced a design of a set, asking me what effect certain knobs had. He said the set had been taken from an aircraft. I told him I knew very little about Monica and could not tell him what he wanted to know...

(Author's note: Monica was a tail warning radar for RAF bombers. It was used to detect approaching German night fighters in 1942, but as Hughes stated, the enemy soon obtained a captured set and developed the Flensburg radar. This allowed German night fighters to 'home-in' on the Monica's radar waves. By the summer of 1944, the RAF realised the Germans were homing in on their bombers' Monica radar and it was withdrawn from service.)

Hughes's statement continued…

'He also asked me about Master of Ceremonies and in connection with this, he mentioned the name of Group Captain Wilson. I think he said that Group Captain Wilson was the first Master of Ceremonies they had captured and that he had been very helpful to them from the point of view of Pathfinder technique.'

(Author's note: Pathfinder raids used what was termed a Master of Ceremonies. A senior and experienced bombing leader would transmit radio directions to the following bombers, advising them about conditions over the target. Target indicators and flares would be dropped to aid the bombing, while directions would be given by the Master of Ceremonies to correct the aiming point etc. The issue with the Hughes statement and Group Captain Wilson, is that he appears to be referring to Group Captain Ernest Wilson of the Royal Australian Air Force. He will be covered in a later chapter, but he was not a Pathfinder and not a Master of Ceremonies, so either Hughes was making the account up, or the German officer was trying to trick him. Wilson had been detained at Dulag Luft between August and September 1943 while Hughes was in the camp). Hughes continued…

'On 1 September, or it may have been the day before, I was visited by Oberst Leutnant Tobler who said he had instructions from the Camp Commandant to visit a night fighter wing. I asked him about getting me better clothing, as I was in the uniform I was shot down in. He said that could not be done, as it would have to be done through the Red Cross officials at the camp and the German authorities did not want them to know I was there.

'About 4 o'clock on 1 September, I was taken out of my cell to a field adjoining the camp by Leutnant Tobler and there we boarded a Fiesler Storch aircraft. The only other person was the pilot, a Major in the German Luftwaffe. I was flown to a field near a castle slightly south of Bonn. (Author: possibly Godesburg Castle?) *I know we were in this area, as I recognised the Rhine and on asking them, they told me I was near Bonn.*

'I was taken to the castle and interviewed by a German officer with the rank of Oberst Leutnant who could not speak English. Tobler interpreted. I was first asked about the food situation in Britain. I told him it was alright, he said there was plenty of food in Germany and called in some other officers and instructed them to get some food ready. We were later shown into a large dining room where the tables were laid with plenty of chicken, champagne etc. I had a meal there. After the meal, I did not get any further interrogation.

'There were a number of German pilots there and some of them asked me various questions in conversation to the effect of what I thought of the Focke-Wulf 190, whether I had been in any fights and I told them I had destroyed one and a half the night I was shot down. Some of them said they were there at the time. I was not asked anything of importance. The whole of the time I was there, everything was of a friendly nature, as if I was a stranger just visiting the Mess.

'Whilst in this Mess the air raid warning sounded and a number of pilots left. I was told that the raid was by Mosquitos flying in the direction of Berlin. I remained at the castle that night and slept in a room with two others and Leutnant Tobler. I was not asked any further questions and left by aircraft with Tobler the following morning and went back to Dulag.'

(Author's note: according to the Bomber Command diaries, on the night of 31 August to 1 September 1943, nine Mosquitos were part of a heavy raid on Berlin. This therefore appears to corroborate this statement.)

What is odd, is the fact a Sergeant air gunner was dispatched and wined and dined at a Luftwaffe Night Fighters Officers' Mess. While some renowned airmen such as Douglas Bader are known to have visited Luftwaffe bases, it would appear the Luftwaffe believed this rather innocuous Sergeant air-gunner would give them something in return.

The identity of the Oberst Leutnant and his pilots is unknown. The fact they spoke of Focke-Wulf 190 night fighters tends to point towards the Wild Boar fighters of JG300, JG301 and JG302. However, JG300 were only recently operational at the time, based in Deelen in Holland and the other two units were not fully operational on 1 September 1943. (Was this a fabrication?)

Hughes continued in his statement:

> *'On the first day I was able to get out of my cell, the American Trix and the Pole Zuromski came to my cell and in conversation I asked them where they got the civilian suits. They told me they got them from a shed outside the building, where there were a number of British suits which had been taken from British airmen. There was no guard on the shed and in their company I selected a blue double breasted large check lounge suit, also a pair of brown thin striped sports trousers and a brownish sports jacket. I wrapped these clothes in brown paper and took them back to my cell. I started wearing the sports trousers that evening and as the Germans took no notice of it, I got into a full set of civilian clothes, including a shirt which I also got from the shed.*
>
> *'I was not able to find any boots or shoes at the shed and only possessing a badly worn pair of brogues and needing shoes, I joined a party going into the Red Cross store, where I obtained a pair of boots and some underwear which I signed for. The person in charge of the store, I didn't know his name, but it might have been Hardy. Later, when I was in Stalag Luft IIIA (after my liberation), Squadron Leader Dudley-Craig asked me if I knew Hardy, in charge of the Red Cross store at Dulag.'*

Flight Lieutenant Richard Hardy was an associate of Pilot Officer Benson Freeman and Squadron Leader Elliott at Dulag Luft. He was a signatory to one of the infamous Freeman letters and it appears there was some suspicion about him, especially as he was part of the Dulag Luft permanent staff and in charge of the clothing store. In fact, having arrived in late 1940, he was still there on 1 November 1943, when the Red Cross visited the camp and made a note that he was a member of the camp's permanent staff, along with Squadron Leader Eric Douglas Elliott and Flight Lieutenant David W. Thomas. (See National Archives file WO224/67.)

> *'I was in the same cell at Dulag all the time, which was No.2. A Group Captain Wilson, Squadron Leader Boyd-Carpenter and Lieutenant Byanant, at different times occupied No.1. A Lieutenant Colonel Dean and a Pilot Officer, I don't know his name, occupied No.3. Staff Sergeant Trix and a Sergeant air gunner Alcock RAF occupied rooms on the other side of the corridor.'*

The comments above appear to indicate and identify those prisoners who may have been employed by the Germans in nefarious activities. Group Captain Wilson, Squadron Leader Carpenter, Staff Sergeant Trix (Tricks) and Sergeant Alcock all feature in this book, while Lieutenant Colonel Dean is mentioned. Lieutenant Byanant may be an error and may have been the US Ambassador's son 1st Lieutenant John Winant jr.

> *'After I obtained some freedom in Dulag, I was asked by the Germans whether I would like to do something. I volunteered to take round Red Cross letter forms to cells for other prisoners to use for writing. I hoped in this way to get in touch with the other members of my crew whom I thought might still be there themselves. I was given this job and used to take round these letters once a day. I only went to the cells of junior officers and other ranks which had bolts on the outside of the doors. I did not meet any of my crew. The cells of the higher officers were locked with a key.'*

These comments may appear believable, but this was not what other repatriated prisoners and even Luftwaffe officers said about Hughes and his activities at Dulag Luft. It is clear Hughes was contorting the truth and knew he would be called to account for various accusations. This was apparent in his next comments…

> *'When delivering these letters, one day I recognised a Pilot Officer Smith of my squadron. His Christian name was Jeff. He told me he was very hungry and I told him that I would come back again at eight o'clock that evening and collect his letter. The cells where Smith was located were guarded by old men and at eight o'clock that evening, I went to Smith's cell in a very official manner. I opened the door, called him out and took him past the guard up to my cell, where I gave him a good meal, which consisted of soup, bread and potatoes, which I had saved during the day and some Red Cross food which Squadron Leader Carpenter had given me.'*

Jeff Smith, as we have already seen, spoke with Pilot Officer Dixon, the captain of Hughes' aircraft and a fellow member of 467 Squadron. Flight

Lieutenant David W. Thomas also spoke with Smith, but neither were given this account and both men heard of Hughes 'interrogating' fellow prisoners with his Red Cross forms.

> *'By this time, I was getting to know Squadron Leader Carpenter very well and told me all about himself. I used to do what I could for him, almost like his batman. I also got to know Sergeant Alcock, but did not have much to do with him, because I did not like him as he was a coarse type.*
>
> *'Squadron Leader Carpenter asked me where I got my civilian clothes. I told him I got them from the shed mentioned and at his request, I got him a suit of clothes, or I think it was only a sports jacket and a tie.*
>
> *'As time went on I got more freedom and I was able to get about almost every part of the building, including the offices and registries. In the registries there were files containing particulars of groups, stations, squadrons, and crews in this country, American and English, including the names of commanders, flight commanders and the crews and the names of Intelligence Officers at the home stations. There were also particulars of different types of aircraft, including Spitfires and Typhoons. A lot of the information was photographic copies. The general correspondence was in German, but the photographic copies were in English. At times when I was alone, I examined these records and I particularly searched for something about my own station and squadron.'*

Hughes, a character previously described by his school and the local police as cunning, deceitful and boastful, appeared to be portraying all of these attributes in his statement. Clearly, his intellect did not allow him to realise that others may have given statements undermining these claims and his claims were too unbelievable to be the actions of an innocent prisoner. Hughes continued to dig a deeper hole for himself…

> *'I was stationed at Bottesford. A Wing Commander Gomm was the OC of my squadron. About a fortnight before I was shot down, he took off on a special mission with another aircraft piloted by an Australian. Neither of these aircraft returned to the station. I found in the records that Wing Commander*

> *Gomm had been killed and that only one member of the crew had been captured...'*

These comments from Hughes about Wing Commander Gomm appear to be completely false. Gomm took off with other aircraft from the squadron on a 199 aircraft raid to Milan, on the night of 15-16 August 1943 – three days, not a fortnight before Hughes was shot down. In addition, the entire crew of seven were killed. Clearly, the information given by Hughes needed to be checked in every detail…

> *'When talking with one of the girl clerks one day, I asked her how they got all this information. She told me that their spies in England took photographic evidence of documents and sent them back by radio photography. I also found a book giving particulars of all the defences in Western Germany, including the Ruhr, which included flak, searchlights, night fighter aerodromes etc.*
>
> *'I informed Squadron Leader Boyd-Carpenter of all this information and two of the photographic documents I took to his room and showed him. They were particulars about the Typhoon and the four bladed Spitfire. The particulars were in English and after Squadron Leader Boyd-Carpenter had seen them, he told me to put them back where I had found them.*
>
> *'Squadron Leader Boyd-Carpenter and I often discussed the possibility of escaping and we intended, if possible, to take the book showing the defences of the Ruhr with us.*
>
> *'One day, a German officer sent for me and asked if I would assist in getting Red Cross interrogation forms filled in. He practically told me to do it. He also told me that it would be better if I was known as Herr Becker. From then on, I was also known in the name of Becker and called Becker by the German staff. I was still known as Hughes by the British who knew me in the camp. The reason for using Becker was because I was more likely to be accepted as a German.*
>
> *'I started taking round these Red Cross forms and more or less, I had to go to particular cells, in some cases to get further particulars on the forms, which had not been properly completed by the prisoners, such as names of their crew, squadrons, group and commands and particularly their home*

address. When I would interview a prisoner who had not completed his particulars, I would ask him if there were any of his crew in the camp. If he told me there was, I would go to that person, ask him if he had been interrogated and if he had, I would get his interrogation sheet and from that, I would copy any particulars he had given on to a piece of paper. I would then go back to the person I had been directed to see and tell him the known particulars. He would then usually fill in everything required. It was difficult at times to get their home address, but as prisoners were allowed to write home, the addresses could be obtained from their letters.'

It would appear Hughes believed, or would like others to believe, that he was not doing anything wrong and was actually assisting other prisoners. However, not only was he filling in the fake Red Cross forms for the Germans, he was also cross referencing details which could have led to all manner of problems for the prisoners themselves at a later date. Again, it appears his actions were deliberately to assist the enemy, while his subsequent explanation varied from being boastful to poorly judged.

'I did not tell Squadron Leader Boyd-Carpenter I was doing this until two days after I started it. He warned me to be careful that I did not assist the enemy more than I could help. I also told him that they had told me to use the name Becker. I don't remember what his comment was on this, but he knew I was known by that name from then onwards.

'During this period, the Germans had mentioned to me about going on parole. I spoke with Squadron Leader Boyd-Carpenter about this. He told me that it was permitted for an NCO to use parole, if it was for his own benefit and not in the interests of the enemy. He pointed out that my circumstances were exceptional.'

Why and what was exceptional about Hughes' circumstances is unclear. Carpenter was now being referred to as Boyd-Carpenter. Why this change was made is unknown.

'On or about 1 October 1943, Squadron Leader Boyd-Carpenter and the Polish officer Zuromski were taken away

> *from the camp by Leutnant Boninghaus. I saw them leave in civvy clothes with packs on their backs. I did not know where they were going, except that Carpenter had mentioned a couple of days before, that he might be leaving and I did not know where they were being taken. As Carpenter was leaving, he waved to me saying, "See you later".*
>
> *'After Carpenter left, I carried on with the job with the Red Cross forms...*
>
> *'I got rather depressed after Squadron Leader Carpenter had gone, as I rather looked up to him as an advisor and friend. I lost interest in the work I was doing and didn't feel like carrying it on but continued for a short while. I then told Leutnant Boninghaus and Dr Haase that I wasn't going to do anymore work with the Red Cross forms or anything else and that I wanted to be sent to a camp. Leutnant Boninghaus told me that could not be done, as I knew too much.*
>
> *'On 14 October, Lieutenant Wynnat arrived there and was placed in cell No.1 next to mine. Through the bars of his cell, I asked him who he was and he gave me his name and told me he was the son of the American Ambassador to Britain. He seemed very nervous and in conversation said, what's to stop them from taking me out and shooting me? I told him they wouldn't do that.'*

Hughes stated that he got Wynnat out of his cell with a key from the guardroom and took him back to his own cell for a meal. This food he claimed to have taken from the German officials' kitchen, as well as some beer from the German Officers' canteen. Hughes claimed that Oberst Leutnant Koch had told him if he wanted beer, he could get it from the canteen and put it down against Koch's name. Hughes took ten bottles and gave some to Sergeants Trix and Alcock.

Hughes also claimed that on a number of occasions he stole food for other prisoners and Squadron Leader Carpenter assisted in stealing cucumbers and tomatoes.

Hughes seemed to have a very good memory for dates and he recalled on 16 October 1943, telling some newly arrived American airmen to stop talking about their operations and remember what they had been told back home. As the statement progressed, it seems as if Hughes was trying to make out that he was some sort of a patriotic hero. At about 3pm that same afternoon, Hauptmann Offerman told Hughes to get packed as he was going to another camp on the orders of the Commandant. He was then taken by car to the prison in Frankfurt am Main and placed in a cell.

The next day the Germans removed Hughes' civilian clothes and gave him his own RAF uniform. Two days later, he was again given civilian clothes, told to dress and bring his RAF uniform with him. He was taken to the railway station and on to Berlin.

In Berlin he was met by Leutnant Boninghaus from Dulag Luft. He greeted him by stating, 'Well Becker, do you remember that little conversation we had at Dulag Luft, when you said you didn't like communism? You will have a chance to fight against it now.'

Boninghaus took him to his own flat at Wittenberg-Platz-U-Bahn-Station. After making some telephone calls, Boninghaus told him, 'Where you are going today, you will meet two old friends of yours, Boyd-Carpenter and Zuromski.' Hughes was told to forget those two names as they were now known as Herr Carter and Herr Kowalski.

Leutnant Boninghaus then took Hughes to the office of Major Heimpel the Security Officer for the Stalag SD (Gestapo). Hughes was lectured about trying to escape, told not to fraternise with Germans and that he would receive a Red Cross parcel every Monday. He was now to be known as John Charles Baker.

Hughes claimed that Major Heimpel searched his personal property and destroyed anything that could identify him as Raymond Hughes. He then told him that Hughes no longer existed.

Hughes was taken to the Auto Hotel, Aldernstrasse 5-7, Charlottenburg, and in room 16 he met Squadron Leader Carpenter. Flying Officer Zuromski was in room 15. Hughes claimed that Carpenter warned him about Zuromski and a Channel Islander (Charles Patrick Gilbert? known as Kenneth James). Carpenter also warned Hughes that the Germans would try and get him to make propaganda broadcasts. Carpenter told him never to do anything unless he consulted him first.

After a few days, Hughes was called by the Channel Islander to the Reichs Rundfunk. They tested his voice for broadcasting, but Hughes claims he took advantage of a missing tooth which would cause his voice to make a hissing noise. Later the Channel Islander brought some ration books and 50 Reichsmarks for Hughes.

The following week, Hughes claims he was told to go to the Saarland Strasse office in the German Foreign Ministry and report to Professor

Haferkorn. Haferkorn told him his voice was unsuitable for the radio, but they would test his writing abilities…

> *'The same day, I was introduced to Baillie-Stewart, a man called Hewitt, a man called Royston, a Professor Mahr, a man named Vernon, a man named Boldey and a man named McCarthy.'*

These people were renowned traitors – Norman Baillie-Stewart, Gerald Percy Hewitt, Pilot Officer Benson Freeman, Edward Salvin Bowlby and possibly Sergeant Frank McLardy.

> *'In getting back to my billet, I told Carpenter all about my experience that day and that I was supposed to go the following morning. He told me to carry on and to let him know what was happening.*
>
> *'There was a raid on Berlin that night and owing to damage, I did not report as directed until three days later, when I was put in a small office which I had to clean up; and which was next to one occupied by Baillie-Stewart…*
>
> *'Haferkorn told me he wanted me to write some talks for broadcasting, principally concerning the Jews and Russians. He showed me some specimens which had been written by Baillie-Stewart and others, and I told him that I had no experience or knowledge of that sort of thing, that I was certain I could not do it there, but I might be able to do something in a different atmosphere, such as at my hotel. He agreed to let me do it at the hotel and when I got there, I told Squadron Leader Carpenter all about it. The attitude the squadron leader adapted was that it was wise for me to be amiable to the Germans, so that I could go back to meet them at any time and as I had been kicked out of Rundfunk, he would help me write something which would not be much good in my new job.*
>
> *'Together we wrote some papers on the subject of Jews, using it on the lines of the talks that had been given by Joyce (William Joyce), such as the Jews in Britain run newspapers, the banks and all the big business concerns. It was not punctuated, it had a lot of unusual words selected*

by Carpenter from the dictionary and after handing it in to Professor Haferkorn, I later learned that it was not much good and they thought my education standard was low and that it might improve. In all, assisted by Carpenter, I wrote three or four of these talks and got a lot of material out of the book "John Amery speaks".

'The reason why we started to write the talks in the William Joyce style, was because he was a man very much hated in Germany for his bombastic manner during the bombing of England. The only person who supported him was Goebbels.

'At the time I was working in the Ministry, Squadron Leader Carpenter was doing practically nothing to my knowledge. Berlin was being bombed at that time and at night Carpenter and I went out and destroyed telephone communications in street kiosks by breaking the wires. In all, we estimated that we had destroyed 432. I also took a number of distributors from the lorries at a Bosch factory at Reidefeld. The distributors I threw into the Teltow Canal.'

Carpenter was a strange character who will be covered in the next chapter. He appears to have been trusted by Hughes, although the squadron leader appears, according to the Welshman, to have done little in the way of assisting the Germans. If this was true, how did he manage to stay at Dulag Luft and in Berlin for so long?

Hughes continued:

'During the bombing, my room was destroyed and I had to clear out to another address at Robert-Bosch Platz 5, Klein-Machow, Berlin Zehlendorlf 4. Squadron Leader Carpenter's room was not badly damaged and he stayed there...

'I was still attending the Foreign Office, where they told me, or at least a Doctor Mertner did, that I was no bloody good, but I would have to hang around as they would probably find me another job. I used to go into Baillie-Stewart's office. He was engaged in writing broadcast material for various stations and he himself, used to broadcast.

'Baillie-Stewart used to broadcast cross talks with Royston (Pilot Officer Freeman). I have never seen them broadcast or make records, but I have heard their broadcasts over the air.

I knew the voices of them both well and could identify them. Royston used to come to the Foreign Office almost daily as a visitor. He had an office there and often did writing there. I have been in his office and seen him writing there.

'John Amery also visited the Foreign Office and had long conversations with a man named Hewitt who used to come there on special missions from Paris, Baillie-Stewart and Professor Haferkorn were always present at these conversations. I was never present myself. I would get to know about what was discussed through Royston, who would be told by Baillie-Stewart as they were great friends. The subject of these conversations was usually about communism and the raising and mustering of a British Free Corps. John Amery was the prime mover in the Free Corps.

'Another person who used to visit the Foreign Office was a man named Wallace, whose real name I afterwards found out was Purdy. He belonged to the Royal Navy and was captured at Narvik, at least that is what he told me. He was a broadcaster at the Reichssportfeld and also at Rundfunk.

'After Squadron Leader Carpenter and I were separated due to the bombing and had different addresses, at my suggestion we adopted the use of code numbers for the purpose of correspondence and telephone communications. My code number was K39, which I adopted as it appeared on a post card from my girlfriend in Britain. The code number for Carpenter was S4 which just came from a suggestion.

'At this time, Squadron Leader Carpenter and I were so far as we possibly could, obtaining information and checking up on people who we believed to be in German employment. I did not question what work he was doing, but I know he had a pass into the Reichssportfeld, which was used as the main propaganda listening station and also for broadcasting propaganda to Poland. I only went to the Reichsportfeld once to see Carpenter. He discouraged me from going there, as he did not want us to be seen together. Carpenter and I carried on obtaining information until he left Berlin in February 1944. I did not know Carpenter was going and when I made enquiries at his hotel, I was told he had been taken away by the Gestapo.

'I don't know what money Carpenter was being paid, but from December 1943, I was paid by the German Foreign Office 350 Reichsmarks a month. My salary was supposed to be 500 Reichsmarks a month.'

The statement from Hughes was astounding. It was clear to the RAF SIB (as well as MI5 and MI9), that Hughes was a collaborator and yet he was almost boasting about his alleged covert activities with Squadron Leader George Carpenter. What Carpenter would have to say about Hughes' statement remained to be seen.

Hughes, having already admitted being a fake Red Cross man at Dulag Luft and being in the company of some of the main British collaborators in the field of Nazi propaganda, now moved on to the issue of the British Free Corps unit of the Waffen SS:

'Also in December 1943, Baillie-Stewart spoke to me one day and told me that as I was no good for broadcasting and I was particularly dumb at writing, he had brought two friends along who he introduced to me as Courlander and McHardy and said they would like to have a chat with me. Courlander apparently being the principle. They both told me they were two of the "Big Six" in the British Free Corps. The only thing I knew then about the British Free Corps, was what bits I had heard from Baillie-Stewart, Royston (Pilot Officer Benson Freeman) and Professor Haferkorn. So far as I could gather, John Amery and William Joyce were endeavouring to raise a British Free Corps on the lines of the Viking Waffen SS which fought against the Russians on the Russian Front.

'Courlander and McHardy told me that they had come along as representatives of the British Free Corps and acting on instructions, they had been ordered to offer me an immediate commission in the British Free Corps.

'I then asked them what the British Free Corps was, what they were intended for and who was in it? They said it was an organisation controlled by the Big Six and backed up by John Amery and William Joyce. The Corps was for the purpose of propaganda against the Western Allies, inducing them to realise that Russia was the menace and endeavouring to get the Western people to join Germany to fight against the

> *Russians. British Free Corps was not intended to fight in the front lines on the Russian Front, but to fight against partisans who were assisting the Russians. I asked them how they knew the German government was going to accept their proposal. McHardy told me that a letter had been sent to the Führer by the Big Six and had been sent through Gunther Schmidt, the Führer's personal interpreter.*
>
> *'The text of the message was, "We the true soldiers of Britain, wish to swear allegiance to the Führer and German Reich. We volunteer to fight side by side with the Germans and beat the enemies of Europe. For this purpose, we the undersigned, make application for a Corps to be formed and called the British Free Corps." I asked them what uniforms the Corps would wear. They told me that it would be grey field uniform with the swastika and the Union Jack side by side and the words British Free Corps. I told him that it was a matter that would have serious consideration and I asked them how many men were in the Corps and who they were. They told me there were 2,000 men waiting to join the Corps and Brigadier General Patterson of Crete was waiting to take over the Corps, but he would not do so until it had been properly formed and he was a man who would have to be handled with kid gloves.'*

Hughes was clearly still trying to explain away any possible evidence against him from the likes of these two men. He continued to maintain that he was only gathering information, but it was quite evident that this RAF sergeant air gunner was at the centre of a complex system of collaborators and betrayal.

The two men who had apparently visited him were Lance Corporal Roy Courlander (alias Regan), formerly of the 18th New Zealand Battalion and Sergeant Francis George MacLardy (alias Wood) – not McHardy – formerly of the Royal Army Medical Corps. Hughes continued:

> *'I knew what I was doing and to encourage them, I told them I was interested and asked them where they were billeted, as I would like to make an official visit there to see if they were comfortable. They did not know my position in the Foreign Office, but I made it appear to them that I was an important*

person there. They knew me only as Baker. They gave me the address in Pankow, Berlin, the caretaker there was a Frau Rex. This interview was on the Thursday, and they invited me for the following Sunday evening at six o'clock, when they would have everybody there. I strictly warned them that they were not to mention who I was or to give my name, as I was to be introduced to the others as a government official. I asked them whether anyone from the Foreign Office would be there and they told me McCarthy and Bolby (Bowlby) would be there.'

Flight Sergeant Raymond Hughes was out of his depth if this was even remotely true. Bearing in mind these events pre-dated Squadron Leader Carpenter having been arrested and disappearing, Hughes then added:

'The next thing I did was get in touch with Squadron Leader Carpenter, whom I met by appointment at the Underground station. We went to a restaurant and I told him all about it. He was astounded at the information, he told me I was making a good show and that I must get into the Free Corps but be careful that I did not sign any papers, pledge any allegiance or wear German uniform. He took down all the particulars and gave me the task of finding out the names of everybody in the Corps.

'When I got back to my office, I spoke to Baillie-Stewart about the Corps and asked him what he knew about it. He told me he did not know much, except that John Amery was at the head of it.

'The bombing of Berlin was then increasing to its maximum and I had wanted to get into the German Air Ministry, hoping that I might find a Britisher there. I mentioned to Baillie-Stewart that I had not been interrogated respecting British bombing tactics and that the German Air Ministry did not know whether I had any information which could assist them. I told him I had been in Berlin during twenty raids and watched how late German fighters arrived on the scene, and the effect of the flak, and convinced him that a target was always attacked from the south. I know that this was not the case, as I had done twenty-one operations over Germany, but it excited him. He called in Royston (Freeman) and also telephoned Professor

Haferkorn. They discussed the matter and informed Gunther Schmidt who was the Führer's interpreter.

'The same day I was taken by car, accompanied by Baillie-Stewart and two German Luftwaffe officers, one an Oberst Leutnant, to the German Chancellery and interviewed by the Oberst Leutnant in the presence of Gunther Schmidt, who acted as an interpreter as I spoke English. Baillie-Stewart was not present during the interview.

'During the interview, Goebbels came into the room. I had not seen him before except by photographs and Gunther Schmidt mentioned who he was. During the interview, I mentioned that I had not been interviewed respecting bombing tactics. They were very surprised and excited, and asked me what I had to say about the bombing. I told them that the flak was nowhere near the aircraft and the night fighters did not get up until the bombers were on their way home. I said the flak batteries were not in proper positions, as the flak appeared miles in front or miles behind the aircraft. I also mentioned that the pendant lights should be left on as a guide to the night fighter pilots, as the Oberst Leutnant had mentioned communications to the night fighters got jammed and the pilots got lost. I had in mind that the pendant lights would be of great assistance to the bombing pilots. They told me that some of the faults mentioned by me had been already noticed and they were concerned about it.'

The propensity for Hughes to apparently brag and overstate his comments is clearly visible in this account. Had he really seen Josef Goebbels or was it an embellishment to enhance his story? He continued to probably overstate his involvement, thereby providing more and more evidence against himself:

'After that interview, I was taken back to my office by car, accompanied by Baillie-Stewart, and I think Baillie-Stewart must have mentioned in the office that I had exceptional knowledge regarding British bombing tactics, because a number of officials used to visit me for advice as to whether there would be a raid that night. The Germans were getting very nervous at the time.

> *'The next thing is I kept the appointment on Sunday at the billet of the British Free Corps. I was first met at the railway station by a Canadian who I later knew as Corporal Martin. Another man was with him who also spoke English, whose name I forget.'*

Hughes explained that at the Billet he did not see Courlander and McHardy. Hughes kept up the pretence that he was from the German Foreign Ministry and was introduced by Martin (Private Edwin Barnard Martin, alias Bartlett of the Essex Scottish, Canadian army), to another alleged member of the so-called Big Six called Sergeant Wilson (John Eric Wilson alias Montgomery of No. 3 Commando). Hughes said there were ten or twelve men present in the meeting. He addressed them, pointing out that it was a serious step and that he did not know what the British Government would think of it. He ended his speech by allegedly stating:

> *'Remember, being anti-communist does not mean you must be pro-fascist. If you think you are doing the right thing, I wish you the best of luck.'*

He was then taken back to the railway station by Sergeant John Eric Wilson.

> *'Sergeant Wilson accompanied me to the railway station. On the way he questioned me as to who I was, he seemed worried. I told him he was in a sticky mess and that I wanted him to get me the correct false names and service particulars of all the people in the Free Corps and that I would see him at 10am in two days. He said he had no money and I gave him 30 Reichsmarks.*
>
> *'I told Squadron Leader Carpenter all about this meeting and the appointment I had with Wilson. He decided that he would also meet Wilson. I met Wilson as agreed and took him to the Excelsior Hotel where we joined Carpenter at a table. We questioned Wilson about the Free Corps and himself. He told us about the Big Six, that there were several in the Corps, and that they were recruiting at concentration camps for more, that Hauptsturmführer Roepka of the Waffen SS, who was later officer in command of the Viking Division, was in command. I gave Wilson the code numbers K69 and S4 of Squadron*

Leader Carpenter and myself, telling him to use them only in extreme urgency, if he wanted to get in touch with us.'

Hughes appeared to now be in the realms of fantasy, his story faltered on the premise that a good liar has to have a good memory. This can be seen by his error of changing his own code in the statement of K39 to K69. The RAF SIB officers allowed his ramble to continue. As any police detective will tell you, once the suspect starts talking, let him tell you his account, especially if you know it's a load of rubbish and you can dismantle it later.

Hughes did appear to be an experienced liar, by using known and genuine facts he weaved an elaborate account, but his memory was not great and many of the facts were too outrageous to be believable. The best cover stories are not sensational, they are mundane and believable. In this case Hughes gave a correct statement with Hauptsturmführer Hans Werner Roepka commanding the unit from September 1943 until November 1944.

'Through the German SS, I obtained an appointment and met Hauptsturmführer Roepka. He told me he was taking charge of the Free Corps and was going to train at Hildesheim near Hannover. He showed me a design of uniform which had been selected. I told him the reason for my enquiries was because I had been offered a commission in it, that my name was Baker and I was an official in the Foreign Office. He asked me if I was accepting a commission. I told him I was very busy at my office at the time and would have to think it over. He spoke to me in German, to which I replied in German, and he told me that if I took a commission, I would have a good rank.

'I continued to pay visits to the Free Corps billet. I found Wilson had let me down by giving my name and code number away, but from a small fellow whose name I don't remember, I eventually got the names and particulars of everybody in the Free Corps, which he obtained from their pay books.

'I asked this chap why he joined the Free Corps. He told me he had been seen in a camp, Luckenwalde, and been interrogated by Corporal Martin who asked him to join, he was treated very badly by a man named Buecher – an Englishman named Butcher – until he consented to join the Free Corps. He

> *also told me that Martin was the interrogator of prisoners at Luckenwalde interrogation camp.'*

Hughes went on to say that he tried to obtain the signatures of everyone in the camp. This was to be achieved by a card system and money which he advanced to them. He claimed this money was 300 Reichsmarks from his own pocket, but he spent more over time as he took some of the men out for meals.

> *'I kept in touch with the Free Corps until 28 March 1944, when I was arrested by the Gestapo to which I will refer later. I did not see anything of the British Free Corps after this.*
>
> *'By January 1944, I had got a number of Free Corps to demand to go back to camp. The Free Corps came under the jurisdiction of Stalag IIIA, which was under the charge of Major Heimpel (SD). He started making enquiries as to why these men were being returned to camp and who had been visiting them at their billet. The interpreter at the billet was Doctor Hans Schultze and it was he who probably informed them I had been visiting there. As mentioned, I collected my Red Cross parcel from Stalag IIIA and when going for it one day, I was seen by Major Heimpel and told not to visit the Free Corps billet any more. I did not report this to anyone but kept away from the billets of the men of the Free Corps, but sometimes met them away from the billet. So far as I know, the British Free Corps did not obtain any uniforms or do any drilling whilst at Berlin, but I understand they moved to Hildesheim.*
>
> *'After Christmas 1943, Squadron Leader Carpenter and I were getting into a bad way for civilian clothes and shoes. I had been offered chits authorising me to buy clothes but refused to accept them. One day in January, Squadron Leader Carpenter and I went to the Quartermasters Dept at Tiergarten, which is a second-hand clothing store. I had obtained authority to obtain a second-hand overcoat. I got a coat and Carpenter got one which I pinched in the dressing room and handed it to him in the corridor. He put it on under his Macintosh and we left the shop.*
>
> *'I had agreed to meet Squadron Leader Carpenter at two o'clock the following day, but he did not turn up and when*

I telephoned his hotel, they told me he had been arrested by the Gestapo at six o'clock that morning. I made enquiries about him at the Foreign Office and was told that he had been shot.

'About this time, I was transferred from the Foreign Office to Professor Marr, who was head of the Irish Legation in Berlin. He told me that I had finished with professor Haferkorn's department and that I should have to do something.'

Hughes explained that he was given a script written by a Briton called Vernon and taken to the Rundfunk Haus where he tried to make a recording of the script. However, his voice caused problems again and the recording was unsatisfactory.

Hughes claimed that William Joyce and Dr Dietze were there and things were not so easy for him. They lectured him about speaking into a microphone and told him that Carpenter had been shot. A few days later, Hughes claimed he made a recording from another Vernon script. Hughes claimed to have met with the likes of McCarthy, Wallace and Purdy and another man called Humphreys at the Rundfunk Haus in Berlin. He claimed to have made another record with Professor Marr and on another occasion he met with Bolby (Edwin S. Bowlby).

'I had a heart-to-heart talk with Bolby regarding the British Free Corps. I had by that time got three revolvers from a Dutchman which I got handed to members of the Free Corps. Corporal Martin got one. I mentioned to Bolby that there would possibly be trouble in the Free Corps, as some of them had got arms and it would be possible that they would be turning against the Germans. Bolby got excited about this and went and saw William Joyce about it. After this he telephoned a friend of his in the Gestapo – Herr Bucker – and on the following morning Bolby and I went to Bucker's office where I related my story. They thanked me for the information. I heard that the Free Corps billets had been raided and that a number had been sent back to camp – including Corporal Martin.'

In a later chapter, we shall see the statements of a number of these British Free Corps men, they show that Hughes' account was not quite the story recounted by them.

Hughes claimed that on 24 March 1944, he had visited the Robert Bosch factory, where he removed distributors from wagons and a blockbuster bomb landed and collapsed the shelter he was inside. He was rescued but arrested by the civilian police and placed in a cell. He was then handed over to the Gestapo and placed in a cell with thirty-eight other men at Borzestrasse prison. He remained there until 10 April, listening to prisoners being tortured or beaten.

Eventually, he was released and went to see Dr Hans Schultze in Berlin. Schultze told him that he had finished with the British Free Corps and was leaving for Rome, (this was the man in Rome Hughes had written to, the copy of which the investigators now held). Schultze offered Hughes the use of his flat in Berlin if he paid the rent.

Hughes moved to the Radio Metropole station at Wansee. The electric cables had been damaged by the allied bombing and Hughes said he did nothing for a month. Eventually, he started to 'announce musical records' on the radio station, he also claimed to have a few small speaking parts in radio plays.

> *'After I had been there for a time, I told them I spoke Welsh and as there were Welsh regiments in Italy and Africa, I suggested that I should do a broadcast in Welsh. It was a direct broadcast as no records were played there.*
>
> *'I wrote a script in Welsh with the national anthem of Wales "Land of our fathers", then I gave an address which included the Lord's Prayer. In the middle of the Lord's Prayer, I put in, "You know where I am, give the sports place a good clout, it is being used as a place for talking over the air", I also put over news items, nonpolitical, such as the death of Lloyd George and other matters affecting Welsh people, which information I got from the* Daily Express. *These programmes were all in Welsh, it was a feature programme and lasted fifteen minutes.*
>
> *'At Radio Metropole my salary was 600 Reichsmarks a month, but I only drew 400, the remainder going in taxes.'*

Hughes claimed he asked for a holiday which was refused. He took one regardless and was arrested and questioned upon his return, by the SD man Major Heimpel. He was asked where he had been for a week and his flat was searched by police/Gestapo. Hughes claimed his hidden documents, strapped to the underside of the coffee table had not been discovered, so he paid Frau Brunne the rent. He then gave her an additional 6,000 Reichsmarks to look after the documents, telling her to only give these to him or a senior British officer. He was then taken back to the police station.

On 22 August 1944, Hughes says he was taken to the air force prisoner of war camp and interviewed by Pilot Officer Thompson and Warrant Officer George Edwards of the South African Air Force. Hughes told them everything about the past year, but he believed Thompson did not believe him. Hughes could now speak fluent German and became the advanced German language instructor in the camp.

On 19 January 1945, with the Soviet advance, the prisoners were force-marched away from the Russians and he was part of a party looking after sick men. Eventually he ended up in Sagan (Stalag Luft III).

> *'I met Squadron Leader Carpenter again at Sagan. We had a chat about what had been happening, but nothing special. He did warn me to refuse an interview with Group Captain Wilson. He can tell you the reasons why himself.'*

This was undoubtedly Group Captain Douglas Ernest Wilson RAAF who is covered later in this book.

A few days after arriving at Sagan, Hughes claims he was given a party of over fifty men, including officers, to take to Luckenwalde by rail. They arrived at the camp and were liberated on 22 April 1945. Hughes claimed he then drew a map of Berlin showing all the places which had not been blitzed and the radio, gas and power stations etc.

Hughes continued his statement:

> *'When I was in Berlin with Squadron Leader Carpenter, he wrote a number of letters to his cousin in England in code. I saw one of the letters. The code was, as I remember, that if you took the words with capital letters and put them together, they formed a sentence. The letter I saw referred to the Free Corps and that the Reichssportfeld was undamaged and an important centre of German broadcast propaganda.'*

The code referred to by Hughes, appears to be too simple to be genuine. In recent years, academics have discovered and unravelled one of the

MI9 POW codes. This was much more complex and relied upon the letter's author taking the first letter of every word in groups of three, before moving onto a three-dimensional matrix. Prisoners would include subtle cues to indicate to the British censor that the letter contained coded intelligence. This might be as simple as the author underlining his signature. Such a complex and detailed code appears on face value, to have been too much for Hughes to comprehend and the statement regarding Carpenter's code, may have been another fabrication.

Hughes concluded his statement:

> *'Whilst in Berlin, I got to know that not well guarded lorries conveying dynamite for destroying dangerous buildings, were travelling about the city and I spoke to Sergeant Wilson of the Free Corps about this. He said he was an expert and asked him to get me some, but he never did so. I also met a Sergeant Blackman in the Free Corps who had been captured at Leros, He knew me as Hughes and as K39. He was one I managed to get back to camp.*
>
> *'In January 1944, I wrecked a train in Berlin. It was one which brought workers and material from a tar factory at Sehlendorf. The train ran through a wood. I jammed the points with a brick after having turned the lever which was secured by a wire. I am informed the train had gone over an embankment and sixty-three people were killed. Squadron Leader Carpenter also knew about it.'*

Raymond Hughes' statement was detailed, but while many facts were corroborated by other witness statements and documents, some of his claims appeared to be too good to be true, while others were clearly incorrect.

Hughes also provided lists of British collaborators (see file: KV2/262 enclosure 78b). He provided a sketch map of the Berlin area, its buildings and defences. This was examined by Major Douglas Packer of Military Intelligence. In his report concerning this map he stated:

> *'The sketch map and key is supposed to refer to the location of buildings and anti-aircraft defences in and around Berlin. I have compared these sketch plans with records of the anti-aircraft defences of Berlin during the last six months of 1944, as recorded in my section.*

> *'The plan can only be considered as a schematic representation of the air defences and had it been received by us at the time of its preparation, it would not materially have assisted us in the detailed pinpointing of the defences.*
>
> *'While some of the positions noted on the plan correspond roughly with our information, a great many other known positions are not recorded.'*

It appears that Raymond Hughes was something of a Walter Mitty, although a man who was at the heart of Dulag Luft, Radio Propaganda and the British Free Corps.

The RAF Special Investigation Branch now needed to check his statement in detail, finding corroboration or evidence that would dismiss his claims.

From an investigators point of view, one of the men they desperately needed to interview was Squadron Leader George Robert Carpenter, a man alternatively known as Boyd-Carpenter, or Herr Carter to the Germans in Berlin. What was his role and what would he say about Flight Sergeant Raymond Hughes? Similarly, what about the other man at Dulag Luft and the radio service – Polish Flying Officer Julius Zuromski alias Kowalski?

Chapter 8

Squadron Leader George R. CARPENTER No. 85924 and Flying Officer Julian ZUROMSKI No. P0350

One of the great conundrums is the role of Squadron Leader George Robert Carpenter, Serial Number 85924 and to a lesser extent, Polish Flying Officer Julian Zuromski Serial Number P0350.

George Carpenter was born in February 1900, in Wadhurst, East Sussex. He joined the Royal Air Force shortly after its conception in April 1918 and trained to be a pilot. From the records held in The National Archives, it appears he was too late to see combat and eventually left the service post-war. (See his personnel file in the archives ref: WO416/58/18.)

It is believed Carpenter moved to South Africa and remained there for a number of years.

With a 'new' war in Europe, on 28 May 1940, Carpenter applied to join the RAF Volunteer Reserve. It has long been alleged, but not confirmed, that his initial application was turned down because he was well into his thirties, but he altered his birth certificate and was eventually accepted and re-commissioned.

What Carpenter did for the first part of the Second World War is something of a mystery, but he joined 103 Squadron with his crew from 1662 Heavy Conversion Unit on 14 June 1943. By this time he was a Flight Lieutenant and later an acting Squadron Leader. He was somewhat older than his young crew, who were mostly around twenty years of age.

Carpenter and his crew flew eight operational sorties, before they were shot down on the night of 24-25 July 1943, on a raid to Essen. Only Carpenter, the bomb aimer, and their wireless operator survived.

Carpenter and Sergeant Brazil, his wireless operator, managed to evade capture and ended up in a safe house in Brussels, but they were betrayed and Carpenter was held in the notorious St. Gilles Prison in Brussels. He was then moved after three weeks of interrogation to Dulag Luft. Why he was held for three weeks before being transferred to Dulag Luft is unclear, but as we shall see, there were some suspicions about his activities while in the prison. There is also no mention of him being beaten or tortured at St Gilles Prison.

Part of the reason Carpenter is such an enigma is his apparent involvement in collaborative activities, but there is a lack of files dedicated to him in the UK National Archives. There are no MI5, MI9 or RAF files relating directly to George Robert Carpenter's activities in Germany, or under his pseudonym Herr Carter. The only snippets of information and evidence available come from the files of other collaborators such as Hughes and Alcock, or in later biographical books.

As we have seen, Sergeant Raymond Hughes continually mentioned Squadron Leader Carpenter throughout his statement, both at Dulag Luft and in Berlin. He claims he was a friend and in a form of conspiracy to undermine the Germans. Hughes even asked the RAF post-war for assistance in locating his 'friend' Carpenter for whom he believed he was a form of batman. Later, we shall see that Flight Sergeant Jack Alcock also mentioned knowing Squadron Leader Carpenter who gave his parole at Dulag Luft.

Professor Haferkorn mentioned in his statement that both Hughes and Freeman probably met with Herr Carter (Carpenter) at the radio station in Berlin.

In early July 1945, the RAF Special Investigation Branch sent a Secret memorandum requesting information be sought from German POWs in relation to Freeman, Hughes, Carpenter, Zuromski and another suspect, Sergeant Whillock. (See National Archives file KV2/262 enclosure 80b.)

RAF SIB clearly knew of links between Peter Adami, who served under Professor Haferkorn and Carpenter. Adami was said to have been present with Leutnant Boninghaus when the subject of Carpenter broadcasting was discussed. Boninghaus also transported Carpenter to Berlin.

The SIB also sought information about Carpenter from Dr Hetzler, the man in charge of the Reichssportfeld Propaganda radio station.

In the *After the Battle* magazine edition No. 106 (Dulag Luft), there is a comment from Sergeant Frederick Jackson, shot down on the night of 10-11 August 1943, in a 97 Squadron Lancaster. He had been captured and imprisoned at St Gilles Prison in Brussels with Squadron Leader Carpenter and Sergeant T. Froats RCAF for seven days on 24 August 1943. He claimed Carpenter recognised his name as soon as they met and even told Jackson that his navigator, Flying Officer John Canham DFC, had been in the cell the previous week. Jackson had no idea how Carpenter could have known this information and visually recognised him when he arrived in the cell. In the magazine a suspicious Sergeant Jackson said:

> *'At first, Carpenter talked a lot about himself and his influential friends in South Africa and also about his own considerable wealth and motor cars. He also told me that he had been betrayed about two weeks before I arrived, in a similar way to my own betrayal, except he had been picked up by a helper in a car in Brussels, which however, had driven him straight to the prison. He asked me about my helpers and the organisation I had been with, and about usual service questions. He also told me about his flying achievements and how he had been shot down on a raid on Essen at the end of May. Our third (Froats), although present, kept quiet.'*

This comment from Sergeant Jackson appears to be valid. Carpenter had been betrayed and he had been on a raid to Essen when he was shot down. The issue is how he knew Jackson's name, that of his navigator, and why he was asking so many questions? Was he working under the direction of the Gestapo and did this cell have a hidden microphone? In addition, the boasting of Carpenter is similar to that of Hughes and the other prisoners we have examined so far. It is also worth noting that Jackson says Carpenter had been shot down at the end of May, when in reality it was the night of 24-25 July.

In his biography of Wing Commander Harry 'Wings' Day, Sydney Smith, on page 160-162 refers to a Squadron Leader Fitz-Boyd arriving at Stalag Luft III in Sagan. There is no doubt this is *our* Squadron Leader George Robert Carpenter, and it appears this was a deliberately misleading name, used by Day and or Smith, but it was similar to the name Boyd-Carpenter used by Hughes at times. It appears a pseudonym was utilised, like that used to identify Benson Freeman earlier in the same book.

Day had been at Dulag Luft, but he had moved on before Carpenter arrived in 1943. When he arrived at Sagan in early 1944, the three tunnels for the so-called Great Escape were under construction. Smith states in the book:

> *'Early in 1944 a Squadron Leader Fitz-Boyd arrived in the camp under special escort by a member of Goebbels Propaganda Ministry. Wings had been on the lookout for him*

for months, ever since receiving a report from Dulag Luft that he had been kept a long time in the interrogation centre and supplied with generous Red Cross rations, before eventually disappearing with a Luftwaffe escort to Berlin.

'Fitz-Boyd, a stocky swarthy man in his late thirties with a cultured voice and appearance, was a night fighter intruder pilot. (Author's comment: This information about him being a night fighter intruder is obviously incorrect.)

'The Germans had soon caught onto Fitz-Boyd's greatest weakness: he could not stop talking and when he talked he could not stop boasting. He spent several months in Berlin attached to a group of renegades, helping as ineffectively as possible with German broadcasts to the Allies. Eventually he was arrested by the criminal police for a series of shoplifting escapades with an English accomplice. The object of the felony was to pawn their loot to buy extra rations of schnapps.

'Fitz-Boyd was tried in a Berlin Magistrates Court and found guilty. His sentence was suspended on condition that he was returned to a proper prisoner of war camp. The moment he was released by the Germans into the Sagan North compound, he was put under barrack arrest. Roger Bushell (also ex-Dulag Luft), as the best lawyer in the camp led the chief interrogation at an official RAF prison camp Court of Inquiry ordered by "Wings" Day. Fitz-Boyd claimed that he had played along with the Germans simply to try and pick up details of the German night fighter system. He had allowed them to send him to Berlin for that reason, but with the intention of escaping at the first opportunity. This he had done he said, but he had been recaptured and ...well...here he was.

'It was decided that he should remain under barrack arrest, permanently escorted and watched day and night by appointed officers, at least until the tunnel "Harry" had broken (the surface).

'To "Wings" Day, the Fitz-Boyd (Carpenter) incident was the clue he needed to his own escape. He spent many hours with him and learned a vast amount of valuable detail on local railway travel in and around Berlin.

'Fitz-Boyd, not the kind to be abashed by any situation, showed no especial signs of gloom at being obliged to live like

a pariah among his fellow airmen in an enemy prison camp. He chatted away cheerfully with Wings on how to survive.'

Once again, the facts appear to corroborate other statements. Who was the English shoplifting accomplice of Carpenter? Was it Hughes? Although he came from North Wales he may have not had a distinct Welsh accent.

In the book *Footsteps on the sands of time* by Oliver Clutton-Brock, he cites a comment by Flight Lieutenant William Willatt, who was also in Stalag Luft III and held in Hut 106 with Carpenter. The comment comes from another book *The Lonely Path to Freedom* by Derek Thrower. Willatt recalls Carpenter:

'His story described his arrest and transport to Berlin where he was asked to broadcast to England. He said that he was tempted to agree, so that he could subtly include valuable information about Germany in his broadcasts. He said he thought better of this and refused the Germans' request, resulting in an immediate transfer to prison camp.'

There must be a file dedicated to Squadron Leader Carpenter somewhere, as in Hughes' file (KV2/262 enclosure 69c), there is an extract from a statement taken from George Robert Carpenter on 22 May 1945. This reads verbatim from that file:

'(Dulag Luft 1943) ...and he took me out into a Summer House and asked me to promise not to escape if he left me alone for a little while. He left me alone for two hours, which I appreciated after having been in close confinement for about a month. In the same block while I was there was a Sergeant Hughes, who said he was helping our prisoners by giving them cigarettes and other things.

'Hughes arrived in Berlin after me. Hughes told me he had been put in a Gestapo Prison for giving cigarettes to prisoners in Dulag Luft and they let him out to come to Berlin. He was dressed in civilian clothes and claimed he was going to sabotage against the Germans. He said he had been asked to join the British Free Corps with a black uniform with a bulldog on the lapel. Five or six days later, he said he had been to a meeting at Rhuleben where McCarthy made a speech

in a barrack, with about 200 men who had been brought out of Prisoner of War camp solitary cells to join the Free Corps. They were to fight against the Russians. There was also supposed to be a British Lieutenant Colonel coming from Austria with 2,000 men. The Lieutenant Colonel had been captured in Finland. They also spoke of organising Air Force people to fly captured Halifaxes and Lancasters to get in the bomber stream and open fire on RAF machines. But there was little reaction to this idea.

'He suggested that I should get an aircraft and he would come as my gunner and we could escape to Russia or England. But I didn't attach much importance to the idea, although I said I'd try it. Hughes claimed he had put a stone in the points near Zylandorf and wrecked a train carrying Russian workmen, but he didn't know they were Russians till he saw the wreckage...

While this extract from a longer unlocated statement, clearly corroborates some of Raymond Hughes claimed activities, it does not contain anything to incriminate Carpenter himself; apart that is from him possibly giving his parole for more freedom.

On 30 June 1945, Squadron Leader Carpenter provided another statement, this time contained within file KV2/259 enclosure 23 (the file for Sub-Lieutenant Roy Walter Purdy another collaborator). The full statement read:

'I was shot down over Holland on 24 July 1943, and later taken to a prisoner of war camp, Dulag Luft. I remained there until 30 September 1943 and was then taken to Berlin under guard. After having been in Berlin a few days, I was taken to a radio station where I saw a German official named Adami. Adami was chief assistant to Professor Haferkorn, whom I also met. Both were German Foreign Office officials.

'I was asked by Adami to broadcast to England to say that I was all right, but I refused. I was then asked to read an article to see if my voice was suitable for broadcasting, but again I refused. The paper I was asked to read dealt with the question of inadequate wages paid to miners in England. Despite the persuasions of the German officials, I persistently refused to work as a broadcaster or translator. In fact, I have never done any work for the Germans.

'Whilst in Berlin, I was dressed in American khaki trousers, a RAF blue shirt and a civilian jacket and was referred to by the Germans as "Carter".

'The German officials often tried to persuade me to work for them, but I always refused.

'Whilst in Berlin, apart from the first few days, I lived at the Auto Hotel in Berlin and was allowed to move around freely, although I was often kept under observation. I was given money by Adami to pay my hotel bills. This would amount to 200, or sometimes more, Reichmarks a month.

'I remained in Berlin from 30 September 1943 until 28 January 1944, when I was returned to Stalag Luft III at Sagan. Adami told me the reason I was being kept in Berlin so long, was that my papers had been burned in an air raid. Adami and his associates were also under the impression that I was related to Mr Churchill and for that reason every endeavour was made to make me work for the enemy, but as I have already stated, I refused.

'During the period I was in Berlin, I used to go to the Reichssportfeld between 11am and noon each day to report to Adami. I went into the studio on about two or three dozen times, but only on one occasion did I go to the underground studio where the broadcasting and recording was actually carried on.

'I was taken to the underground studio as mentioned above by the man named Adami, who was still trying to persuade me to broadcast or work for him. This was in about October 1943. During this last visit, I stood and watched and heard a Naval Lieutenant whom I know as Wallace (and whose photograph I have now picked out), and a man named McCarthy (whose photograph I also identified) making a joint recording.'

(Author's comment: his German alias name was Wallace, but he was Sub-Lieutenant Roy Walter Purdy RNVR, detained and charged by the British authorities after the war).

'Wallace was speaking into a microphone and said, "This is British Radio National – the only uncensored radio station run by Englishmen." After Wallace had said this, McCarthy then commenced to speak into the microphone.

'Wallace remained with McCarthy throughout the talk. McCarthy's talk dealt with persuading mothers to refuse to let their sons fight and included, "Did you bring up your sons to die on the beaches?" I cannot, of course remember the exact words, but the effect of the recording was as I have indicated above.

'I have been shown a note of a broadcast which took place on 21 October 1943, and can positively identify it as the talk I heard being recorded in the underground studio, referred to above. The recording was done jointly by Wallace and McCarthy.

'I spoke to Wallace on a number of occasions. He was a most conceited and loud-mouthed individual. I asked him how he had come to do this type of work (meaning broadcasting) and he replied that he was at a camp near Bremen and the Senior British Officer there, (a naval Captain) had got on his nerves and he was willing to do anything to get away from behind barbed wire. I have no doubt in my mind from what I saw and what he told me, that Wallace was a most willing worker. He always seemed to have plenty of clothes and women friends. Wallace told me on several occasions that he was a first-class broadcaster and was much sought after by other German radio stations; and added that he was known as the "Man with the golden voice."

'On one occasion, Wallace said to me, "Look here, I believe you are a spy" and I told him he was talking nonsense. He never at any time suggested that he was committing acts of sabotage. In view of his general ways and behaviour, I would not have believed him if he said so.

'Wallace did not seem to be ashamed of the work he was doing for the Germans. In fact, he was most boastful about it, always emphasising how good a broadcaster he was and always appeared to be quite prosperous.'

Wallace, or rather Sub-Lieutenant Roy Walter Purdy RNVR, admitted in his statements that he had been working in broadcasting, but also engaged in acts of sabotage.

On 29 May 1945 in his statement, Purdy admitted being allowed to roam around Berlin and meeting William Joyce. As a result, he was known as

Ronald Wallace. He stated that he knew Royston (Pilot Officer Freeman) and his work, but Carter or Boyd-Carpenter was always at the Buro Concordia and didn't do any work.

At the end of Purdy's file (ref: KV2/259) there is a comment from MI5 that, 'Squadron Leader G.R. Carpenter must be regarded as a tainted witness, but whose statement appears reliable.'

There is an issue with the 'tainted' Squadron Leader George Robert Carpenter. Here was a man who had been held in St Gillies Prison for at least two weeks, his behaviour leading to suspicion among the other prisoners. Then he spent about a month at Dulag Luft, where he was given a place in the special cells and quarters of the Stone House, used by the likes of Hughes and others. Hughes states they, 'Both had civvy suits and money and were under no obligations' and yet Hughes admits he was engaged with the completion of the Red Cross forms.

Carpenter was sent on to Berlin and 'asked' to engage in broadcasting, but he refused to do so. Yet he was housed in a paid for hotel and allowed to move around freely, but under some observation. He claims the Germans believed he was related to Winston Churchill, but there is no evidence of this from anyone else. On 28 January 1944, Carpenter was sent to Stalag Luft III at Sagan (allegedly because of theft), where he was placed under barrack arrest and subjected to an internal inquiry.

Can we really believe the Germans and the Nazi regime were happy to allow a Squadron Leader to lounge around wearing civilian clothes for six months in a paid for hotel in Berlin? A man who had to attend the recording studios and saw other collaborators betraying their country? Or was it more expedient for the British authorities to use Carpenter as a prosecution witness?

Professor Reinhard Haferkorn made a statement dated 13 July 1945 (reference: file KV2/826 enclosure 49a). In it he describes his personal view of Carpenter, a description that could have possibly saved the Squadron Leader:

> *'I do not know why this officer was brought to Berlin, but it was at the suggestion of a Leutnant of the Luftwaffe, whose name I forget, from Dulag Luft. I now know that the officer was Leutnant Boninghaus.*
>
> *'I interviewed Carpenter upon his arrival in Berlin and as a result of this interview, was left in no doubt that he would not collaborate with us. I accordingly asked that he should*

> *be returned to Dulag Luft immediately, but certain difficulties arose to prevent this being done, and for that reason Carpenter, who was known as Carter, was kept in Berlin.*
>
> *'I do not know who paid his expenses whilst he was there. His retention in Berlin was due to the fact that we could not arrange for his return and for no other reason. In fact, after a while, we had definite suspicions that he was a British agent.*
>
> *'At the interview in Berlin, Adami was also present. Neither of us could understand why Carpenter had been selected as a possible candidate for this type of work. I do not know why Carpenter was known as Carter.'*

Perhaps the last word on Squadron Leader Carpenter should go to Pilot Officer Benson Freeman (Royston). In Dr Hetzler's archives file, there is a memorandum from Flying Officer F.R. Wickham of the RAF Special Investigation Branch. He had been directed to make further enquiries with Freeman concerning Flying Officer Zuromski (who we shall look at shortly).

In the memorandum, Flying Officer Wickham states that Freeman asked him a direct question as to what was being done about Carpenter? who he alleged he had dealt with in Berlin. He refused to make a further statement about Carpenter or Zuromski but named Dr Hetzler as their direct employer (see the chapter on courts martial for more details).

After his time at St Gilles Prison and Dulag Luft, there must have been some reason why the Luftwaffe thought Carpenter could assist their war and propaganda efforts. It is clear there was more than a whiff of suspicion about Squadron Leader Carpenter, but would this be enough for the authorities to charge him with assisting the enemy?

In the files there is one other prisoner's name both at Dulag Luft and the radio stations, continually linked to Squadron Leader Carpenter. That is the name of Polish pilot, Flying Officer Julius Zuromski.

Zuromski was born on 6 November 1918, in the town of Borysoglebsk. He joined the Polish Air Force before heading to England and joining the RAF with the service number P0350.

In 1940, it is believed he may have served with the French Air Force and engaged with the Luftwaffe, before being evacuated to England. Once in Britain he was trained to fly Spitfires and served with two Polish squadrons before joining 66 Squadron.

On 30 July 1943, at 07:10 hours, he was shot down and wounded in a Spitfire Mk. Vb, serial number BL436, while on a 'Ramrod' escort mission to Holland. He sustained burns to his face and came down near Domburg, Zeeland, in Holland.

Zuromski ended up in Dulag Luft and within a few weeks, it seems he was already either assisting the Luftwaffe or being groomed to assist them; this was because Raymond Hughes recalls meeting him and Staff Sergeant Tricks in the last weeks of August, walking around the camp in civilian clothing.

Hughes said he spoke with them and asked how Zuromski and Tricks were able to walk around the camp. They told him all he had to do was ask the guard to leave the cell door open. Later they were together with Carpenter, Alcock, and others in the special accommodation cell block. What Zuromski was doing to get this treatment is unclear from Hughes, but if Hughes was taking fake Red Cross forms to prisoners, then it is highly probable the other occupants of the improved accommodation and living standards were also engaged in something similar.

Hughes states that on 1 October 1943, Zuromski and Carpenter left Dulag Luft with Leutnant Boninghaus. Hughes claimed in his statement that he went to Zuromski's cell and found talks written in his handwriting mostly in Polish, but one or two in English making statements against the Jews and Russia.

Hughes says that Zuromski talked a lot about RAF Biggin Hill, but he never saw his documents in the registry. Zuromski's face had been badly burned and he had a beard.

When Raymond Hughes arrived in Berlin, he met both Zuromski and Carpenter in the Auto Hotel, but now they were to be called Herr Carter and Herr Kowalski or Kovalski. Zuromski, according to Hughes, '*Looked every bit a Nazi when he put a monocle to his eye*' and '*Was without doubt hand in hand with the Nazis and I warned the Squadron Leader to be careful what he said to him.*'

In Berlin, Zuromski appears to have worked for the Polish station of German propaganda. Signalman William Colledge stated in his statement that Kowalski was an acquaintance of Carter and worked on the Polish station. He was a Flying Officer in the RAF, a very brave man, but broadcast on Buro Concordia. He was, however, described as pro-British and anti-Russian.

Lance Corporal Ronald Spillman said, '*Kowalski was known as Warsaw Willi. A Polish fighter pilot with the RAF who was a prisoner of war. He came in the summer of 1944 (actually 1943). He wrote and spoke on the Polish Station of Concordia. I don't know what propaganda line he adopted.*

I don't know what happened to him. He had a mind of his own and used to stand outside during air raids and describe the raid to those in the cellars.'

Professor Haferkorn, in his statement, stated that as Zuromski was a Pole he was passed on to the Polish section having arrived with Carter. He also mentioned Zuromski was known as 'Warsaw Willi' and Peter Adami, Major Heimpel, Dr Hetzler and Leutnant Boninghaus would have known him.

Sergeant Jack Alcock, who was also at Dulag Luft, remembers being detained in a special block with Carpenter, Hughes and Tricks, as well as a Polish officer whose name he could not remember.

What happened to Flying Officer Zuromski at the end of the war is shrouded in almost as much mystery as that of Squadron Leader George Carpenter. It has been alleged that he escaped from a prisoner of war camp and joined some partisans.

There is a returning POW questionnaire in the name of Zuromski, dated 25 August 1945. There is also a scribbled note on the form stating 're-interrogated', but he seems to have dropped off the Special Investigation Branch radar and in 1948, he signed a contract to fly fighters for the embryonic Pakistan Air Force. He signed a three year contract and served with a number of squadrons, before finally returning to the United Kingdom.

He is believed to have continued flying and possibly worked as an aerial survey pilot in the Mediterranean and North Africa in the 1960s.

He died in May 1999 in Surbiton, Surrey, where he was buried. It appears Flying Officer Zuromski took a good number of secrets to the grave, as we still do not have a clear picture of what he was doing in Berlin. Perhaps if the authorities had sought the answers to these questions from the likes of William Joyce, John Amery and Baillie-Stewart, we might know why no action was taken against Zuromski.

Wing Commander Harry 'Wings' Day, first SBO at Dulag Luft 1939-41 with Ersatz the cat. (*Charles Rollings originally in Der Adler military magazine in 1940*)

Dulag Luft's Commandant's office. (*Charles Rollings*)

Above: The Stone House cell block for collaborator and VIP prisoners, with the Commandant's Office to the right. (*Charles Rollings*)

Left: Pilot Officer Benson Railton Metcalf Freeman. (*Copyright unknown freely available*)

Above left: Flight Sergeant Raymond Davies Hughes. (*Copyright unknown*)

Above right: Sergeant Jack Alcock via *Daily Mail* 3 November 1945.

Above left: Squadron Leader George Robert Carpenter. (*David Fell - northlincsweb.net*)

Above right: Flying Officer Julian K. Zuromski 66 Squadron. (*Piotr Hodyka/ Krzystka's list*)

RAF POWs being entertained away from Dulag Luft by the Luftwaffe. (*Charles Collings*)

The Wuppertal War Crimes Trial for Dulag Luft. Left to right: Lt. Gustav Bauer-Schlictegroll, Lt. Henrich Eberhardt, Boehringer, Major Junge and Lt. Oberst Erich Killinger. (*Charles Collings*)

Norman Baillie-Stewart post-war.
(*Public domain, copyright unknown*)

The two Dulag Luft Commandants: Erich Killinger and Theodor Rumpel. (*Charles Collings*)

Roger Bushell, Lt. Eberhardt and Vincent 'Paddy' Byrne. (*Charles Collings*)

Horst Barth. (*Public domain, copyright unknown*)

Above left and above right: Hermann Hakerhorn left and Dr Fritz Hesse. (*UK. Nat. Archives*)

Chapter 9

The British Free Corps (Waffen SS) and other Collaborator Witnesses

As we have seen in the first chapters of this book, the RAF prisoners who were delivered to the German propaganda services in Berlin and beyond soon came in to contact with other non-RAF collaborators.

There were many British collaborators working within the propaganda services who were not prisoners of war, these included William Joyce, John Amery and Edwin S. Bowlby. Others were ex-military such as Norman Baillie-Stewart and Vivian Stranders, while some, such as Charles Patrick Gilbert and Pearl Vardon, had been resident in the Channel Islands before they were occupied.

This group split themselves between the various departments at the propaganda service, but they soon came into contact with the likes of Freeman, Hughes, Carpenter and Zuromski. In addition, they also started to encounter men from the British and Commonwealth armies who were being used as propaganda and those seeking to join the British Free Corps.

The likes of Benson Freeman and Norman Baillie-Stewart, as well as Vivian Stranders, were heavily engaged with this new unit and by association, these contacts started to include the four RAF radio collaborators in Berlin.

A review of the various files in the British National Archives for the non-military collaborators in Berlin sheds little evidence regarding the RAF men and their collaborative activities at the Reichssportfeld establishment. In fact, the Security Service interrogators and investigators seem to have been more interested in gathering evidence on the collective group, which included the likes of Joyce, Amery, Bowlby, Purdy, Baillie-Stewart, Stranders and others as their main targets. In the archive files of these suspects, which are open to the public, there is little, if any direct evidence against the RAF or British Free Corps men. There is also no apparent evidence of the British authorities trying to seek information about the activities of the RAF collaborators from these traitors.

What evidence there is in relation to Freeman, Hughes, Carpenter and Zuromski comes mainly from the British Free Corps suspects themselves and two civilians, Arthur Chapple, a civilian ex-NAAFI manager and Reginald Humphries, who was a teacher in Germany before the war. Both men were similarly involved in propaganda at the Reichssportfeld in Berlin.

Although Reginald Humphries does not go into detail in his statement (see Archives file KV2/258), he names other British speakers at the radio station as Wallace, Carter (Carpenter), McCarthy, Lang and Murphy. Humphries highlighted the fact that these names were all assumed names and he did not know their real names.

Arthur Chapple had been captured in 1940 in France. He was a NAAFI manager and was detained and sent to a prisoner of war camp. After writing the camp magazine and showing some anti-conservative tendencies, he ended up working for Peter Adami and Dr Hetzler in Berlin.

In his statement (Archives file reference: KV2/443), Chapple admits making broadcasts himself on Radio National with the alias of Arthur Lang. He also states that all the speakers were British prisoners of war or internees like himself. He named Purdy, alias Wallace, Humphreys, Maton and in July 1944, an Irishman named Murphy as broadcasting. He added:

> *'Another was Squadron Leader Boyd-Carpenter, but he only attempted to write scripts. He came almost daily from October to December 1943 or January 1944. Some of his scripts might have been used by Maton or Humphreys.'*

Despite admitting to making broadcasts himself, Arthur Chapple stated that he refused to be introduced to the likes of William Joyce, Norman Baillie-Stewart and Benson Freeman. He added:

> *'Regarding my relations with the other Englishmen in Buro Concordia, I would like to state that I had very little to do with them and never passed my free time with them or spoke more than the time of day with them for many months. I think they did not agree with my views and they said that our station was a complete farce.*
>
> *'When Boyd-Carpenter arrived in Buro Concordia, I did not think he was pro-German. He being a British officer, I helped him with money, as he was very short and when he saw that the Germans would not send him back to a prison*

> *camp, I offered to assist him by getting him railway tickets etc. Adami had given the order that Boyd-Carpenter had not to be allowed to read the British news, when he asked to go back to the camp.'*

Other repatriated and arrested men had differing views on Squadron Leader Carpenter.

Signalman William Colledge, of the North Somerset Yeomanry, had been captured in Crete in 1941 and was recruited by the Germans to assist in covertly obtaining information from fellow prisoners. Performing poorly, he was sent to Dr Hetzler and the propaganda radio services. In his statement in Dr Hetzler's file in the UK National Archives (ref: KV2/2861), William Colledge states:

> *'About this time, a man I know as Carter (Carpenter), who was a Squadron Leader in the RAF, a thorough gentleman arrived and was an acquaintance of Kowalski (Zuromski), who worked on the Polish station. I am pretty sure that Carter did not broadcast for the Germans but may have done other work which would not be known to me, as I kept out of the office.*
>
> *'Carter gave the impression that he was a member of the British Intelligence Service. He did little work that I know of. He later disappeared. He was the whitest man I ever knew.'*

Another statement in Dr Hetzler's file came from Lance Corporal Ronald Spillman. He had also been detained in Crete and ended up at the Buro Concordia in Berlin. He stated that he knew Carpenter:

> *'Carter (Carpenter), who had been in an official position in the RAF, I think he was a prisoner of war. He used to write programmes and spoke on the Fascist Station Concordia. We all thought he was arrested. He disappeared anyhow. I didn't ever hear any of his Fascist Station broadcasts.'*

It was clear that Freeman and Hughes were complicit in propaganda broadcasts and more, but the issue with Carpenter and Zuromski was far from clear, as further statements continued to give a varying picture of their activities – especially those of Carpenter.

Corporal Francis Paul Maton of the 50th Middle East Commando was captured in Crete in 1941 and ended up in a prison camp. He too worked on propaganda at Radio National. In his statement (Archives file reference: KV2/245), he states that he would read the British newspapers in the morning, before making a ten-minute broadcast at 2:30pm for two to three minutes. He also volunteered to join the SS-Standarte Kurt Eggers, a Waffen SS propaganda unit.

He admitted to working with Arthur Chapple – known by the German pseudonym of Arthur Lang, Sub Lieutenant Walter Roy Purdy of the Royal Navy (Wallace), Humphreys and others:

> *'The station had as its main function to be a Fascist station run on the same lines as the British Union of Fascists in England, and for this purpose John Amery, Baillie-Stewart, Joyce and Freeman a Pilot Officer, all worked in the Foreign Office writing talks. Purdy and myself read the talks written by Amery, Baillie-Stewart and Freeman.'*

After describing others at the station, Maton added:

> *'Shortly after I went to Concordia, two other men came, one whose name is acting Wing Commander Carpenter, and who was before the war a personal friend of Goering. The other was a Polish RAF pilot whose real name I do not know, but who calls himself Julien Kowalski. His first real name is actually Julian and he was shot down over Holland when flying a fighter in June 1943. Carpenter was an example of the German's carelessness, because I believe that in a talk to a German officer, he had mentioned the fact that before the war, he had personally met Goering and so the Germans jumped to the conclusion that he was pro-German and sent him to Berlin in civilian clothes.*
>
> *'When he first came, he made it quite clear that he would not broadcast and only after much persuasion did he write some anti-Jewish literature. This was never used by the station. Another example of German bureaucracy is the fact that Carpenter asked to be sent back to his Stalag, but owing to the fact that he had been transferred from the Luftwaffe to the Wehrmacht, his return was delayed for four months, during which time he did absolutely nothing except draw money from*

the German Foreign Office and live a life of comparative luxury in a hotel.

'He was eventually sent away, but to where I do not know. I have heard two stories. The first is that he was shot at Sagan while attempting to escape with the other forty-odd RAF prisoners; and the second is that he did escape.

'The other RAF man, Kowalski, broadcast on a Polish station which has the same function as the English one.'

One of the best statements detailing Zuromski and Carpenter, as well as Hughes, came from Corporal Roy Courlander, a member of the New Zealand army, captured in Greece in 1941. He recruited for the British Free Corps before joining the SS-Standarte Kurt Eggers propaganda unit with Corporal Maton in 1944 and deserting in Belgium to the advancing British forces. He gave an initial statement in late 1944, after the British army picked him up.

Roy Courlander's 1944 statement and a report from a Captain Peebles in February 1945, appear to have been dismissed by a Lieutenant Colonel Seymour of SLB3 (Intelligence). He stated on the bottom of the report: *Note: 'This information in this letter about Carter can hardly be reliable, as it does not seem to fit the previous information about Carter & Carpenter. (Dated 7.2.45).'*

This was quite a sweeping statement considering the war had not yet concluded and there was a plethora of statements about to land on the intelligence services' desks, with prisoners being repatriated and other German prisoners yet to be interrogated.

(Author's comment: As a former Senior Investigating Officer with the police, I can categorically state this was a fundamental error for a senior investigating officer to make. Ignoring fresh evidence which does not corroborate previous information, which has clearly allowed a senior investigating officer to form an opinion, is not only detrimental to the suspect individual and general fairness, but it is fundamentally against the rules and aims of any investigation. So why did he say this?)

In his statemented comments to Captain Peebles, Roy Courlander commented that he had once been given a parcel of French ladies' underwear in Paris to give to an English lady in Berlin:

'Close neighbours to this woman, though not probably next door, were Carter and a Polish officer, who were together for

a month – October/November 1943. Carter was certainly on propaganda under Baillie-Stewart. Carter was a South African and was engaged on South African broadcasts.'

Courlander was quite definite about this point and was actually present at the recording of one of Carter's radio talks. He added:

'The only object in using Carter on the Empire Zone, was him being a South African.'

Courlander was asked if he had heard of Carter undertaking any other particular form of activity. He said that when Carter was approached to join the British Free Corps, which was done by Norman Baillie-Stewart, he gave a reply via Baker (Sergeant Raymond Hughes). He said he could not join, as he was waiting to join the special flying squadron when it was formed.

The other officer was a Polish officer and Courlander could not recall his name, but he was able to describe him as a fighter pilot, shot down in June/July 1943. He was flying one of the latest types of Spitfire and returning from strafing over Northern Germany when he received a direct hit by flak and bailed out right over the coast of Holland.

'He is said to be very well-in with the Luftwaffe and to have given a demonstration in a Spitfire, constructed in Germany from parts recovered, copies etc. His outlook was coloured by the fact he was told and believed, that his father had been murdered by the Russians at Katyn.'

(The Katyn Forest massacre saw the murder of over 20,000 Polish military officers, academics and others deemed members of the Polish intelligentsia by Stalin. When a German advance uncovered the massed graves, Goebbels and the Nazi propaganda machine were quick to use this information in a bid to divide the Allies in 1943.)

The Polish officer, according to Courlander, had a very badly burned face and by October 1943 the burns were not completely healed. Part of his moustache was burned and no hair grew again on half of his upper lip. He was only with Carter about a month and then disappeared from the scene.

In a previous full statement dated 23 September 1944, Lance Corporal Courlander had also stated:

'During the first half of September 1943, a Sergeant John Wilson came to Genshagen. Wilson and myself, as a result of increased suspicion in Genshagen, were moved to the Schleiffen-Ufer near Lehrbahnhof. This house was used for members of the Mission Scapini and for various Russian propagandists such as Lieutenant Trotsky, son of Leon Trotsky. While we were at this house, Major Heimpel, the SD Intelligence Officer at Stalag IIID, who had always displayed a very suspicious attitude towards me, asked me to work on the German Uberseesender under Dr Bohringer. After having put him off a couple of times, it became evident that the only way to allay his suspicions was to do a certain amount of work. I therefore wrote and broadcast four talks on colonial affairs and five on Prisoner of War reminiscences during October 1943.

'During this period, I met the following people: Percival and Dr Stranders, who were both working as freelancers on the German Radio generally; Baillie-Stewart, Flying Officer Royston (Freeman) and Flight Sergeant Baker, (Hughes) who were working in the Foreign Office propaganda section. The latest pamphlets dropped, showing Hamburg horrors, is Royston's work.

'Also at this time in Schleiffen-Ufer were Squadron Leader Carter (Carpenter) who stayed for about three days and was then given a flat in Berlin.'

This statement is quite revealing for a number of reasons. The Mission Scapini was set up by a French Vichy diplomat called Georges Scapini in 1940, to look after the affairs of prisoners of war. Later it was used to house some of the more important prisoners and those assisting the Nazis. With Carpenter being housed in the Mission Scapini house at Schleiffen-Ufer, this again raises the question of what he was doing there?

As we have already seen, Freeman and Hughes were heavily involved in the propaganda side of things in Berlin, but what was the role of Carpenter, and did he really make recordings for South African troops? If he did, where are the recordings and did British intelligence services record such broadcasts?

James Arthur Cryderman, a British army POW and member of the Waffen SS British Free Corps, also supplied a statement dated 13 May

1945. An extract from this is contained within Hughes' National Archives file KV2/262. In the extract, Cryderman states:

> *'On the Sunday before I left Pankow (Berlin), Kipling and myself were taken on a trip around Berlin. The man in charge was named Baker, who said he was an Englishman and a Flight Sergeant in the RAF. He told me that his proper name was Hughes. He is the subject of photograph No.98 shown me by Captain Spooner. When we got by the radio building, he said that was where his office was. He told us we were wise in getting out of the Free Corps.* (This would appear to have been about December 1943.)'

In the same file, KV2/262, enclosure 69d contains a statement from Private Edwin Barnard Martin, another army POW and member of the Free Corps. After joining in February 1944, he was allowed to move around with some freedom. He states in the statement taken on 13 and 16 May 1945:

> *'I first asked to be allowed to go to Berlin to see some people I knew, but they refused. I had it in my mind to see an RAF Sergeant named Hughes, who had visited Pankow several times, I believe with the object of breaking up the Free Corps.*
>
> *'I next called at the German Foreign Office to see Flight Sergeant Hughes, alias Baker, who was working in the Irish redaction. I told him that I'd been forced to sign the papers to join the British Free Corps and he said that perhaps it was just as well, as "they" had been preparing some unpleasant things for me. At this meeting (or when he had called at Pankow earlier), he gave me his address on a piece of paper from my notebook. I produce this exhibit showing "Herrn. Heinrich Griener, Berlin-Zehlendorf 4, Robert Bosch Platz 5, Klein Machow. Bus 33 to End Station."*
>
> *'The writing "Sergeant J. Hughes = Baker' is mine".*
>
> *'Hughes had an office of his own, with the name Baker on the door, but I don't know what his work was. He said he got somebody to write material for him for use on the radio, instead of doing it himself, which he was supposed to do.*
>
> *'Hughes introduced me to a man named Royce (phonetic and actually Royston – Freeman), who said he was in the RAF,*

but had been shot down in France in a Hurricane in 1940. I only met him for a minute and don't know what his work was.

'Hughes' office was situated on either the 2nd or 3rd floor at the front of the building, at the head of the main stairway, and he took me to an office at the back of the building where there was a typist.

'About a month after I got to Dronnewitz, Bowler (Edwin S. Bowlby) and I got chatting and he used the expression, "Do you like good music?" I remembered that Hughes in Berlin had used the same expression and as I trusted Hughes, I thought that he and Bowler belonged to the same organisation. I then decided to be open with Bowler and gave him some photographs of different people in the British Free Corps and information concerning the BFC, also of the happenings at Luckenwalde, The reason I told Bowler was that I hoped the information might get through to some right British people.

'The last occasion I was in Berlin, that is when I was leaving for Boissow, Blackman and Leigh told me that Flight Sergeant Hughes, alias Baker, was supposed to come and see them that day and pay them for broadcasting on German radio. I asked them why they had done it after I had warned them to get back to Stalag. They said that Bowler (Bowlby) had got them onto the radio and they didn't think this would make much difference, as they had only broadcast one or two lines in a play.'

Martin's comments about Bowlby and Hughes were backed up by Fusilier Leigh of the Lancashire Fusiliers, in his statement dated 21 July 1945. This was taken a good six to seven weeks after Martin had provided his statement:

'After the play, Blackburn and I were taken to Pankow again. Bowlby told me that I would get eighty marks for the broadcast. I was given a cheque to go and draw the money, but I gave it to Baker and told him he could have it, as I was going back to Stalag, Baker, I think, was a Flight Sergeant in the RAF. The first time I met him was at Pankow. He was wearing civvy trousers, overcoat and trilby, but an RAF battle blouse. He was working for the Rundfunk Broadcasting. I saw him there when I went up to make my broadcast. He told me then that

> *he was broadcasting propaganda to England. He advised the lads at Pankow to get out of the BFC.'*

Blackburn was Harry Charles Blackman, a Sergeant in the Essex Regiment, Service Number 6010228. He left Pankow in December 1943.

Gunner Tom Blake Kipling Service Number 1123187, also gave a statement on 18 July 1945. *(See KV2/262 enclosure 87AB)*:

> *'When I was in Berlin, I met an RAF man who was a rear-gunner and whose name was Sergeant Hughes, alias John Baker, and who came from Lancashire. He told me that he had broadcast several times over German radio.'*

Sergeant Frank George McLardy of the Royal Army Medical Corps, Service Number 7522956, gave a statement on 1-2 June 1945 (ref: KV2/262 enclosure 71a). The soldier was another member of the British Free Corps at Pankow. One extract from his statement said:

> *'Sergeant Baker, an RAF Sergeant who told me he was working as Rundfunkabteilung of the German Foreign Office with Squadron Leader Carter, came to Pankow several times. He couldn't make up his mind whether to join us or not.'*

Finally, there is the statement of Trooper John Eric Wilson of No. 3 Commando and a member of the British Free Corps. In his statement, dated 29 July and 1 August 1945, the grammar is poor and perhaps a reflection of the educational standard of the witness. He said:

> *'It was about this time that Flight Sergeant Baker made his appearance at Pankow. Courlander said Baker wanted to join the Free Corps. Baker asked me to go for a walk with him. He said that the Legion (Free Corps) was a lot of "cock" and should be stopped. I asked him why he told me that, because for all he knew I might be whole heartedly in the Corps and may report him for what he had said. He replied that he knew men when he was picking them and wanted me to help him. He said that if I proved myself of any use, he would introduce me to the chief of his organisation. I asked him what his organisation was, but he evaded the question.*

> *'My first impressions of Baker was that he was an educated chap and I thought he really was speaking truthfully. I told him that before seeing him I already intended to get rid of as many men as possible and never let it get thirty strong; and to continue to do that until the idea of the Legion was given up and by this means I would also get back. I saw Baker once or twice after this at Pankow and once went to Baker's office at Saarland Strasse, where he had a room in the German Foreign Office. He told he his job there was to correct English.*
>
> *'I later met Squadron Leader Carter who Baker told me was a Wing Commander and leader of his organisation. Carter and I went to the Excelsior Hotel to dine. While at the Excelsior, Carter told me that Baker was a young irresponsible person who lived in the clouds, or words to that effect. He said that the Germans wanted him (i.e. Carter) to work, but he wouldn't. I didn't ask him what he was doing there and he never told me. Carter said he had, as yet, no contact with any British Intelligence, but that he hoped to get it soon. I explained to him how I came to be in the Legion of St. George (British Free Corps) and why I had decided to stay. He said that I was doing right and that he would keep me informed as to how he got on.*
>
> *'At a later meeting with Carter, he told me about lorries which were going around with explosives to blow up bombed out houses and that these lorries were very carelessly guarded. He suggested that I stole a few sticks of explosive as they might come in useful at a later date. He also said that whenever I could, I was to "snip" telephone communication wires. This I did on a couple of occasions, but I never saw the type of lorries which Carter had spoken about.'*

John Wilson went on to explain that after Christmas 1943, a number of men were returned from the British Free Corps to Luckenwalde prison camp. This was because they wanted to return and get away from the Corps. At this juncture in time, he felt he was being followed and under surveillance by the Gestapo. He continued:

> *'My observations proved correct, as the next day I was called to Major Heimpel's office and reprimanded for being out after ten o'clock. This practice of shadowing us continued*

and we complained to Major Heimpel because there was a man outside the billet at almost every hour of the day. I never met with Carter again and ceased connections with Baker because he put a report in to Roepke (Author's comment: SS-Hauptsturmführer Hans Werner Roepke head of the British Free Corps), *saying that most members of the BFC were only out to commit sabotage.*

'I met Baker once again and tackled him with this, but he denied it. I know it was true because Roepke told me. I hadn't trusted Baker for some time because I heard from Courlander and other people that he was speaking on the Irish redaction. Having found Baker out and lost all contact with Carter, I began to lose hope of ever getting any contact and worried about the position I was in, having still done nothing to justify being where I was.

'I would like to say that at Luckenwalde, I was swindled into the BFC and then when I got to Pankow. I met so many people like Baker and Carter, that lent a mysterious spy aspect to the show, that I got taken up with the idea and gave myself to it; thinking that something could have materialised out of it and that I should have been able to work on those lines.'

If there is one thing these statements illustrate, it is that there were many stories surrounding Freeman, Hughes, Carpenter and Zuromski. There were allegedly a number of conflicting comments attributed to the likes of Hughes and Carpenter. The question for the British authorities was which statements and reported verbal comments were true and could be corroborated?

If we compare the statements in this chapter, we start to get a clearer picture of which comments were repeated by different witnesses and therefore corroborated one another. In addition, we can check them against the statements of Hughes, Freeman, Carpenter and Zuromski.

According to a number of these witnesses, Flight Sergeant Raymond Hughes (alias Baker), clearly worked at the Radio station and the German Foreign Office propaganda section. In addition, Hewitt claimed Hughes had openly stated to him that he hated Jews and admitted providing the Germans with plans of aerodromes, factories and ammunition dumps.

A number of the men stated that they had seen Hughes' office in the radio station complex, while another said, he had been paid 80 Reichsmarks for making a broadcast himself, but gave the money to Hughes when he was sent back to a prison camp.

There was a clear link between Raymond Hughes and the British Free Corps, with Martin stating that Hughes had told him it was just as well he (Martin) had signed the paperwork to join the Free Corps, as the Germans '*were preparing some unpleasant things*' for Martin.

McLardy also claimed that Hughes could not make his mind up whether to join the British Free Corps, while John Wilson claimed that Hughes had gone to Pankow and wanted to join the Free Corps. However, he also said, Hughes had told him the Free Corps was a lot of 'cock' before moving on to an apparent attempt to 'recruit' Wilson to an unspecified organisation. Wilson somewhat confusingly believed this may have been linked to the British Intelligence Service until Carter (Carpenter) told him he had not had any contact yet with British Intelligence.

John Wilson also claimed that Hughes had told SS-Sturmbahnführer Roepke that the Free Corps recruits were engaged in acts of sabotage, leading to a number being returned to prison camps. Wilson claimed he had challenged Hughes about this, but he had denied the accusation.

This collection of statements, together with those in previous chapters and Raymond Hughes' own statement clearly show that he was employed by the German Foreign Office on radio propaganda duties. However, there is a major question over exactly what he was trying to achieve with the British Free Corps and its recruits. In addition to this, what exactly was his relationship with Squadron Leader Carter (Carpenter)? Carpenter said Hughes' head was in the clouds and he was irresponsible, add this to the earlier comments about him being deceitful and boastful and it appears he was living in a very dangerous cloud cuckoo land.

Pilot Officer Benson Freeman (alias Royston) was also identified as working for the propaganda services, according to Colledge he appeared to have many privileges and good connections. He also heard that Freeman had joined the British Free Corps, something that was admitted by Freeman.

Maton claimed that Freeman wrote scripts for broadcasting and earned over 1,000 Reichsmarks per month.

New Zealander Roy Courlander also confirmed that Freeman worked at the propaganda office and Martin, who met him once, says that Freeman told him he was a Hurricane pilot shot down in 1940.

Once again, the evidence against Freeman from all the witnesses in this book seems to be quite compelling, especially when added to his own statement of evidence. Again, like Hughes, he seems to be boastful and deceitful about his own background.

Flying Officer Julian Zuromski (alias Kowalski) is the one suspect about whom little is known from the accounts of these men, but what information there is, is pretty damning.

Colledge, Spillman, Maton and Courlander all allege that Zuromski worked for the Germany propaganda radio services, some specifically mentioning the Polish radio section. He was deemed to be anti-Russian and Roy Courlander states this was due to his belief that the Russians had killed his father at Katyn. He also added that the Pole was 'well-in' with the Luftwaffe and flew a demonstration flight in a Spitfire, built from recovered parts.

Squadron Leader George Robert Carpenter (alias Carter) was still something of a mystery. Previous witnesses, including Professor Haferkorn, had suspected he could be a British agent, now John Wilson claimed that while dining with the pilot at the Excelsior Hotel in Berlin, he informed him that Hughes was young and irresponsible. Carpenter then added that he had no contact at that time from British Intelligence, but hoped he would have contact soon. Colledge had also said he had the impression Carpenter was working for British intelligence.

Squadron Leader Carpenter had told John Wilson that the Germans wanted him to work for them, but he would not do this. He then spoke to Wilson about lorries filled with explosives in Berlin and the cutting of telephone wires. The telephone wires and sabotage claim was in many ways, similar to the claims made by Hughes in his own statement, when he said he went out with Carpenter committing acts of sabotage in Berlin.

These acts of sabotage on the one hand appear brave and perhaps reckless, but the question is why do this if you are living in comparative luxury and why involve Hughes – a man he thought irresponsible? Was Carpenter trying to mastermind a network of saboteurs which included Hughes and John Wilson?

The fact Carpenter appears to have been stealing with Hughes and then allegedly later detained for theft, makes one wonder why he would do this?

In addition to the claims of sabotage and being an agent, Roy Courlander claimed that Carpenter had initially been housed at the Schlieffen-Ufer, a Mission Scapini house in Berlin. This location housed 'special prisoners', allegedly including Leon Trotsky's son. At the same time, Maton claimed that Carpenter had been a personal friend of Herman Goering, the head of the Luftwaffe before the war. Add to this Carpenter's own statement, when he claimed Peter Adami and the other German officials believed he was related to Winston Churchill, and we have a very confusing story; but one which would explain him being housed in the Schlieffen-Ufer and then the Excelsior Hotel while apparently not doing much work! This apparent double-crossing and differing explanations is reminiscent of the Alastair McLean novel '*Where Eagles Dare*', but was Carpenter/Carter a British agent or a man who played confidence tricks on others to further his own future?

However, there were witnesses as we have seen, who claim that Carpenter was working for the German propaganda services. Courlander had also claimed that Carpenter worked under Norman Baillie-Stewart on propaganda, as well as broadcasting on the South African radio broadcasts.

Colledge claimed Carpenter did not broadcast, but maybe did other work for the Germans, while on the contrary, Humphries said he did speak on the radio.

Arthur Chapple claimed Carpenter had attempted to write radio scripts and was at the radio station on an almost daily basis, between October and December 1943 or January 1944. Chapple also recalled that after Carpenter wanted to return to Stalag, Peter Adami had directed that he was not to read anything on the radio. Is this another indication that he had already made some broadcasts?

Maton added that the Germans were careless with Carpenter and inefficient – something most Britons do not normally associate with Germany. Maton claimed that as the Luftwaffe had transferred responsibility for Carpenter to the Wehrmacht, they could not send him back to a Luftwaffe controlled Stalag. As a result, he lived a life of comparative luxury in a hotel in Berlin, paid for by the Germany state.

However, Maton claims that after some persuasion from the Germans, Carpenter did write some anti-Jewish literature, but it was never used in radio broadcasts.

Finally, to return to Roy Courlander's statement, he claimed that Carpenter had been asked to join the British Free Corps. He had declined via Hughes, stating that he was waiting to join a special flying unit which had not yet been formed. Add to this the statement of McLardy, which states Carpenter visited Pankow with Hughes and it raises some questions about what he was actually doing and what his aims were.

These claims about Carpenter are quite varied, in some cases extreme and without corroboration, but there is a continuing theme running through them: that Carpenter did little or no work, was engaged in or encouraging sabotage and was believed to be either related to Churchill or a friend of Goering. It appears he was happy to admit the Churchill line himself and that he had been somewhere else for his first few days in Berlin, although he did not specify where he was or that it was the Schleiffen-Ufer house. He then said he had stayed at the Auto Hotel.

While Hughes and Freeman were without doubt traitors and Zuromski likely to have been a radio broadcaster, the question is whether there was sufficient evidence to indict Carpenter.

Here lies the issue with an apparent lack of evidence and questioning of the main traitors such as William Joyce, Norman Baillie-Stewart, John Amery, Vivian Stranders etc. Could these men have provided evidence against these RAF airmen or are there other closed files that do contain such evidence?

Finally, could Squadron Leader George Robert Carpenter have actually been a member of British Intelligence? It seems highly unlikely, for the sole reason that he was shot down in mid-1943 and it is inconceivable that was a planned event.

It would appear Carpenter made the most of his predicament and possibly used those around him, playing the system. A system that could easily have dispensed with him at any point in time.

Chapter 10

Flight Sergeant Jack ALCOCK No. 1480577

Flight Sergeant Jack Alcock would be deemed to have been a collaborator by the RAF and the British authorities, but he was somewhat different to the four airmen described so far.

Born in Manchester in January 1913, he joined the Royal Air Force in April 1941 Service Number 1480577 and trained as an air gunner. He was posted to 51 Squadron at RAF Snaith, between York and Doncaster, in the summer of 1943 and began operations shortly after his arrival.

Just a few weeks after arriving at RAF Snaith, on the night of 5-6 September 1943, Jack Alcock and his crew took off in their Halifax, serial number JD263 to bomb Mannheim.

At about 00:44 local time, they were intercepted at over 11,000 feet by a night fighter, probably a Focke-Wulf 190 Wild Boar of JG300, flown by Oberfeldwebel Karl-Heinz Seeler. The Halifax was shot down and appears to have exploded in mid-air, but not before Alcock and another crewman parachuted to safety. Sadly, the remaining five members of the crew were reported missing believed killed and they are commemorated on the RAF Memorial at Runnymede.

Jack Alcock was soon captured and sent to Dulag Luft at Oberursel. Although Raymond Hughes identified Jack Alcock as residing in the same improved stone house cells at Oberursel with himself, Carpenter, Zuromski, Tricks and Group Captain Wilson, there was little in the way of evidence against him. Very little evidence was supplied by other prisoners of war, while Hughes described giving Alcock and the American Tricks, some of his bottles of beer.

Alcock appears to have been his own worst enemy, both at Dulag Luft and later, when the RAF Special Investigation Branch (SIB) team started to ask questions about his time in captivity.

Apart from Hughes, the main prosecution evidence came from Leutnant Gustav Bauer Schlichtegroll, who would later provide a statement in June 1945, as well as Jack Alcock himself.

Leutnant Bauer Schlichtegroll had given a lengthy statement to the SIB team investigating the actions of collaborators at Dulag Luft and the Propaganda radio services in Berlin. He had worked at Dulag Luft from February 1942 to March 1945.

In relation to Sergeant Jack Alcock, Bauer Schlichtegroll said he worked as an interrogator at Dulag Luft and met Alcock when he came in for interrogation in the late summer or the beginning of autumn 1943. Alcock was interrogated in Bauer Schlichtegroll's own office after another officer went away temporarily, but he did not know if a previous interrogation had taken place.

He asked Alcock for details of his squadron, group and home station. Initially, Alcock had not given any details, but eventually he provided them when he was told he would have to stay in his cell for some time. Alcock complained that he had been in solitary confinement for some time and asked how long this would continue. Bauer Schlichtegroll informed him that he was in quarantine for health reasons and it might take some time. Alcock replied, saying he wanted to get out of his cell and asked Bauer Schlichtegroll what he wanted to know. The interviewer asked Jack Alcock for his squadron and various other details which were then freely provided by the airman.

The next day, Bauer Schlichtegroll interrogated Alcock again, but he could not remember the precise questions he asked. Bauer Schlichtegroll recalled Alcock mentioning that he worked in an aircraft factory, so he passed him on to the engineering interrogation officer Leutnant Tobler, who would try and get some technical answers from him. Leutnant Tobler interrogated Alcock twice.

After Tobler had completed his interrogations, Bauer Schlichtegroll interviewed Alcock again with some extra questions, probably about RAF organisation. From this renewed interrogation, Bauer Schlichtegroll managed to get information about 51 Squadron and Alcock's home airfield at Snaith, although he told the British investigators that after so much time, he could not remember the details. He also could not recall whether this was original information or just confirmation of previous intelligence gleaned from other sources.

Bauer Schlichtegroll could not remember whether he interrogated Alcock while dressed in civilian clothes or if he told the prisoner he was a member of the Luftwaffe. However, he was certain that if he had introduced himself to Alcock (which was standard procedure), he would have said he was acting on behalf of the Luftwaffe.

Jack Alcock asked Bauer Schlichtegroll if he could go to a POW camp and the German said he could go. However, the Luftwaffe officer made Alcock a proposal asking him, '*You can go to a prisoner of war camp, but would you consider having some more freedom in our place and doing some jobs for us?*'

All Alcock had to do was take Red Cross forms to prisoners and have them fill in the answers to several questions. These were the forms that Alcock had already partially filled in himself. Alcock knew the content and nature of these forms, questionnaires which airmen were briefed to look out for during their security briefings in Britain.

The forms contained the usual questions such as name, rank number, home address, squadron, aerodrome, crew details and so on. It also included time and place shot down. Some forms had a Red Cross emblem on them, but later forms did not contain the emblem – unauthorised use of which was a war crime.

Alcock initially asked for time to consider the offer, but after a day, Bauer-Schlichtegroll asked him if he had made a decision. Alcock asked what the *freedom* amounted to. It was explained, this included being allowed to wear civilian clothes and an ability to move around the camp at Oberursel. Bauer Schlichtegroll added, that Alcock was also told, '*There was hardly anything of military value contained on the sheet, apart from possibly the squadron, or station which we mostly knew anyway.*'

Eventually, Jack Alcock agreed to the offer and was given civilian clothes and better quarters in the Stone House.

According to Bauer Schlichtegroll, over the next two months, Alcock went about the camp with the forms, trying to get recently arrived airmen to fill in the answers to the questions. Bauer Schlichtegroll recalled the first form Alcock was given, was possibly one with a Red Cross emblem on it. In addition, Bauer Schlichtegroll could listen in to some of the meetings between Alcock and the new prisoners via a series of hidden microphones in the solitary confinement cells.

Bauer Schlichtegroll thought Alcock's line of questioning to be clumsy and more likely to cause suspicion among the prisoners. Alcock would say phrases like, '*Come on sign this, it's all above board.*' When he introduced himself to the prisoners, Alcock would say, '*Well I've taken on this work now, it's mostly Red Cross or connected with notifying the relatives.*'

Alcock was given freedom of movement around a limited area. This was about five miles from the centre of the Dulag Luft camp. His quarters were in a stone house near the Commandant's office and he was housed with other prisoners, with a little mess room and sleeping quarters. Bauer Schlichtegroll confirmed that some of the other prisoners housed in the stone house were also working for the Dulag Luft staff. Those not working for the Germans but housed in the block were often high-ranking prisoners.

In time, Alcock became apprehensive and did not like the work anymore. According to Bauer Schlichtegroll, Alcock did the Red Cross form work for about seven to eight weeks. Eventually, he was sent on to another prisoner of war camp.

This was the initial evidence against Jack Alcock and led to him being marked as a possible collaborator and suspect. After the war concluded, he was repatriated and returned to England in May 1945, being housed in London.

It appears from records held within the UK National Archives that Jack Alcock did not have the most distinguished of career records prior to being captured. He had previously been charged with being absent without leave, being absent from parade and while on sentry duty, being insufficiently on alert.

On 18 May 1945, Flight Lieutenant G.E.T. Nicholls DFC DFM, attended the Endsleigh Hotel in Euston with Flight Sergeant Inglis of the RAF Special Investigation Branch. There they located Jack Alcock.

Flight Lieutenant Nicholls told Alcock that they were making enquiries regarding activities of certain persons whilst they were prisoners of war in Germany. Nicholls then suggested that they return to his office in South Kensington, where they could continue to discuss the matter. Alcock agreed to this and all three men returned to the SIB office.

At the office, Nicholls asked Alcock if he would care to tell him what had happened to him from the time he was shot down, until he was repatriated. Alcock agreed and then related an account which bore '*no outstanding incidents of note, other than those you would have expected of a shot down airman*.'

Flight Lieutenant Nicholls told Alcock that he had received information about a Sergeant Alcock who had collaborated with the Germans at Dulag Luft. Nicholls did not go into detail about this collaboration at this point in time.

Nicholls reported in his later statement, that Alcock became very emotional and with the greatest of effort, restrained himself from crying.

Nicholls asked if he was the same Sergeant Alcock and Jack Alcock said he was. Flight Lieutenant Nicholls immediately cautioned Alcock by saying, '*You do not have to say anything unless you wish to do so, but anything you do say will be taken down in writing and may be given in evidence.*'

Alcock immediately told Nicholls and Sergeant Inglis that he would tell them all about it, but he had been tricked into this by the Germans. He then dictated a statement which was written down by Nicholls as follows:

> *'I am an air gunner and in September 1943, I was a member of 51 Squadron stationed at Snaith. On 5 September 1943, I was detailed for an operation with Mannheim as the target. I was the mid-upper gunner in Halifax 'L'. When over the target, we were attacked by a fighter and ordered to bail-out by the pilot, Flight Sergeant King. I bailed out and landed safely.*
>
> *'I landed to the west and after landing, later found a bike near Mannheim. I was cycling along and ran into a roadblock and was captured.*
>
> *'I was taken by the German police to an aerodrome and then on to Dulag Luft. I met my navigator Sergeant Barnett at the aerodrome, but we were separated at Dulag Luft and I did not see him again until I reached Stalag Luft IVB.*
>
> *'At Dulag Luft I was put in a room with two other airmen, I don't know their names. After six or seven days, I was put in a room on my own. After another four or five days, a man speaking English without an accent and dressed in civvy clothes came in to see me. He said he was from the Red Cross and asked me to fill in a long form. I answered the questions of name, rank, number, next of kin, full names of my crew.*
>
> *'Two days later, he came back and asked me to fill in details of my squadron, type of aircraft and target. I filled the details in and afterwards he asked me if I would like better quarters. I said "Yes". He said, he would let me have them if I gave him details of aircraft and operations and he would let me have my parole to go outside the camp.*
>
> *'I agreed to this and answered questions regarding the Halifax, its speed, armament, bomb load, endurance, height of flying to the target and details of "Monica". He asked about the Gee box and other gadgets, but I couldn't tell him anything about them.*

'I told him the number of planes in the squadron and number of planes of my squadron on the raid.

'I was then moved to a better room in another block. I was given a civvy jacket and civilian shoes and I received better food and toothpaste, soap and a shaving kit. I was given parole and I signed a slip of paper to this effect, and I was allowed to wander about the camp from dawn to dark.

'While I was there, I helped the man I believed to be a Red Cross official by getting, on different occasions, British aircrew prisoners of war to fill in the false Red Cross forms. I didn't encourage them to fill in all the detail and when I had finished, I gave them back to the Red Cross man. He never said anything about my not getting all the answers. That is all the work I did for the Germans.

'While I was at Dulag Luft in the special block, I met Squadron Leader Carpenter, Sergeant Hughes, Staff Sergeant Trick of the USAAF and a Polish officer whose name I cannot remember. Squadron Leader Carpenter was wearing civilian clothes and had given his parole, he wandered about the camp. Carpenter told me that he went to tea in a large house nearby. I saw the woman from this house in the garden once when I was with Carpenter. The woman spoke perfect English and Carpenter told me she was English. (Author's comment: who this woman was is unknown.)

'Hughes also wore civilian clothes and I have seen him with a folder of Red Cross forms under his arm. He also told me in the presence of Trick, that the Germans had offered him a job on the radio and he was going to take it.

'Later, Carpenter and Hughes both left for Berlin and told me they were going.

'After I saw the Red Cross man in German uniform, I realised what a fool I had been and demanded to be sent to a Stalag Camp.

'Trick was able to get beer on two occasions and told me that the Germans wanted him to go to an aerodrome and show them over an American aircraft. I don't know if he went.

'Soon after I left for Stalag IVB, I remained there until I was released by the Russians on 23 April 1945. Whilst at this camp I changed identity disks and clothing with Private

> *(unclear) and got on a working party and tried to escape. I got away from the working party but got caught by the military when I was only twenty kilometres away. I got ten days solitary confinement, but I eventually did twenty-eight days in a cell.'*

Sergeant Alcock may have been tricked, but he broke all the rules for a prisoner by discussing not only routine matters, but technical issues such as the Monica tail warning radar system. There was no need for him to have disclosed these issues and by his own admission, it was done to facilitate a better lifestyle while in captivity.

Squadron Leader Hugh Hardwick Oak-Rhind Service Number 133934 from the Air Ministry Intelligence made a statement concerning the issue of Monica:

> *'I am attached to Air Intelligence Security One (A.I.{S}1) and I have been in this department since December 1942. The formation of A.I.(S)1 is the security and records of compromise of classified equipment. Classified equipment covers everything from Top Secret to Restricted.*
>
> *'Monica is the name of a piece of radar equipment. This was in use by September 1943, it was then still Secret and remained Secret for at least six months after that. So far as our records go, the Germans had some knowledge of it in the last four months of the year. We were uncertain of the exact extent of their knowledge, but there was evidence to show they were concerned to obtain further details of it.*
>
> *'Whether information given to the Germans about Monica at this time would have been of use to them, would depend upon the nature of the information given.'*

While the RAF SIB had no specific evidence of exactly what Jack Alock disclosed in relation to Monica, it was clear they were very concerned and there was the possibility that he had increased the Germans' knowledge of the system. With hindsight, we now know the German scientists had developed an electronic system of their own, which was deployed in early 1944 – the passive radar receiver called the Flensberg FuG 227. This allowed their night fighters to home in on the tail of British bombers fitted with Monica. It is highly unlikely that Alcock would have known or even been aware of the technical abilities and frequencies of the Monica system.

However, he would have been aware of the system and how it worked, warning them of an approaching night fighter. Having been captured in September 1943 and interrogated by Leutnant Tobler, it is possible he gave them some useful information, no matter how small, which assisted them and ultimately led to the development of the FuG 227. That could have indirectly led to the deaths of many allied airmen.

On 27 July 1945, Squadron Leader William Percy Thomas from the RAF Special Investigation Branch and Sergeant William John Hicks, met with Alcock in the Main Guard Room of RAF Cosford, where he was now stationed.

Sergeant Hicks read two charges of assisting the enemy to Alcock and cautioned him. Alcock replied, *'As I said in my statement when I came back to England, I made a fool of myself, I was tricked into it by the German Intelligence Staff. When I found out I had made a mistake, I demanded to be sent to a prison camp.'*

Alcock was then conveyed under close arrest to RAF Uxbridge to await court martial. In his statement Sergeant Hicks said that en route to Uxbridge Alcock made one or two remarks which he later recorded in his notebook. He could not do this contemporaneously, as he was driving the car at the time. Alcock had said he was worried about the matter and was sorry it had happened. He said that as Squadron Leader Carpenter was doing the same thing as himself, he thought it was alright to give his parole.

Squadron Leader George Robert Carpenter, as previously stated, was an intriguing character in all of these accounts. The man appears to have been in and around Dulag Luft before moving on to join other collaborators at the German Radio propaganda in Berlin, allegedly without doing anything of benefit for the enemy.

While Carpenter had not been indicted, Flight Sergeant Jack Alcock was now preparing himself for a court martial.

Chapter 11

Wing Commander Harry 'Wings' DAY No. 5175 and Group Captain Douglas E. WILSON RAAF No. A16

During the course of my research for this book, I found three senior officers who were claimed, at times, to be collaborators of one sort or another. Freeman and Hughes certainly had a lot to say about these men, as did Squadron Leader Carpenter.

Wing Commander Harry 'Wings' Day was a career RAF officer and commanded No. 57 Squadron in 1939. On 13 October 1939, he became one of the RAF's first casualties in France when his Bristol Blenheim was shot down by a Messerschmitt 109E. Injured in the process and suffering burns to his hands and face, he was captured and received medical treatment before being sent to Spangenberg Castle POW camp, which was Wehrmacht controlled. Before he arrived at Spangenberg Castle, Day was interrogated and was one of the first men to see the fake Red Cross forms. Clearly believing it to be a phoney intelligence form, he chose not to fill it in – other than with his name, rank and service number.

When Dulag Luft was opened at Oberursel by the Luftwaffe, Day was one of the first prisoners to be transferred to the new site and by Christmas 1939, he was part of the new British permanent staff.

The camp commandant, Theodor Rumpel, tried to make the facilities as comfortable as possible and in early 1940 he gave Harry Day a gift – a pet cat. A German propaganda team arrived at the camp and took photographs, one of which featured Day and the cat. The image was posted in the German military magazine *Der Alder* and was undoubtedly seen in Britain by the Intelligence services and in other prison camps. This in many ways was the start of problems for 'Wings' Day. (The image is included in the photographic section of this book.)

Ill feeling towards Day and the other permanent prisoners at Dulag Luft started in early 1940, with the allegation that Red Cross parcels were not being sent on to Barth from Dulag Luft. Squadron Leader Stevenson and Lieutenant Fanshaw (Royal Navy) sent a report to England complaining about this, but this was later rectified, as parcels should have been requested via Geneva, not Dulag Luft at Oberursel.

There was an official British decree that prisoners of war should not give their word not to escape. However, when Theodor Rumpel and his officers offered walks in the nearby woods on the proviso the airmen gave their parole (word) not to attempt to escape, Day agreed to this. His later explanation was that the confined camp justified 'parole walks' for the good of the prisoner's mental health. On these walks, an armed guard always followed the escorting Luftwaffe officer and the prisoner, they would talk freely and sometimes stop for a glass of beer. This, on occasion, undoubtedly loosened tongues.

Word soon got out to the prison camps about these walks and the easy-going camp management at Oberursel. This, as can be imagined, started to cause some bad feeling among the prisoners at other camps.

Unknown to Harry Day, the Luftwaffe were starting to develop their system of interrogation and intelligence gathering, and the use of fake Red Cross forms would become commonplace.

One prisoner who had been at Dulag Luft for some time was Pilot Officer Benson Freeman. As we have already seen, he was a former British Union of Fascists member who could not contain his views. Squadron Leader Roger Bushell asked his commanding officer to order Freeman to keep his fascist views to himself, but Day thought Freeman would make this known to Eberhardt and Rumpel and they would use it in anti-British propaganda.

In addition, Day also had Major John 'Johnnie' Dodge, a distant relative of Winston Churchill in his camp. Dodge had been initially captured in Normandy in June 1940 before escaping. He was recaptured by the Luftwaffe and although he was a soldier, he was sent to the Luftwaffe camp at Dulag Luft.

It was claimed that Dodge tried to deceive the Germans by claiming that he could be exchanged for German prisoners. He wrote home, knowing the German censors would read his letters, stating his admiration for Adolf Hitler. He also, like many other members of the permanent staff under Day, regularly chatted with the camps' German officers. This once again did not go unnoticed by prisoners heading to other camps and word soon spread of these 'collaborating' officers, overseen by an apparently compliant Wing Commander Harry Day.

In the summer of 1940, unknown to most prisoners, Day was sending coded messages home to MI9, using the code a recently arrived prisoner had taught him. In London, it seemed to MI9 and the RAF, that Day was a Senior British Officer who was sending back valued intelligence. However, they would soon start to receive coded messages from other camps in relation to the activities at Oberursel.

Day had a permanent staff at the camp, so he started to give these men responsibilities. Unknown to him at the time, many of these men would feature in later collaboration reports and allegations. Among others, he made Flight Lieutenant Richard Hardy the Messing Officer, Pilot Officer Benson Freeman the Clothing Officer, Sergeant John Slowey was President of the Mess and Sergeant Michael Joyce the storeman responsible for Red Cross parcels. All of these men would come under suspicion and all on Days 'watch' as the Senior British Officer, therefore some started to doubt Harry Day's allegiance.

In September 1940, three Irishmen – Flying Officer Vincent Byrne, Flight Lieutenant Mike Casey and Sergeant Michael Joyce – were invited by the Germans to be interviewed by a panel of supposed Irish nationals. The three airmen had Irish connections and were questioned about camp conditions and their knowledge of Dublin, but it was clear this was the first step to recruiting them as collaborators.

Mike Casey dismissed the matter out of hand, but Paddy Byrne spoke with 'Wings' Day and proposed a plan to make the Germans think he was an Irish nationalist. He hoped to gain their confidence and then escape, while identifying other renegades. Day agreed and through the coded message system, he received authority from MI9 to go ahead with the plan. It took two months for this to get the go-ahead, and in order to preserve the cover, only Byrne, Day and Roger Bushell, the head of escape intelligence, knew of the plan. As we have seen, the plan did not reach fruition and Byrne later managed to get repatriated via his faked mental illness.

The third member of the trio, Michael Joyce, did become a collaborator and is covered in Chapter 13.

In January 1941, there were increasing numbers of RAF prisoners in Germany, and most had passed through the Dulag Luft establishment. They did not like what they saw and heard and were quick to make their feelings known when they arrived at the other prison camps.

The Dulag Luft permanent staff lived two to a room with books, lamp shades and apparently had plenty of food, alcohol sometimes provided by the Commandant and their Red Cross parcels. In comparison, the men at

Stalag Luft I at Barth had not received any Red Cross parcels in months. They were cold, hungry and most wore the same clothes they had been shot down in, months before.

The Senior British Officer at Barth, believed to have been Squadron Leader Brian Paddon, sent a letter through German channels to Dulag Luft, accusing Harry Day of diverting Red Cross parcels for the use of himself and his permanent staff.

In the book *'Wings' Day*, a biography of Harry Day, Sydney Smith recounts the episode:

> *'One day Rumpel received a letter from Stalag Luft I at Barth, addressed to Wings. It was signed by the Senior British Officer, a Squadron Leader and being a POW's letter it was opened. Eberhardt stood and watched while Wings read it. It was expressed in terms that were more than simply impertinent. It implied quite clearly, that Wings was responsible for diverting – to put it bluntly, stealing – personal and Red Cross parcels for the use of himself and the Dulag Permanent Staff. Still holding the letter, Wings looked up, trembling with shock and fury. Eberhardt, who knew the injustice of the accusation, was embarrassed and said, "They don't seem to like you much up there Wing Commander." Wings replied, "My compliments to Major Rumpel. I shall not be replying to the letter," and turned away.'*

Harry Day was disgusted by the impertinence of this officer and even more angry with the fact he had sought to send it via the Luftwaffe, knowing only too well it would be read by them.

The problem for Day was that thanks to coded letters from other camps, aircrew were now being briefed to be wary of Dulag Luft and the permanent staff there. In effect, although Day was sending coded information of his own to MI9, they were receiving a lot more information about Day and his permanent staff.

Day did not know it at the time, but the RAF/MI9 directed two Squadron Leaders at Barth to conduct an inquiry into Day and his activities. They interviewed a large number of officers who had passed through Dulag Luft. The report which was said to have taken six months to compile, exonerated Day, but neither he or his staff were told of the result and an element of suspicion remained.

In June 1941, a number of officers escaped from Dulag Luft and a few months later, Rumpel was replaced by a new commandant – Erich Killinger. Harry Day was sent on to Stalag Luft I at Barth, the last place he must have wanted to be.

The arrival of Harry Day and a number of his permanent staff at Barth caused a commotion. As they arrived, the prisoners were lined up for the final count of heads for the day. There were some boos and a few unpleasant remarks, but Day held his nerve as he walked past them.

Later, in his quarters, Day asked Squadron Leader David Torrens where the officer who had written the accusation was. He was told the officer had been sent to Colditz. Although Smith and Day never name the officer in their book, this appears to confirm that the accusing officer was Brian Paddon, who was sent to Colditz Castle in May 1941, just before the escape attempt from Oberursel and Day's arrival at Barth.

(Brian Paddon would actually escape in 1942 and make a 'homerun' back to Britain via Sweden. He was awarded the Distinguished Service Order and remained in the RAF post-war, reaching the rank of Group Captain. Whether Day and Paddon ever met after the war is unknown.)

Squadron Leader David Torrens advised Day that the allegation that Dulag Luft staff took parcels and collaborated was just a general feeling across the camp which just grew out of control.

News soon spread around Barth that Day and the others had only arrived because of the escape attempt. This improved feelings towards Day, but some suspicion remained. This was probably not helped when Harry Day dealt with the issue of another alleged collaborator, Flying Officer Peter Casenove (see the next chapter).

Despite the suspicion that some still held, Day ensured that new prisoners were debriefed and information sent back home via the coded letters. He also oversaw a series of escape attempts and tunnels, but in April 1942, Day and a large number of officers were transferred to a new camp – the infamous Stalag Luft III at Sagan.

Harry Day was the initial SBO at Sagan, but he passed the baton on to Group Captain Massey in September 1942.

In Chapter 8, we saw how Harry Day dealt with George Robert Carpenter when he arrived at Sagan. As time passed by, it was clear suspicion started to decrease and Harry Day regained respect.

Harry Day was at Sagan when the Great Escape took place. He managed to escape with fellow Dulag Luft airmen Roger Bushell and Mike Casey who were recaptured and murdered by the Gestapo.

Day escaped dressed as a British Colonel, he was supposed to be under armed guard by a German soldier, in reality a Polish airman called Flying Officer Pawel Tobolski. The two men made their way to Stettin but were betrayed and arrested. Day was conveyed to Berlin and interviewed by Arthur Nebe of the Gestapo – the man who chose the fifty airmen to be executed on the orders of Adolf Hitler. Sadly, Bushell, Casey and Pawel Tobolski were among the fifty men murdered by the Gestapo.

Day was not executed, he was sent to Sachsenhausen concentration camp and then Dachau in 1945. He was in effect under sentence of death but managed to escape to Allied lines. He was repatriated and awarded the Distinguished Service Order (DSO) and the Order of the British Empire (OBE). He remained in the RAF until 1950, reaching the rank of Group Captain.

Harry 'Wings' Day spent a considerable amount of time in German captivity. As a Senior British Officer, he always sought to do the right thing for his men. In many ways, he played a 'wise hand' and did just enough to satisfy his captors. To many, he may have looked like a collaborator, but he could not divulge everything he knew and did at the time. The fact he assisted in so many escapes, wrote coded letters and assisted other prisoners was not lost on the authorities in 1945. However, it is clear there was an element of suspicion during the early years of the war.

* * *

Group Captain Douglas Ernest Lancelot Wilson of the Royal Australian Air Force, Service Number A16, served as an acting Air Commodore and was part of the Supreme Command for South-East Asia until January 1943. He was then attached to the RAF and posted as a Group Captain to Bomber Command. Wilson was station commander at RAF Wyton before moving on to command RAF Linton-on-Ouse and finally RAF Holme on Spalding Moor.

In 1943, the Bomber Command casualty rates were high, and it is said Wilson's attitude towards his aircrews was not entirely sympathetic. In fact, he is believed to have been universally disliked, especially as he had not flown one bombing sortie over Europe himself.

In the book *Flying Into the Flames of Hell* by Martin W. Bowman, on page 192, one of Group Captain Wilson's pilots, Flight Lieutenant Ron Read states:

> *'Wilson was a dry humourless Australian, who had mainly engaged in training and had no experience whatever in*

> *operations. What made him very unpopular was his attitude in his first couple of briefings, telling us, most all veterans of many ops, how we should press on more than we do and not be slow to attack the heavy Ruhr targets, which we were doing two or three times a week in some cases.'*

Ron Read added that Wing Commander Smith, the new CO of 76 Squadron and Wing Commander Warner suggested to Wilson that he should fly an operation himself, believing he might change his attitude. '*Perhaps he would not be so critical, and we slyly thought he might go for the chop himself.*'

Group Captain Wilson flew just the once on the night of 22-23 June 1943. He flew as a second pilot in a Halifax of 76 Squadron, their target being Mulheim in Germany.

Unfortunately for Wilson and his crew, they were shot down by a night fighter over Holland. The entire crew, including Wilson, bailed out and survived, except the unfortunate flight engineer.

Wilson and two of the crew, managed to make contact with a Dutch escape line and they were passed down to the famous Comet Line in Belgium and on into France. Unfortunately, they were captured in Paris and ended up at Dulag Luft.

As already mentioned in the chapter on Sergeant Raymond Hughes, he recalled in his statement, an interrogation with Leutnant Boninghaus:

> *'He also asked me about Master of Ceremonies and in connection with this, he mentioned the name of Group Captain Wilson. I think he said that Group Captain Wilson was the first Master of Ceremonies they had captured and that he had been very helpful to them from the point of view of Pathfinder technique.'*

As previously stated, Group Captain Douglas E.L. Wilson was not a Pathfinder, so this may have been some form of trickery by Leutnant Boninghaus, however, both Hughes and Sergeant Alcock confirmed that Group Captain Wilson had been housed in the special prisoners' block along with the two Sergeants, Carpenter and Zuromski. To be housed in this block, there was a suspicion Wilson had done something to assist the enemy, although it was also said senior officer POWs were held in the house.

In September 1943, after his arrival at Dulag Luft, Wilson was moved to Stalag Luft III at Sagan, replacing (because of his higher rank) Harry

'Wings' Day as the Senior British Officer at the camp. This was around the same time Carpenter, Hughes and Zuromski were moved on to the propaganda services in Berlin, so the question must be considered, was Wilson co-operating with the Germans?

Sergeant Raymond Hughes added that when he got to Sagan:

> *'I met Carpenter again ... he did warn me to refuse an interview with Group Captain Wilson – he can tell you the reasons why himself.'*

What was meant by this comment and whether it was ever explained or fully explored, is unclear. Like the concerns with both Carpenter and Zuromski, it appears to have been left unexplained.

While Wilson was at Sagan, the Great Escape took place. He managed to get a list out via the Swiss Red Cross back to Britain, detailing the fifty men murdered by the Gestapo.

After the war, the accusations of both Sergeants Hughes and Alcock that Wilson had collaborated with the Germans led to a formal SIB inquiry, but the Judge Advocate General found no evidence. The inquiry was closed on 4 July 1945.

It is possible that Group Captain Wilson had tried to mislead his interrogators at Dulag Luft and they believed him to be a Pathfinder Master of Ceremonies. If this was the case, they probably tried to induce him to assist them further, but he was soon found wanting and sent on to Stalag Luft III at Sagan.

However, between 23 June and late September 1943, Wilson was reported as missing in action. No one knew he was alive or that he was held at Dulag Luft, Oberursel. He had in fact been detained in Paris on 4 August 1943 by the Gestapo, who probably did not inform the Luftwaffe of his detention. Bearing in mind that we know he was in Oberursel and that prisoners were given false names and in many ways removed from the official system, did the Germans expect more from Wilson?

In the file in the Australian National Archives (reference: NAA:A705, 166/43/232), there is a telegram message sent to Wilson's wife in September 1943. This states:

> *'Desire to inform you that department of Information advises that a message, purporting to be from your husband Group Captain Douglas Ernest Lancelot Wilson, was received by the*

> *Australian Broadcasting Commission in a Berlin Broadcast, on 5 September 1943. Message states he is a prisoner of war. Request treat with considerable caution.'*

A further Royal Australian Air Force (RAAF) report in the file, dated 11 September 1943 adds:

> *'Group Captain D.E.L. Wilson Aus. 16, enquiry made with International Red Cross Geneva for confirmation. Will advise further broadcast heard this country, 20:00 hours September 8, states that Group Captain Wilson in perfect health....'*

The broadcast on the 5th and apparently a second one on 8 September were part of the Anzac Tattoo propaganda radio programme made by the Buro Concordia in Berlin.

A letter dated 20 September 1943 and sent to Wilson's wife from the RAAF Casualty Section, states that the information should be treated with considerable reserve, as the message was broadcast as part of an enemy propaganda programme.

On 24 September 1943, the Red Cross in Geneva confirmed by telegram to the POW Unit in Melbourne, Australia, that Wilson was alive and a POW, having been captured on 23 June 1945 (although this is actually the date he was shot down). A further report arrived, confirming this on 12 October 1943.

The question is whether Wilson had been so apparently forthcoming with fake information about Pathfinder techniques, the Germans had sought to recruit him for propaganda services and also sent him to Berlin? Once there, had he made an initial recording thinking this was acceptable and would only confirm to his family he was alive? Did he then realise his error and get passed on to Sagan?

In addition to these questions, why did Squadron Leader Carpenter warn Sergeant Hughes about talking to Group Captain Wilson at Sagan? If the radio recordings were made in the first week of September, it would appear impossible for Carpenter to have witnessed anything in Berlin. As we have already seen, in his own statement, Carpenter told RAF SIB:

> *'I was shot down over Holland on 24 July 1943 and later taken to a prisoner of war camp, Dulag Luft. I remained there until 30 September 1943 and was then taken to Berlin under guard.*

> *After having been in Berlin a few days, I was taken to a radio station... I remained in Berlin from 30 September 1943 until 28 January 1944, when I was returned to Stalag Luft III at Sagan.'*

Carpenter could not have seen Wilson in Berlin, but he may have been aware he made a propaganda radio recording. Carpenter would have only seen Wilson at Dulag Luft for a few days in late August and the first few days of September. And why was Carpenter apparently not asked about this, or was this another fabrication from Hughes? If he was asked about this, where is that evidence?

After repatriation in 1945, Group Captain Wilson returned to Australia. MI9 asked that he be 'fully interrogated' about his flight, capture, details of assistance, as well as details of RAF, RAAF and RCAF personnel he met during captivity.

A statement was prepared and is held in the Australian Archives file. Wilson gave details of being shot down and captured in Paris on 4 August 1943 by the Gestapo; but it does not give any detail of his interrogation by the Gestapo or at Dulag Luft. Neither does it detail his radio recordings and broadcasting in Berlin. In fact, the statement is quite short and lacking in detail.

With Carpenter being a South African and Zuromski a Polish pilot, did the fact Wilson was an Australian and not British have any bearing upon this? On face value, the SIB investigation appears to have been lacking in detail and evidence.

There is no apparent or publicly available evidence from Carpenter or any of the mainstream radio collaborators, such as Baillie-Stewart, Amery, Joyce etc., or even the Dulag Luft staff regarding Wilson. The Judge Advocate General discontinued the inquiry only a few weeks after the war's conclusion, the only evidence apparently being from two confirmed traitors Hughes and Alcock.

In October 1945, Wilson was appointed commander of the Western Area RAAF, but he retired in March 1946. He lived and died in New South Wales in August 1950.

Chapter 12

Squadron Leader Eric Douglas ELLIOTT No. 24205 and Sergeant John SLOWEY No. 516838

Squadron Leader Eric Douglas Elliott, Service Number 24205 was born on 1 December 1908, in Tenterden, Kent. He joined the Royal Air Force in 1930 and was promoted to Squadron Leader in October 1938.

In early 1940, he commanded 253 Squadron flying Hawker Hurricanes. On 21 May 1940, he was shot down in Hurricane serial number P3552 over Arras in the Pas de Calais area. Injured during the incident, he spent a number of months in a military hospital in Hirson near Aisne, before eventually arriving at Dulag Luft in October 1940.

There has always been some doubt about what happened to Elliott that day in May 1940, some believe he was shot down by a Messerschmitt 110 of ZG/76, while the official file in the National Archives (AIR 81/481) states that he was hit by anti-aircraft fire and bailed out near Douai. (National Archives file WO344/101/2 states that according to Elliott's liberation questionnaire, he was shot down and burnt in the process.)

John Greenwood, who flew with 253 Squadron in 1940, states on page 39 of his autobiography '*One of Churchill's Own*', that Elliott had not been shot down and had deliberately landed and surrendered, because he did not want to fight in the war.

In his own statement to the RAF Special Investigation Branch in 1946, Elliott stated he was shot down by flak and his aircraft caught fire. He spent three months in hospital before finally ending up at Dulag Luft on 20 October 1940. He remained at Dulag Luft until September 1943, having taken over from Harry 'Wings' Day as Senior British Officer on 19 May 1941.

As we have seen, there was an element of suspicion about Dulag Luft and in particular the permanent staff there. After Harry 'Wings' Day moved to Barth and was eventually exonerated, there was continuing resentment and suspicion surrounding Dulag Luft under the new Senior British Officer – Squadron Leader Eric Douglas Elliott. Coded messages continued to be sent back to MI9, stating there were issues at Oberursel. The following statements and comments are listed in a National Archives file on Elliott (reference number AIR 40/2305), some of these statements were given while in German custody to senior British officers.

On 25 July 1943, Sergeant Charles Edward McDonald RCAF was interrogated by MI9 following his escape. In his report (National Archives ref: WO208/3314), he states that he had been interrogated by Squadron Leader Elliott upon arrival at Dulag Luft in September 1941. Elliott asked him various questions while claiming to be looking after British interests in the camp and had the ability to pass messages to England. Sergeant McDonald also claimed that when he told Wing Commander Douglas Bader about Elliott, the renowned legless pilot warned him that the SBO was suspected of being a stool-pigeon.

On 18 July 1944, a statement was provided by Flying Officer Thomas, an equipment officer. He stated that he had heard the following charges against Elliott and these were 'common currency at Stalag Luft III':

1. That Elliott was in the habit of telling new prisoners of war at Dulag Luft before their interrogation; 'The enemy knew everything in any case and concealment was useless.'
2. Elliott asked prisoners of war questions himself and that his interrogation was as thorough as the Germans.
3. Elliott discourages any attempt to escape from Dulag Luft.

Squadron Leader Eric D. Elliott also came to the attention of the British authorities when Flight Lieutenant Paddy Byrne was repatriated in mid-1944. He immediately gave a statement during his debriefing with MI9 and stated at the beginning of his account:

> *'I wish to make it understood that my report on all officers and NCOs, with the exception of Flight Lieutenant Freeman and in a minor degree Squadron Leader Elliott and Sergeant Slowey, is entirely my personal opinion and should be treated as such.'*

Byrne went on to give evidence against Benson Freeman, but sadly did not develop the issue of Elliott or Slowey by giving any information about any alleged wrongdoing.

Harry 'Wings' Day spoke of Elliott being at Dulag Luft and managing the entrance to the tunnel, the night there was a large-scale escape from the camp in 1941. Elliott would later replace Day as the Senior British Officer at Dulag Luft, when Day moved to Barth. These were hardly the actions of a collaborator.

On 11 February 1944, Warrant Officer James was noted as being rather bitter about Squadron Leader Elliott. He stated that while detained in the Dulag hospital with 'bad eyes', Elliott visited him and advised him not to make any escape attempt. James confirmed that he could not have escaped because of his condition at that time, and the interviewing SIB officer suggested that Elliott had said this for some special purpose.

On 9 May 1944, Aircraftsman Jacob Gewelber stated that Squadron Leader Elliott gave an opening speech to new arrivals, in which no useful information was given regarding the status and duties of prisoners of war, but he said prisoners would be well treated and were to salute German officers. No warning was given against parole, but would-be escapers were referred to the Escape Committee. Permanent Staff had better food at a different table to other prisoners of war. Some new arrivals complained of this, as Red Cross parcels were pooled in the camp, but Elliott told them, '*We chaps have been here a long time. Your turn will come – it depends on length of confinement.*'

AC1 Gewelber noted that Wing Commander Douglas Bader had also quarrelled with Elliott. This was believed to be due to what Bader regarded as his half-heartedness, particularly in the encouragement of escape attempts.

Later, once the war had concluded, MI9 debriefed prisoners and were inundated with allegations about Squadron Leader Elliott. Here is a selection from the file:

> *Wing Commander Harry Melville Day of 57 Squadron considered Elliott's conduct to be foolish, rather than wilfully disloyal, and added that a Court of Inquiry had been held about Elliott at Stalag Luft III in his absence. Elliott was exonerated, although Harry Melville Day believed the Court of Inquiry left much to be desired and many witnesses were personally unavailable to give evidence.*

> *Warrant Officer 971165 Toynbee-Clarke of 218 Squadron stated, 'Squadron Leader Elliott and Warrant Officer Slowey,*

at one time permanent staff at Dulag Luft, were both very pro-Nazi, particularly Warrant Officer Slowey. He attempted to insinuate Nazi propaganda to new prisoners, in May 1942.' (More on Slowey later in this chapter).

Flight Lieutenant Reid J. Gordon of 37 Squadron, stated that he met Squadron Leader Ingrham at Dulag Luft and told him what had happened to him when shot down and captured. Gordon refused to tell Elliott anything, having been warned not to give him any information. Elliott, he said, lived in 'peculiar circumstances, having a furnished room complete with radio.' Elliott had approached him, but Gordon refused to give him any information.

Warrant Officer Thomas L. Nickson of 115 Squadron, stated that Elliott and Slowey should be enquired into re-misappropriation of articles out of Red Cross parcels.

Leading Aircraftsman E.D. Ross stated that on his arrival at Dulag Luft in August 1941, he was interrogated by Squadron Leader Elliott who was the SBO. He wrote down all the information given by Ross in a book. Ross had been informed there were microphones in Dulag Luft and every time he gave an answer, Elliott repeated it in a loud voice (as if for the listeners).

Elliott had privileges in the camp which other prisoners did not share and he seemed to be on very friendly terms with the German guards. The Germans would be seen in Elliott's room where the book containing all the debriefing information was openly kept. Sergeant Slowey also worked in the same manner. He would go into the billets at night and ask questions, making notes in a book. One day, Ross went to Slowey's room and there was a German officer with him and the same book was open on the table next to them.

Despite these reports, the National Archives file reference WO344/101/2 contains a report that Squadron Leader Elliott be recommended for an award for communicating with MI9 by coded letters while imprisoned in Germany. However, on 26 April 1946, a further report states there are current on-going enquiries concerning his conduct when a prisoner of war.

On 23 May 1946, Warrant Officer Thomas Henry Sutton gave a statement to SIB. In it he claimed to have seen Elliott frequently walking and talking to German officers, particularly the interrogators. In September 1943, he recalled Elliott giving a talk and gave the prisoners the understanding that all orders from the Germans were to be implicitly obeyed. He also recalled that Red Cross parcels seemed to be short on cigarettes and yet the Germans seemed to have a lot of British and American cigarettes.

On 25 May 1946, Flight Lieutenant Wilfred Palmer made a statement. He arrived at Dulag Luft in mid-April 1942, where he met fellow prisoner Flight Lieutenant Marshall.

Marshall had a plan to escape by hiding in a hut on the camp playing field and then getting away under cover of darkness. Only a few prisoners knew of the plan. On the day of the escape, a Non-Commissioned Officer took Marshall's place at roll call. Squadron Leader Elliott found out what was going on and asked Palmer where Marshall was. He then added that he and the Germans knew where he was hiding.

Palmer knew the Germans could not have found out so soon and he told Elliott this. He then went to see Squadron Leader Phipps and told him the story. Palmer and Phipps approached Elliott and in no uncertain terms told him that if anything happened to Marshall, he was for it and that the only way the Germans could find out was if he (Elliott) told them. The Germans did not find out and Marshall managed to escape.

Palmer also recalled seeing Elliott going out of the camp and into the German area with Heinrich Eberhardt and other Germans with whom he seemed to be friendly.

On another occasion at Dulag Luft, Palmer says he approached Elliott for help with his own escape plan. Elliott told him, '*If I were you I wouldn't try to escape from here, I'd wait until you get to your new camp.*' Elliott once gave him a map, but he asked him to return it!

As well as having a disagreement with Douglas Bader, it appears Elliott also fell foul of another renowned fighter ace – Wing Commander Robert Stanford Tuck.

Robert Stanford Tuck gave a statement on 4 June 1946 which stated:

> *'I was shot down on 28/1/42 and arrived at Dulag Luft 2/2/42. I did not see Squadron Leader Elliott until I came out of the "cooler" six or seven days after my arrival there. I then approached Elliott for assistance in an escape attempt, as the camp struck me as having rather good escape possibilities.*

> *Elliott informed me that he was more concerned with the welfare of officers there, that is food, clothing and general morale, than he was with escape, because if an escape took place it would have meant curtailment of the comfort and facilities for which he had been working. After about half an hour's conversation with this officer, I began to realise that the help he would afford me in an escape direction was negligible.*
>
> *'I later approached Major Killinger (actually Oberst Leutnant), the German Commandant, with the request that as I was senior officer to Elliott, I take over the post of SBO, to which Killinger replied, "For all the rice in China I would not keep you here. I have a perfectly good Squadron Leader".'*

The statements kept on coming…

Flight Lieutenant Mortimer Crane Love, on 5 June 1946, stated that he arrived at Dulag Luft on 15 September 1943. He was in solitary confinement for about a week and then met Squadron Leader Elliott the SBO.

Love had been on a diet of four slices of bread a day while in solitary confinement and was very hungry. He therefore went to the cookhouse to get some food, but someone reported him to Elliott. Elliott told him he could not have any more food and threatened to have the Germans throw him in the brig.

A couple of days later, Love suggested to Elliott that he might hide in the clothing store which was outside the camp. He could then escape when the Germans moved away. Elliott told him this plan had been under consideration and people who had been there longer than Love would have the right to go first. No one ever tried to use this plan and when Love questioned Elliott again, he was told that if he didn't stop causing trouble, he'd have the Germans put him in the brig.

Later, Love and Flight Lieutenant Greenway RAAF planned to escape by hiding in a pile of old furniture in the dining room. Elliott and Thomas, his adjutant, (see the chapter about him later) were told that they were going to escape, but details were not given to them.

That night they hid under the furniture, but they were discovered by Germans who entered the room and walked straight over to the pile of furniture.

Love said the only people who knew of this plan were Elliott, Thomas and Flight Lieutenant Richard Hardy. When they told Elliott of the plan, he was alleged to have said it would not be successful. Later, after their discovery, he just said, '*Hard luck.*'

Lieutenant Marius Eriksen of the Royal Norwegian Air Force stated that he was shot down in flames on 2 May 1943. After being burned, he ended up in the Hohemark Hospital at Dulag Luft.

He was visited by the SBO, Squadron Leader Elliott, who produced a book and asked him to sign it. He explained this was a parole book which would enable Eriksen to go for walks in the area. Ericksen signed but regretted this when told very few other prisoners had signed the book.

Ericksen and another Norwegian, Lieutenant Strand, planned to escape and assembled an escape kit with maps, a compass and food. Ericksen asked Squadron Leader Elliott to remove his name from the parole book, but the SBO told him he was to stay in the hospital another week. Elliott asked why he wanted his name removed, but Ericksen did not mention the escape plan, only that few other prisoners had signed the book.

Despite having been told by Elliott that he would remain in hospital another week, the SBO returned the same day with a German guard and told Ericksen he was moving into the camp. As Eriksen packed his things, he could not take his escape kit with the guard watching him. Eventually, as he left, leaving the escape kit under the mattress of the hospital bed, he claimed Elliott walked over and lifted the mattress exposing the kit to the guard. Nothing was said, but the kit was lost.

There were many more statements like those above, but on 27 June 1946, Squadron Leader George Roger Tench Service Number 70669 gave SIB a statement. This would explain the letters detailed in the chapters on Benson Freeman.

Tench reported being captured in March 1942 and ending up at Dulag Luft on about 4 April. The SBO did not meet him or ask to see him, so he met Squadron Leader Ian Cross (murdered by the Gestapo after the Great Escape in March 1944), Squadron Leader Hogarth and Wing Commander Anthony Eyre (killed in a flying accident in February 1946).

Over the course of the next few days, Tench became aware of Benson Freeman and his behaviour and pro-Nazi tendencies. Tench believed his words and behaviour were not conducive to good camp morale and conditions, so this group of senior officers went to see Squadron Leader Elliott.

Wing Commander Eyre, who acted as the spokesman, told Elliott that Freeman and a Sergeant (Eric Galloway) must sign an application to the Germans to move to another camp. This was the first letter, dated 5 March 1942:

> *The following prisoners of war at Dulag Luft request to go to another camp with the next transport:*
>
> *B.R.H. Freeman*
> *E.A. Galloway*
> *E. Hill.*

Wing Commander Eyre, in front of Tench and the other senior officers, was told that he too must sign a similar application. This one read:

> *In view of the above and the existing feeling within the camp itself, the undersigned officers request to be included:*
>
> *E.D. Elliott, Squadron Leader*
> *John Cotton, Lt. Commander RN.*

Tench added to his statement, saying he took these steps with a view to counteracting any effect which such conduct might have upon the moral of new POWs. In fact, none of these people were moved by the Germans until a year or so after this time. Tench believed Elliott was an ineffectual and inefficient Senior British Officer. Tench only remained at Dulag Luft a week before he was sent to Stalag Luft III at Sagan. Therefore, Elliott remained at Oberursel long after he had departed.

As already discussed in the chapters on Benson Freeman, further evidence came in the form of a letter to Oberst Leutnant Erich Killinger, the camp commandant, dated 23 June 1942. This letter stated:

> *Dear Oberst Lt. Killinger,*
> *We send this note to thank you very much indeed for granting us the facility of such a marvellous walk, together with the much appreciated 'Betrlebsöl'.*
>
> *Your countryside is so beautiful that we shall not want to leave it when the war ends.*
>
> *I hope that you will agree with us, and decide that such walks are also most beneficial for the health and potential energy of Luftwaffe officers!*
>
> *Yours sincerely,*
> *E.D Elliott, B.R.H. Freeman and R. Hardy.*

Clearly, Squadron Leader Elliott, Benson Freeman and Pilot Officer Richard Hardy were on very good terms with the Camp Commandant and undertaking long walks. The use of the German word Betriebsöl translates as 'Operating Oil', but what did they actually mean by this? Did it have a metaphorical meaning as far as Elliott and the others were concerned?

On 9 May 1946, Squadron Leader W.H.N. Turner, Service Number 26216, gave a statement. He recalled 'Wings' Day and a number of Dulag Luft personnel arriving at Barth following their massed escape.

In October or November 1940, he received an instruction from the Air Ministry to carry out a Court of Inquiry into Dulag Luft. He carried out his instructions with Squadron Leaders Torrens and Pritchard, interviewing Lieutenant Fanshaw (RN) and Squadron Leader Donald MacDonnell. MacDonnell had concerns as we have already seen, describing Dulag Luft as being far too free and easy, with ample supplies of cigarettes, French wine, brandy and cigars. However, Turner stated that neither MacDonnell or Fanshaw could produce any witnesses to support their own claims.

Turner added that from June 1941 (after the mass escape), Freeman, Casson and others were left at Dulag Luft as the permanent staff, with Squadron Leader Elliott as the Senior British Officer. Further complaints about the camp were soon circulating, the majority about a shortage of food in the camp hospital and a lack of interest in escaping.

In July 1942, Group Captain Herbert Massey DSO MC, a very respected officer ordered a further Court of Inquiry regarding the running of Dulag Luft. (He had been shot down on the night of 1-2 June 1942 in a Short Stirling of 7 Squadron.) The investigation was undertaken by Wing Commander John Charles MacDonald of 105 Squadron. He had been shot down on 2 July 1942 and spent the previous two weeks at Oberursel before being given the task.

Turner claimed that he believed the report had cleared Elliott, but Group Captain Massey tried to persuade the Germans to make him SBO at Dulag Luft. They turned him down.

While he was at Barth (Stalag Luft I), Turner and Massey heard a continual flow of complaints about Dulag Luft and its permanent staff. These were similar to the earlier complaints received when Day was in command.

On 24 October 1946, Eric D. Elliott, now a Group Captain, was questioned and provided a statement to the RAF Special Investigation Branch.

After confirming how he ended up at Dulag Luft, Elliott sought to explain some of the statements listed in this book.

He claimed that; '*At the beginning of 1941, there were about eight officers at the camp (the permanent staff), all of whom were trying to run it and things were not happy.*'

Pilot Officer Benson Freeman was an embarrassment to Elliott and the camp commander Oberst Leutnant Killinger, who told him he was receiving too many complaints from too many sources, and he would have to clear the camp. Elliott said he told Killinger that if he remained in charge as SBO he only wanted an Adjutant and a Mess Officer. As a result of this conversation, Elliott claimed he was left with Pilot Officer Benson Freeman, Flight Lieutenant Richard Hardy and Flight Lieutenant David W. Thomas.

Elliott added that he had been taught the code for communicating with Britain by Lieutenant Commander Casson and used this to send twenty-six messages home, all of which he claimed were acknowledged by MI9.

Elliott also claimed that Flight Lieutenant 'Paddy' Byrne had been responsible for assisting escapees, but Pilot Officer Marcus Marsh took over from him. When Marsh left the camp in February 1942, Elliott took on the role himself.

He claimed that Killinger, the Camp Commandant, was a difficult man to deal with, being an extreme disciplinarian. In June 1942, Killinger allowed Elliott and others to go for a walk with a German officer escort. After the first walk, Elliott said he thought it polite to write and thank Killinger, while ensuring future walks. (This was the note mentioning *the much appreciated 'Betriebsöl'.)* Elliott tried to explain that the bottle of wine described as Betriebsol in the letter, was obtained by bribing their escort – none other than Leutnant Heinrich Eberhardt – with cigarettes, but why would he tell the Camp Commandant that they had been given a drink – possibly by bribing a German officer?

Elliott also stated that the final paragraph of the letter stating:

> *Your countryside is so beautiful that we shall not want to leave it when the war ends.*
>
> *I hope that you will agree with us and decide that such walks are also most beneficial for the health and potential energy of Luftwaffe officers!*

…was just a piece of flattery for Killinger.

Elliott stated that he remembered Wing Commander Eyre complaining about Pilot Officer Benson Freeman and Sergeant Eric Galloway. He said Eyre had suggested having the men sign an application to transfer to another camp and that Elliott should do likewise.

He also recalled Wing Commander Standford-Tuck asking the Camp Commandant to make him Senior British Officer at Dulag Luft. He could also remember Standford-Tuck approaching him for assistance in an escape attempt. Although Elliott did not say what he did or did not do in response to the request, he stated that the weather at the time was not suitable for an escape bid.

Elliott denied ever telling prisoners to obey German orders implicitly. He also added that it was natural for him to be seen with German officers, as they reported to him frequently on prisoner issues.

On the subject of Squadron Leader Marshall's escape attempt, Elliott confirmed the prisoner did not ask for his assistance in his escape attempt. He claimed he heard rumours that the Germans knew where Marshall was hiding and he tracked these down to the cookhouse. Having assured himself that the Germans did not know where he was (he did not say how he knew this), he did no more. Elliott claimed that no one had ever claimed he had told the Germans of Marshall's location and if anyone had done so, he would have been very angry with them.

On the subject of Love and his Australian friend's attempt to escape, Elliott stated that he remembered being told of two officers caught trying to escape. The only conversation he had with them was after they had been captured. He merely said, '*Hard luck, try again.*'

Elliott also recalled Lieutenant Eriksen in the camp hospital. He agreed that they had spoken, but he claimed the Norwegian had asked to be returned to the camp as his burns had healed. Elliott denied ever asking him to sign the parole book. He also denied ever lifting the mattress off the hospital bed, exposing the escape kit to the German guard.

With regard to the radio left by Harry 'Wings' Day in his room when he moved to Barth, Elliott said this was taken away by Killinger in July 1943. Elliott claimed he was glad it was taken, as it was a nuisance and prisoners would listen to it in his room, although it had remained in place two years after Day had moved to Barth.

Elliott also denied ever dining with Killinger or being out of the camp unescorted.

On 31 October 1946, the Officer Commanding the Special Investigation Branch (SIB) completed a full report covering the facts related above. His report went further.

He pointed out that the allegations made against Squadron Leader Elliott were detailed and made by a number of officers and senior NCOs. In addition to this, a Mrs Dorothy Van den Bergh made a complaint regarding a post-war cocktail party. Elliott, by this time a Group Captain, had openly stated that he had always been correctly treated by the Germans, they were very efficient, he had a good time with them and he had no complaints against the Germans. Most damningly of all, in relation to the fifty airmen murdered by the Gestapo in 1944, she claimed he had said, '*What else can you expect if you try to escape, you're asking for trouble*.' Finally, Elliott had stated that Germany was more efficient than England.

In response to these claims, Elliott admitted being at the party and taking part in the debate, but he pointed out that everyone had too much to drink. He admitted that his views were apparently held to be too tolerant. He added that he had been correctly treated as a POW, believed many farmers in Germany loathed the war, war criminals should be executed as soon as possible and it would be excellent if all members of the Gestapo were exterminated. He also said he may have said it was very dangerous to escape with the Gestapo holding such power and those that did were very brave – clearly a differing explanation.

Information had also indicated that Elliott had been in contact with a German woman at Dulag Luft called Margaret Krammerer. He was known to have received two letters from the woman, but when asked about the letters, he refused to disclose their contents on the grounds that he did not think it was necessary. The author of the SIB report stated this did not explain Elliott's relationship and communications with a German woman.

The SIB officer also pondered why Freeman had not been removed from the camp at the first opportunity by Elliott. Elliott's explanations for a number of incidents detailed in the statements of officers and NCOs conflicted with his own account and most of the witnesses were available to give evidence if required.

The SIB report accepted that Elliott's coded reports had been checked and it was recognised he had provided information about Sergeant Hughes and Flying Officer Zuromski's treachery. The fact these messages had been sent and contained some useful data, would in the event of any action being taken against Elliott, be used by his defence team to challenge the allegations that he was a collaborator.

In relation to Mrs Van den Bergh's complaint, it was recognised that those present at the party were under the influence of alcohol at the time.

Ms Margaret Krammerer had not been spoken to by RAF investigators. There was no independent evidence of this allegation to corroborate the claim or to explain these communications.

In conclusion, the SIB reporting officer suggested, that before a final decision be taken in this case, Oberst Leutnant Erich Killinger and Leutnant Heinrich Eberhardt should be interrogated.

On 19 December 1946, both Killinger and Eberhardt provided statements to the SIB investigators.

Oberst Leutnant Erich Killinger had been found guilty of mistreatment of prisoners of war in a tribunal, held at Wuppertal and sentenced to five years imprisonment. Surprisingly, he was content to speak with the SIB investigator, but he gave little away.

Killinger stated that he was prepared to swear upon oath that at no time did he or any of his officers receive information, either of intelligence value or regarding prisoner activities from Squadron Leader Elliott. In fact, his greatest concern was that Elliott would discover which prisoners were acting as stool-pigeons.

Killinger said he held the now Group Captain Elliott in the highest regard owing to the manner in which he performed the difficult task of maintaining a correct balance between the German staff and the prisoners.

The SIB officer, in his report, added that Killinger appeared genuinely distressed that allegations of collaboration could have been brought against Group Captain Elliott.

Killinger added that he could well understand how Elliott's contact with the German staff, which was inevitable owing to his duties, may have given rise to unpopularity and even suspicion. He was also unable to recall any of the specific allegations made against Elliott, but stated that if such incidents had occurred, he would have been automatically informed. He then stated emphatically that no such incidents with regard to Elliott had ever occurred.

With regard to the allegation that Elliott caused POWs to sign the parole book, Killinger produced a copy of a letter written to him by Elliott in September 1942. This concerned non-flying RAF personnel being directed to sign for parole and the fact that Elliott in no way condoned this.

Leutnant Heinrich Eberhardt gave a similar account of Elliott at Dulag Luft. He also pointed out that the only escape he could remember being betrayed to the Germans was a case where the prisoners had arranged to leave one of their number half-buried on the field during a rugby match. This plan had been disclosed to the German camp staff by Sergeant Michael Joyce (see later chapter). Eberhardt added that he normally watched these games, but on that occasion he had been persuaded by Elliott to have tea with him, thereby getting him out of the way of the escape attempt.

It was now clear that there were a series of allegations against Elliott, but they were not supported by the two German officers. There was no doubt that Elliott had assisted some escapes and sent coded messages regarding Hughes and Zuromski, but there was still a sense that he was too weak and, in some ways, assisted the German camp staff in ways that may not have been treacherous, but seemingly aimed at making life easier at Dulag Luft.

On 4 November 1946, the Air Commodore in charge of the Judge Advocate General's (JAG) office sent a message to Group Captain Barraclough at the Air Ministry.

He was in an invidious position and stated:

> *'In view of the fact that Group Captain Elliott sent such (coded) messages to the Air Ministry, I do not think a court martial would convict him on any charge of misconduct whilst serving as a prisoner of war.*
>
> *'In view, however, you may consider that Group Captain Elliott is unsuitable to remain in the service. The effect of the letter (to Killinger about the walks) must have been to create a feeling of contempt and ridicule for an RAF officer in the eyes of Oberst Leutnant Killinger. It is difficult to see how a regular RAF officer could at a time when the Germans were seeking the destruction of the British Empire, bring himself to write such a letter. The only explanation Group Captain Elliott can give of this letter, is that he wrote it to flatter the Germans.*
>
> *'Whether or not Group Captain Elliott should remain in the service is, of course, entirely a matter for the Air Council to decide. It seems to me, however, that the only grounds on which it can be decided that Group Captain Elliott should not remain in the service is that of unsuitability, and if the Air Council decided that Group Captain Elliott is not to remain in the service, then it seems to me that the proper authority under which to operate for the termination of Group Captain Elliott's service is King's Regulations & ACI 3538 (3), i.e. that he should be called upon to retire or resign his commission on grounds of unsuitability.'*

The report ended with a paragraph suggesting that if he retired, he would be entitled to retired pay (i.e. a pension). This recommendation, however, seems to have been ignored because Elliott remained in the RAF and served as a Group Captain until he eventually retired in 1955.

* * *

One name linked to Squadron Leader Elliott, as we have seen from a number of witness accounts, was that of Sergeant John Slowey.

Slowey would appear to have first come to the notice of MI9 and the Special Investigation Branch, when he was identified in an International Red Cross visit to Dulag Luft in November 1943. He was listed as a member of the so-called permanent staff, and 'Wings' Day made him President of the Mess. However, Flight Lieutenant Vincent 'Paddy' Byrne stated in his repatriation report, that he had concerns about Freeman and to a lesser degree Slowey and Squadron Leader Elliott. He never expanded upon this in his report, so what did he mean?

Sergeant Harold Bell, captured in late 1941, stated in his liberation questionnaire about collaboration, that while he was held at Dulag Luft, Sergeant John Slowey and Squadron Leader Elliott both asked him detailed questions about his squadron – why?

Upon repatriation in 1945, another witness made a statement against Slowey, this was Warrant Officer Gerald Tipping Service Number 580815. He had been a prisoner of war from September 1940 until 16 April 1945.

He initially recalled that Slowey had collaborated with the Germans by withholding Red Cross parcels and obtaining military information for them. He would go into POWs' rooms and ask them about their squadrons, where they had come from and what they had been doing. Tipping however, could not recall Slowey asking any technical questions, but remembered other POWs '*ticking him off*' for talking, when they had been warned about hidden microphones.

Warrant Officer Tipping added that Slowey was rather friendly with some of the Germans, but he had no proof that he was giving them information.

As we have already seen, Leading Aircraftsman Ross alleged that both Squadron Leader Elliott and Slowey were making notes of discussions with prisoners and allegedly giving them to the Germans.

Post-war, Slowey, now a Warrant Officer, was questioned by SIB and provided a statement about his time at Dulag Luft.

He had been a prisoner since 22 April 1940, when his No. 44 Squadron Hampden was shot down by flak ships near Heiligendamm in Germany when they attacked the port of Kiel.

He was sent to Dulag Luft at Oberursel and remained there until January 1944, when he was moved to the Hohemark hospital for treatment. While in Dulag Luft, he was a member of the permanent staff, first under Wing Commander Day and then Squadron Leader Elliott. He was given the role of checking cleanliness in the camp and this he claimed, caused some bad feeling among the other NCO prisoners who resented him.

Slowey added that doing the role for so long, he got to know the German staff and was friendly with them, as this assisted him to obtain the necessary cleaning materials. He denied ever getting any special advantages beyond those offered to other members of the camp's permanent staff, such as long walks and drinks at Christmas and birthdays.

Slowey denied ever having control of the Red Cross store, except for the drawing of food for the NCO Mess kitchen. He said the store was under the control of Flight Lieutenant Richard Hardy and Flight Lieutenant Milne. He also denied ever obtaining information for the Germans from other prisoners of war.

The only prisoners he had suspicions about were Pilot Officer Freeman and Flight Sergeant Hughes. He recalled two or three other prisoners who wore plain clothes in the camp, but he could not recall their names (probably Carpenter and Zuromski).

The British authorities appear to have left the matter and no action was taken against Slowey. This was probably due to a lack of evidence and no corroboration from any of the German officers such as Eberhardt, Killinger or Bauer-Schlichtegroll, men who had been only too willing to give statements regarding other POWs.

Chapter 13

Flying Officer Peter F. CASENOVE No. 73727

While I was undertaking research for this book, I came across an account in the biography of Wing Commander Harry 'Wings' Day by Sydney Smith. This outlined the fact an RAF officer had apparently been sentenced to death by his colleagues in the prison camp at Barth for collaborating.

As we have seen in the previous chapter, Harry 'Wings' Day was himself considered by some to be too compliant with the Germans and when he left Dulag Luft and arrived at Stalag Luft I at Barth, he found a very antagonistic atmosphere.

In the book, Day recalls that shortly after arriving at Barth, an officer he called Flight Lieutenant Paul Burke came to see him in his quarters. Day described the officer as tall, fair, distinguished looking, with a background difficult to associate with disloyalty. He had been educated at Eton and when the war began, he held a commission in one of the elite RAF Auxiliary Squadrons, he had also been a junior executive in a city firm.

Burke had been shot down in France at the time of Dunkirk and made his way to Calais. He tried to board a ship for England but was handed a rifle by a senior Naval officer and told to go and defend Calais.

As we have seen, Smith and Day, in their book, gave Benson Freeman and Carpenter false names, I therefore suspected Burke to be a false name and set out to identify him.

I checked known losses during the withdrawal from Dunkirk and specifically those that came down near Calais with the pilot being captured. I then considered the fact, Smith/Day had claimed he had been an officer in an Auxiliary Air Force unit. Unfortunately, none of the Auxiliary Air Force losses matched this data, so I expanded my search to pilots who were captured in the stated location and time frame.

Eventually, I found that Flying Officer Peter F. Casenove of 92 Squadron (an old associate of Roger Bushell and Paddy Byrne), had been shot down on

24 May 1940. He force-landed on a beach near Calais and headed into town, in a bid to get home to England. He was an old Etonian, tall, well-built and he had worked as a stockbroker in the City of London before the war. Peter Casenove had originally held a commission in an Auxiliary Squadron before the war (probably 601 City of London Squadron), but when he was declared bankrupt, he resigned his commission. When war was declared in 1939, Peter Casenove rejoined the Royal Air Force and was posted to 92 Squadron.

In addition, confirmation that I had now identified the identity of Paul Burke came from the autobiography of 92 Squadron pilot Flight Lieutenant Tony Bartley (*Smoke trails in the sky*, published by Crecy in 1997). In his book on page 19 he states:

> *'We heard from Pete Casenove, one of our squadron who was shot down and captured at Dunkirk. He tried to get on three destroyers but was turned off each one. The Navy said that all accommodation was reserved for the army and the air force could go f... themselves, gave him a rifle and told him to join the army.'*

To return to the account from 'Wings' Day in Barth…

Paul Burke (Casenove), mindful of hidden microphones, asked if they could go around the circuit. This was a walk around the camp in the open air, but it allowed for a more private conversation.

The young pilot had difficulty expressing himself, but eventually told Day, '*I've been sentenced to death*'. He then explained that there had been a kind of drumhead court martial and he had been sentenced to hang for collaboration with the Germans. He had been friendly with a guard called Hauptman Buckvig (his real name was Oskar Bukwick and he was an Austrian), who was an Abwehr intelligence officer at the camp.

The pilot then explained that he thought they were going to execute him, but the sentence was commuted.

In addition, in one of his first letters home from Dulag Luft before he arrived at Barth, Casenove had told his parents about being shot down and the attitude of the navy. The German censors had quickly picked this up and passed it on to the Foreign Office propaganda unit in Berlin. A short time later, the prisoners at Barth were shocked to see Casanove's account in the local *Frankfurter Zeitung* (Frankfurt newspaper) and coupled with his apparent friendliness towards Hauptman Buckvig, he was deemed to be a collaborator.

In an echo of the situation at Dulag Luft, Burke (Casenove) stated that the Hauptman was not a Nazi, in fact he had even taken the young pilot to his quarters to listen to an escape tunnel being dug through a primitive seismograph. Burke told Day he had reported this to the camp Senior British Officer, but they did not believe him. To make things worse, the Intelligence officer regularly visited Burke in his quarters for a cup of tea or coffee. He also gave advice about hiding compasses and provided some maps according to Burke.

The Senior British Officer and his deputies in the camp could not believe these accounts, or that a German (Austrian) officer would assist them. This view was supported by the fact that all their escape tunnels were being located.

A Squadron Leader (unnamed) warned Burke that a court of inquiry was to be held. The whole camp was assembled and until the findings were made known, Burke was effectively sent to Coventry.

After a week, it was decided that Burke was indeed a collaborator and if he was seen talking to a German again, the Squadron Leader warned him, '*There were ways, even in a POW camp of executing people*'.

'Wings' Day could not believe what he was hearing and decided the whole procedure and inquiry had been highly irregular. He therefore ordered a new court of inquiry led by two trusted officers. The two officers spoke with about one hundred and fifty officers and the final conclusion was that the whole episode was a mass of hearsay, suspicion and pure gossip. This had been caused by boredom, hunger and poor leadership in the camp.

Day summoned the whole camp into a mess hall and according to the book stated:

> *'It is impossible for a proper court of enquiry to be held in the circumstances in which we live as prisoners. However, the present inquiry confirmed that Flight Lieutenant Burke is as loyal as anyone in this room. Therefore, Flight Lieutenant Burke is completely exonerated. The course taken originally by other officers was done with the best and highest of intentions and I pass no criticism on what was judged the correct action based on the available evidence. This matter is now closed.'*

What the prisoners at Barth thought of this decision is not recorded, but together with his time at Dulag Luft, an air of suspicion developed around Harry 'Wings' Day, as we have seen in a previous chapter. This was probably compounded by Harry Day tasking Burke (Peter Casenove) to continue his contacts with the German/Austrian officer.

Day remained deeply suspicious of Hauptman Buckvig, but he continued to compromise himself, bringing all manner of contraband into the camp to exchange for chocolate and coffee. In return, Burke (Casenove) obtained tip-offs and other escape material, but when three prisoners managed to get away from a new tunnel, Buckvig's days were numbered, as the Germans started to suspect his openly cosy contacts with the British airman.

Peter Casenove eventually moved on to Stalag Luft III at Sagan (as did 'Wings' Day and Roger Bushell) and he was due to take part in the Great Escape. Casenove was last in the line to enter the escape tunnel, due to his large build and height, which many feared could lead to him being stuck in the confined tunnel. Fortunately for him, the escape in progress was discovered and he never made it out of the camp. Thankfully, he was not one of the fifty escapees who were captured and murdered by the Gestapo.

Casenove tried on a number of occasions to escape, but he was eventually repatriated and returned home to England. However, it appears his past and his relationship with Buckvig at Barth were still preying on his mind in 1945.

In the National Archives in file WO311/569Q there is a letter dated 6 June 1945, from Peter Casenove to the Air Ministry Intelligence section, in which he states the following:

> *'Sir,*
>
> *'While at Stalag Luft I, Barth, in the early days we received quite a lot of help from an Austrian Hauptman Oskar Buckvig of 197 Hammerling Strasse, Graz, Austria. During the Battle of Britain he daily brought us in our news and was then a decided anti-Nazi and helped us in many other small ways, such as bringing in maps etc. to our escape committee. He later took letters to Rome for us which were sent into our Minister in Vatican City, while he was a courier from Berlin to Rome. I last heard of him in Zagrel in early 1944.*
>
> *'I mention this, not for him to be rewarded, as he had his pound of coffee and cigarettes for all the help he gave us, but because I thought he might be of use to the Military Government there as he hated the Germans with all his heart.'*

It does not appear any further enquiries were made by the RAF Special Investigation Branch or the Intelligence Services regarding Peter Casenove and his time at Stalag Luft I. There is nothing to be found about him or Oskar Buckvig in the National Archive records.

Peter Casenove had been exonerated by Wing Commander 'Wings' Day and his team at Barth, but this case clearly shows how even just talking to a camp guard or an official could lead to an allegation of collaboration. There was no follow-up enquiry when he returned to the United Kingdom post-war.

Peter Casenove later moved to Kenya, but he returned once more, settling on the south coast of England.

Casenove's Spitfire was recovered from the shifting sands on the beach near Calais. It was restored to flying condition and took to the air again in September 2011. Sadly, Peter died just before being told that his old machine had taken to the air.

Chapter 14

Sergeant Michael Joseph JOYCE No. 580715

There have been a good number of strange stories and accounts from the prisoners described within this book, but one that is very odd, is that of Sergeant Michael Joseph Joyce, Service Number 580715; a man said to have been the cousin of the infamous William Joyce (Lord Haw Haw).

Michael Joyce joined the RAF pre-war and volunteered for aircrew duties. On 27 August 1940, the Irishman was part of a 61 Squadron Hampden crew, which made a forced landing on the Isle of Ameland in the Frisian Islands.

According to his own account of his escape, Joyce stated that the crew of four were captured within twenty minutes of landing by about twenty to twenty-five German soldiers. The Germans had initially fired machine guns over their heads causing the crew to stop and surrender.

The crew were taken to a village and given coffee before a Luftwaffe Leutnant arrived and started to question them. He asked which station they came from and what their squadron number was. Flying Officer Tunstall, the pilot and captain of the Hampden, refused to answer the questions, so the interrogator told him they had come from RAF Hemswell and produced a map from their aircraft. This the crew thought had been burned in the aircraft.

The interrogations continued and Joyce said he possessed a piece of rice paper which contained a list of light beacons. He therefore flicked this away in small pieces to avoid detection.

Sergeant Brock, the aircraft's wireless operator, was found to have a letter in his pocket addressed to him with Hemswell written on it. He was asked by the Leutnant why he had destroyed the radio set, but Brock just laughed. According to Joyce none of the crew answered the questions.

Joyce gave a detailed report about how they were moved and housed from the crash site to Terschelling, to Harlingen and on to Amsterdam. Eventually they reached Dulag Luft on 29 August 1940.

Once they arrived, they were separated and put in individual cells. The next morning a Luftwaffe Ober Leutnant called Fuergut came into Joyce's cell and asked him to fill in a form with a Red Cross on it. Joyce said he declined to answer the questions or fill in the form and was eventually taken to the main POW camp at Oberursel. Initially he was in a room with his crew, but ended up with Sergeants Slowey, Galloway and Taylor, as part of the permanent camp staff billeted in two rooms.

About a fortnight after his arrival, Joyce recalled being interviewed by two men and a lady. This interview took place in the Camp Commandant's offices and one man was allegedly Irish, although he did not have an Irish accent. Also interviewed were Flight Lieutenants Vincent 'Paddy' Byrne and Mike Casey. They were asked questions about Ireland, Dublin and what the interviewees thought of the Irish government. (This corroborates what Byrne had reported in his repatriation report.)

Joyce claimed there was a complete IFF (Identification Friend or Foe electronic system) in the camp. He did not see it himself, but Sergeant Galloway, who was an observer, had seen it in November 1940 and told him about its presence.

Joyce also claimed that there were no microphones ever found in the sergeants' block or in the officers' quarters. However, as a rule they never discussed aircraft or operations in the rooms. Joyce added that his escape maps and compass were never removed from his possession at Dulag Luft and remained sown into his uniform. Since his time at Dulag Luft, he had learnt that prisoners' clothes were later thoroughly searched, being taken away for closer examination over two days.

Joyce recalled working in the camp store, issuing Red Cross parcels until January 1941. From that time until May 1942, he claimed to have worked as the camp carpenter.

In May 1942, Joyce said he went into hospital at Kloster Haina with stomach problems. Most of the patients were German soldiers with head wounds from the Russian front. He was given blood tests, injections and various tablets and remained in hospital until September 1942.

As he recovered, Joyce asked the German authorities if he could work on a farm. This was because he intended escaping. When he was discharged, he was sent to a farm at Kaisersesch near Koblenz. He was the only POW working on what was a small family run farm. At night the farmer would lock him in his bedroom, but one night he opened the window and its shutters before climbing down the drainpipe. He then took the farmer's bicycle on 23 September 1942 and headed off towards Bitburg.

The next morning at 06:00 hours, Joyce claimed to have hidden the bike and slept in a wood. At 20:30 hours that night, he recovered the bicycle and cycled off towards Redange in Luxembourg and on to the Belgian frontier. He repeated this process over a number of nights and eventually crossed into France.

On 27 September at about 02:00 hours, he decided to look for food and hoped he might get into a monastery or a convent. He found a building next to a small church and entered it. Later, as he exited the outhouse, he was confronted by a woman he initially thought was a nun. However, the woman, possibly thinking he was a tramp, went inside the house and shut the door. Joyce knocked on the door and the woman spoke French. He said, '*Anglais*' and she asked in English, '*What do you want?*' Joyce told her he wanted food and drink and she told him to wait while she fetched her husband.

After about five minutes, the husband arrived and Joyce was let inside and given soup, bread, butter, meat and coffee.

He stayed with the couple in a spare bedroom, until he was passed on to an organisation which assisted him in leaving the country and getting back via Gibraltar, to the United Kingdom on 1 November 1942. This was the report given by Joyce regarding his escape.

In November 1942, a J.R. Whyte (either MI5 or MI9) completed a report having interrogated the returning Michael Joyce. The report in National Archives file AIR2/13438, states that Joyce was interviewed on 2 November at a transit camp, but Whyte was not satisfied with '*the tale he told*'.

The reasons Whyte was not satisfied were:

1. Joyce had been in Dulag Luft from August 1940 to May 1942, a total of nineteen months in a reception camp.
2. He said he had been sent to a hospital in Thuringen in May 1942, suffering with stomach troubles. He was there three months before going to work on a farm not far from Koblenz.
3. Joyce appeared to regard as thoroughly loyal, individuals with whom we are not completely satisfied, such as Pilot Officer Benson Freeman.

Sergeant Joyce in effect stated that he had never met his first cousin William Joyce, who was commonly called Lord Haw Haw.

Discussing the Irishman and the man and woman who visited the camp in 1940, Whyte believed the first man could have been William Joyce himself, as he fitted the description given by Michael Joyce. However, when a photographic image of William Joyce was shown to Michael, he did not recognise his alleged cousin.

Whyte pondered upon whether William Joyce had come to examine his cousin, but found him to be a loyal patriot and unapproachable. As such, he may have thought it better not to disclose his own identity. (Author: However, why involve Byrne and Casey?) This, Whyte contended, may be the reason why Michael Joyce was kept at Dulag Luft for so long and not moved to another camp.

Whyte stated that Michael Joyce had told him that a few weeks after his arrival, the Camp Commandant sent for him and offered him a glass of whisky. Mentioning his cousin Lord Haw Haw, he asked Joyce if there was anything he could do for him? Joyce said he had told him he did not want Lord Haw Haw to do anything for him at all.

It was because of this that Whyte believed, '*The secret of Sergeant Joyce being kept at Dulag Luft is to be found in his relationship with Lord Haw Haw, and in the camp Commandant being told to make things as easy as possible for Sergeant Joyce.*' That may also have been the explanation why, when he asked to work on a farm, permission was given so freely.

Whyte added that he had the impression that Sergeant Joyce was thoroughly ashamed of the activities of his first cousin and would have nothing to do with him. Sergeant Joyce appeared to him to be thoroughly loyal, but rather bewildered, not only about what had happened to him in Germany, but at the attitude which he had received since his escape.

Michael Joyce's belongings had been carefully searched by the authorities upon his return and Whyte said he was inclined to believe that he had not been recruited by the Germans. He added that any obviously unfair and discriminatory treatment of the escapee would be likely to antagonise Michael Joyce and may make him a 'real danger'.

Finally, Whyte stated that the fact Michael Joyce was a first cousin of William Joyce would probably lead to him being the object of special attention by the British authorities and thus make him, from a German point of view, unsuitable for use as an agent.

In these circumstances, Whyte did not consider there were reasons for suspecting Michael Joyce. He recommended that Joyce be allowed to proceed on leave and '*In the meantime, a special fuss should be made of him*'. When he returns (to duty) the authorities will keep an eye on his activities.

In the space of two pages of typed report, J.R. Whyte had moved from saying he was not satisfied with Michael Joyce's account of his escape, to believing he was not a threat and loyal to the United Kingdom. How wrong he would be!

The file in the National Archives gives no further detail of Michael Joyce's RAF service until August 1944. In the meantime we know he was commissioned to the rank of Pilot Officer in June 1943 and promoted to Flying Officer in September 1943. It appears he was a national hero and awarded the Military Medal.

On 27 August 1944, Joyce was recommended for the Military Medal by none other than the renowned Air Vice-Marshal Ralph Cochrane, AOC of No. 5 Group Bomber Command:

> *'For his persistence and determination to escape at the first available moment in spite of ill health and long imprisonment, and his success and resource in his escape, I recommend that Flying Officer Joyce be awarded the Military Medal.'*

On 6 September 1944, the recommendation was forwarded along the chain of command for submission to King George VI. On 14 November 1944, he was duly awarded the Military Medal. What the staff of Dulag Luft and William Joyce thought of this in Germany, is not recorded.

Less than a year later and things started to unravel for Flying Officer Michael Joyce, as the Allied armies crossed Europe and into Germany.

One of the first indications that something was wrong with Michael Joyce's escape came in June 1945. Warrant Officer Leslie A. Parker gave a statement to the RAF Police SIB detailing his time at Dulag Luft and the actions of Squadron Leaders Elliott and Carpenter, Flight Lieutenant Thomas and Sergeants Hughes and Whillock. He also spoke about Sergeant Michael Joyce:

> *'I remember Sergeant Michael Joyce, he was my roommate in Dulug Luft, he was already in the Dulag when I arrived, he acted as camp carpenter and used to draw his tools from a hut outside the barbed wire. I never had any reason to suspect Joyce of collaborating with the Germans. He never told me that he was related to William "Lord Haw Haw" Joyce.*

> *'In spring 1942, Joyce was suffering from kidney trouble, he was taken by a medical orderly to the hospital believed to be in Bavaria and on making enquiries later from a medical orderly, I was told that Joyce had been very ill, but had got better and had gone to a Stalag at Heidergruge. I never saw him again.'*

While Parker's statement did not reveal anything too concerning, there was the issue of why he had been told that Joyce was taken to another Stalag in 1942.

Soon afterwards another statement was obtained by the Special Investigation Branch, this one came from Dulag Luft's Leutnant Heinrich Eberhardt.

The first prisoner he referred to in his statement, was Sergeant Michael Joyce, who arrived in the camp in the summer of 1940. He stated:

> *'He was interrogated by Major Rumpel. I was not present at the interrogation. It is my impression now that it was just after the interrogation that Major Rumpel, who was the Camp Commandant, confronted me with Joyce and said in effect, that Joyce had agreed to collaborate and that I was to act as a go-between for Joyce and the Camp Commandant.*
>
> *'Joyce was in the Interrogation Centre, I think, for only two days and then went into the Transit Camp. Wing Commander Day was the Senior British Officer of the camp at the time.*
>
> *'Joyce was given the job as carpenter of the Transit Camp and by reason of this, he was able to come out of the camp to the carpenters' shop, which was outside the boundary wire of the camp. When visiting the carpenters' shop, Joyce would have a guard with him, but this gave me an opportunity of seeing him in the shop and away from the other prisoners of war.*
>
> *'In this way I saw Joyce frequently and was able to ask him any questions on matters which the Camp Commandant desired to know. The nature of the information required generally was regarding squadrons, losses in squadrons, new types of aeroplanes etc., and any information which he was obtaining through associating with other prisoners of war.*
>
> *'I obtained certain information from Sergeant Joyce, which was of use to us at the time, as we were building our*

> *records and always did endeavour to keep our records of the Allied Air Force up to date. I cannot now quote anything which stands out in my mind of special importance and reviewing the matter later on I began to realise how futile such information was, as all aircraft carried the index letters of the squadron.'*

Leutnant Eberhardt stated that Joyce collaborated satisfactorily for a time but started to get restless and carried on.

Eberhardt then claimed that in the spring of 1943 Joyce was taken to North Africa. Eberhardt was not involved in the arrangements himself and believed they were made by Major Erich Killinger, the Camp Commandant at that time. Eberhardt believed he was sent to North Africa for some purpose in an Interrogation Centre for prisoners of war like Dulag Luft. However, Joyce contracted malaria and after a few months, he was sent back to the German casualty hospital at Dulag Luft. He was placed in the German hospital because he did not want to go to the Hohemark prisoners' hospital where POWs would be sent.

After he was released from the hospital, Eberhardt spoke with Joyce and says the Irishman told him he had been involved with the interrogation of British POWs in Africa. He also had a false name, but Eberhardt could not remember it.

Once Michael Joyce was fit and well, Eberhardt claimed he was present when Joyce was briefed to go and collaborate with the German Counter-Intelligence authorities in Luxembourg. This was for the purpose of discovering the escape lines and underground movements assisting escaping Allied airmen.

Eberhardt then claimed that some months after Joyce had gone off on this mission, he heard he had escaped.

Michael Joyce had told Eberhardt his cousin was William Joyce, but he could not get on with Lord Haw Haw, who had even called him a traitor for serving in the RAF. As far as Eberhardt knew, William Joyce had never visited Michael at Dulag Luft.

SIB now had the decorated man in their sights, it now appeared this man had not been telling the truth in his 1942 debriefing and Whyte's initial suspicions were correct. Michael Joyce had not only been decorated with the Military Medal, he had been commissioned. As the first cousin of William Joyce, who had already been condemned for treachery at the Old Bailey, it now seemed a major embarrassment was brewing.

To add to the evidence of Leutnant Eberhardt, the Camp Commandant Erich Killinger also made a statement. He stated:

> *'When I took over the command at Dulag Luft, a man named Joyce, a British prisoner of war was employed in the camp as a stool-pigeon. I was informed about Joyce by Major Rumpel, from whom I took over the command of the camp. He told me that Joyce was working very secretly for us and it was very necessary that other people should not get to know about it. He advised that it would be wise to let Joyce be handled by one of our officers who knew him and mentioned Leutnant Eberhardt had been with him and knew him well. I decided to let Leutnant Eberhardt carry on and he continued his interviewing with Joyce.'*

Killinger also explained that Joyce could come and go at will from the camp to the carpenters' shop, allowing meetings with Leutnant Heinrich Eberhardt.

The camp commandant added that the information he received from Joyce was about conditions in England, obtained through his discussions with newly arrived POWs. He was sometimes asked to speak to certain prisoners who the interrogators had found difficult to break down and talk. Killinger, like Eberhardt, could not remember a precise piece of intelligence provided by Joyce and was quick to say that he was certain there was nothing of importance provided by Sergeant Joyce.

Erich Killinger said that some months after he had taken command, Joyce was sent to North Africa near Tobruk. This was to act as a stool-pigeon at a POW camp or Interrogation Centre. He could not remember who made the arrangements for his transfer, but it was possible he had contacted the Intelligence Department in Berlin and told them he had no further use for Joyce.

Michael Joyce, according to Killinger, returned to Oberursel after three to six months, he was ill with, he thought – yellow jaundice. He was placed in the Hohemark hospital for treatment and was very ill for some time.

Killinger stated that once Michael Joyce was well again, he was sent to the neighbourhood of Aix-Le-Chappelle to work under the instructions of the German authorities, trying to discover the escape lines back to England.

Killinger said he was later told that Sergeant Joyce had stayed for a few days at the house of a security agent in that district. At night, he was taken by car and dropped off near a monastery which was suspected of being involved in the escape lines. Joyce, however, escaped and when the German authorities found evidence of an escape line near the Spanish frontier, his name was found to be one of the airmen crossing into Spain.

This evidence against Michael Joyce was quite damning and on 10 July 1945 at South Kensington, London, he was interviewed by Squadron Leader Thomas from SIB.

After being told that enquiries were being made about his time in Germany, Joyce cracked and admitted that his original 1942 account of his escape was incorrect. He sat down and made a new statement.

Straight away, Joyce gave a reason for his initial statement, claiming that he feared an honest account would have prevented him from continuing in the RAF and the war against Germany.

The details of his initial capture were ninety per cent correct, but this time he claimed that they had run out of fuel having become lost and made a forced landing. Joyce and the pilot went off to try and find the identity of their location. The plan was, if they were in enemy territory, they would fire a red Very flare and the other two crewmen would set fire to the Hampden. Unfortunately, when they fired the flare, the crewmen could not set fire to the aircraft, so they smashed all the instruments and the wireless set.

Their capture and removal via Terschelling etc. to Dulag Luft remained the same, but upon arrival at Oberursel, he stated he was visited in his cell by a medical orderly and an interrogator called Viergood (actually Rumpel's adjutant Fiergutt). One or the other produced a form and asked for details. When he did not fill it in, Viergood (Fiergutt) filled in all the answers correctly on the form.

Joyce said Viergood (Fiergutt) had asked about conditions in England and about IFF, but the airman told them he knew nothing about it.

Later, Fiergutt took Joyce to see the Camp Commandant (Rumpel). Wing Commander Day was the Senior British Officer and Joyce was given a role in dealing with Red Cross parcels, but after two months he became the camp carpenter.

Joyce admitted to meeting Leutnant Eberhardt in the carpenters' shop. He would ask Joyce about conditions in the camp, about other prisoners and what they said about conditions in England. Joyce, however, was quick to add that Eberhardt did not ask him very much about service matters. He did once ask Joyce about IFF, but again he said he did not know anything about it.

Access to the carpenters' shop was useful and Joyce claimed that he often provided wood for the escape tunnel pit-props.

Joyce said he continued as the camp carpenter until about May 1942. During that time he was taken to the Commandant's office three or four times and again asked about IFF. He was also questioned about his relationship and knowledge of William Joyce (Lord Haw Haw). The Commandant at that time was Major Theo Rumpel and Joyce again recalled the two men and the woman coming and asking him questions about Ireland.

After the escape of eighteen prisoners, Rumpel was replaced by Killinger, but Joyce said he was never taken to the new Commandant's office.

Joyce confirmed that he was the first cousin of William Joyce and had only met him once, in central London at about the end of 1938. William resented the fact his cousin had volunteered for RAF aircrew duties, especially as he had only been in England six to eight weeks, having arrived from the family home in County Mayo. Michael Joyce said he knew nothing at the time of the fascist movement.

Michael Joyce said he did not meet William in Germany. However, he did state that when talking with Leutnant Eberhardt one day, he mentioned to the German that he thought it funny his cousin had not written to him. Michael Joyce wrote a note to William and gave it to Eberhardt, but he did not know whether his cousin received it, as he never received a reply.

After the escape of the eighteen airmen from Dulag Luft, Squadron Leader Elliott and Squadron Leader Jennings called Joyce to the SBO's room. There he was told that he was a suspect in the camp and aircrew had been told not to talk to him. What he was alleged to have done was never disclosed to him, but he was angry and felt this was linked to the identity of his first cousin in Berlin.

Joyce spoke with Leutnant Eberhardt about what Squadron Leader Elliott had told him and the fact he was under suspicion. Joyce suggested to Eberhardt that he be moved to another camp, but nothing happened.

In about May 1942, feeling fed-up and unwell, Joyce told Eberhardt that he wanted to get out of the camp. At the end of the month, he was suddenly taken by car to the hospital at Hohemark and placed in a room. He could not remember anything being said to him, but shortly after arriving, Leutnant Eberhardt arrived and said, '*You are going places.*' He was told he was going to Munich where someone wanted to meet him. Joyce believed the name 'Konrad' was mentioned by Eberhardt before he was taken by train to Munich.

Joyce said he wore air force uniform to travel and at Munich station he met Major Konrad. He had an escort with him and they took Joyce to a hotel. After a meal, Konrad told Joyce he was being taken to Rome by train.

When they arrived in Rome, Joyce said he was fitted with civilian clothes and stayed in a hotel. He was then flown with Konrad and a guard to Brindisi. After a while, he was flown again, still in civilian clothes and in the company of Major Konrad, to Crete and then on to Derna in North Africa.

Major Konrad told Michael Joyce that he wanted him to act as a Red Cross man and get forms filled in by prisoners of war who were in the transit camp at Derna. He stayed in a house near the headquarters, but he was not allowed out and signed no parole agreement. When Joyce was allowed to go for a walk, it was always accompanied.

Joyce said he realised he was '*Right in it now*' and had to do something to satisfy the Germans. However, he admitted obtaining some information from prisoners and carried on questioning them with the forms, as he knew there would be hidden microphones.

He was given the alias of Willi Schneider by Major Konrad and a Luftwaffe Private's uniform. He was told to use this alias and never to use the name Joyce. Sometimes he would wear his RAF uniform, especially when going into rooms containing RAF prisoners.

After three to four weeks at Derna, Joyce was moved to a place called Fuca in the Western Desert. There he wore his Luftwaffe uniform and was known again as Willi Schneider. He remembered interviewing one officer and an NCO there, telling them he was also a POW. He asked them questions about service matters, but claimed he did not get any information from them; this made Konrad angry when he returned without any intelligence.

Joyce claimed he then became sick with dysentery, so ill he could not do anything. He was flown to Italy and stayed in hospital, before being moved back to Munich by air. However, upon arrival in Germany, he was taken under escort back to Oberursel and put in the hospital with German patients. Leutnant Eberhardt visited Joyce and he told the officer he did not want to go to the POW hospital ward with the other prisoners.

Eberhardt visited the hospital a number of times and Joyce asked if he could work on a farm, but the German said he thought he should go to France instead.

In about September 1942, Leutnant Eberhardt arrived and took Joyce by train to Luxembourg. There he was introduced to Kimmerich, who was head of the local Gestapo. By this time Joyce was quite fluent in German and Kimmerich told him they wanted him to try and discover the underground movement (escape lines) in Holland, Belgium and France. He was to be dressed as a shot down airman and seek assistance to get to England.

Joyce agreed to do this, but pointed out that he would need some sort of identity in the event of him being stopped by the German patrols. Kimmerich therefore gave him an identity paper bearing Joyce's photograph, an official stamp and the German officer's signature.

Joyce was given the alias of Eric Johnstone and another set of identity papers and dog tags bearing that name. Joyce recalled that Leutnant Eberhardt was present throughout this interview.

Dressed in RAF battledress and flying boots, he was taken by car and dropped off by a monastery suspected of being involved in escapes. He hid in a wood and once it was dark, he made his way to the monastery. Joyce now claimed he realised this was his chance to escape, especially with him possessing Kimmerich's pass.

Joyce claimed to have knocked on the door of a building and repeated his earlier 1942 account, of a man and his wife taking him in and assisting him. He was taken into France and passed through St. Jean de Leuse near Bordeaux, over the Pyrenees and into Spain and then Gibraltar. He returned home on 1 November 1942.

Squadron Leader Thomas (RAF SIB), having spoken with Michael Joyce, completed a report dated 13 July 1945, which was sent to the Air Officer Commanding SIB. In the report he stated:

> *'It is evident that the work which Joyce had done for the Germans had been such that it must have inspired great confidence and trust in him, or he would not have been sent into the underground movement without better supervision to prevent his escape. Various considerations arise:*
>
> 1. *Did he get taken too far, that he could not get back to Kimmerich?*
> 2. *As he walked for hours, did he strike a movement other than the monastery?*
> 3. *Did he have an opportunity of getting out of the movement, once he was on his way etc?*
> 4. *It is evident he experienced no difficulties in getting out of German control.*

'In view of the information that Joyce has been awarded the Military Medal for his exceptional work in getting away from German control; and his admission that the story he told was not a true one, this report is submitted for information and consideration in respect of the award.

'Regarding proceedings against Joyce for aiding the enemy, his own story is all the evidence available at present, except that Leutnant Eberhardt stated he was a stool-pigeon and was sent to North Africa. This has also been corroborated by Major Killinger who is now in this country and has been interviewed.'

On 15 September 1945, Major Richard Kimmerich of the Gestapo was interviewed and a statement taken by Squadron Leader Thomas (SIB).

Kimmerich explained that he worked for the German Intelligence Service in Luxembourg. He remembered an English flyer called Michael Joyce being brought to him by Sonderführer (Leutnant) Eberhardt in about September 1942. Kimmerich did not arrange this, instead he received a telephone call from his head office in Wiesbaden, informing him Joyce would arrive for the purpose of discovering the means by which Allied fliers were escaping.

Kimmerich continued stating that Eberhardt and Joyce arrived in civilian clothes, but the Englishman also had flying clothes in a bag. He also had an escape kit in his possession. They discussed things and they stayed the night. They ate their meals in the Officers' Mess and from conversations with Joyce and Eberhardt, Kimmerich knew that the Irishman had been at Oberursel having been shot down over Holland. He also knew that Joyce had been to Tobruk, where he had assisted the German authorities with prisoner interrogations. This was disclosed when Kimmerich questioned the integrity of Michael Joyce and the decision to send him on this new mission.

In answer to this question of integrity, Kimmerich said Joyce gave the impression of reliability and was from Northern Ireland. He was a cousin of the radio announcer William Joyce and had been a member of the Republican Army in Ireland. Joyce also told Kimmerich that he had many privileges in Dulag Luft and often went alone to the cinema or shopping in Frankfurt.

Kimmerich disclosed that Joyce had false papers in the name of Johnstone and if any question arose in respect of his mission, a telephone call should be made to the Chief of Police, Kriminalrat Runge in Luxembourg. The police officer Runge had signed the false identity papers.

The next day Eberhardt left and a car took Joyce and dropped him off near a monastery at Orval in Belgium.

Kimmerich stated that as they drove to the drop-off point, Joyce asked him if he could get right through to the Spanish frontier (by that Kimmerich thought he meant England), should he do so. Kimmerich told Joyce he should not leave German controlled territory and get all the information back to him.

After eight days, Kimmerich had not heard from Joyce and wondered what had happened to him. He made enquiries through the Intelligence Service in Brussels and with Erich Killinger at Oberursel. Kimmerich thought he might even have been identified as a stool-pigeon and shot by the escape line.

Later, upon hearing that Joyce had escaped, Kimmerich believed this was his aim all the time he was with him.

The British authorities and RAF SIB were now in a very difficult position. It was clear that Michael Joyce had assisted the enemy in a number of ways. The SIB file appears to have been shunted around various departments, one of the main problems being that any charges under the Air Force Act were now defunct. This was because, under section 161 of the Air Force Act, 'A person shall not in pursuance of this Act be tried or punished for any offence triable by court-martial committed more than three years before the date at which his trial begins, except in the case of the offence of mutiny, desertion or fraudulent enlistment'. As these offences took place in 1942, the three year period had expired.

The Air Ministry were keen to charge Michael Joyce with a more serious offence and an approach to the Director of Public Prosecutions (DPP) resulted in him saying he would undertake a prosecution if there was sufficient evidence available.

The Director of Public Prosecutions also gave advice on the Military Medal awarded to Joyce in 1944. He said removal of the award or consideration of such an action, would not prejudice the question of a later prosecution of Michael Joyce. The DPP stated that either the medal should be removed now before any further evidence is obtained, or it should be postponed until after a trial, if one takes place.

In May 1946, moves were in progress to withdraw the Military Medal, but on 18 June 1946, information was passed from the Director of Public Prosecutions to the Judge Advocate General's office stating that owing to MI5 being unable to obtain further evidence, the Director is unable to proceed with a prosecution of Joyce. (Author's comment: specific details of what this could have been were not given in the memorandum.)

The Military Medal was withdrawn with the agreement of King George VI and no further action was taken against Michael Joyce. He was called upon to resign his emergency commission and leave the RAF immediately, which he did.

What happened to him in later life is something of a mystery, he escaped justice and may well have headed back to the family home in Ballinrobe, County Mayo.

Chapter 15

Sergeant Edward WHILLOCK No. 1384110 and Flight Lieutenant David W. Thomas No. 45050

Sergeant Edward Whillock was another name the RAF Special Investigation Branch became aware of when other prisoners of war were repatriated at the end of the conflict. His name had already appeared in a number of coded letters during the war and it seemed only a matter of time before he was brought to justice. (See National Archives file AIR40/2295 re: Whillock.)

Edward Whillock was an air gunner with No. 35 Squadron based at RAF Graveley in Cambridgeshire. The unit flew Halifax bombers and on the night of 24-25 August 1942, Whillock and his crew took off in aircraft serial number W7765 for a raid on Frankfurt. The aircraft successfully bombed the target and was on the homeward bound leg of their journey when they were shot down over France by a Messerschmitt 110 night fighter of 7/NJG4, flown by Feldwebel Heinrich Macke. Five of the crew, including Whillock, managed to bail-out successfully, but the pilot and the wireless operator were killed – possibly during the fighter attack.

The surviving crewmen parachuted safely to the ground, but were quickly captured and sent to Dulag Luft, Oberursel.

The primary witness against Whillock was Flight Lieutenant David W. Thomas, the Adjutant at Dulag Luft when he arrived at the camp, although Thomas himself would become a collaboration suspect in time.

Thomas was interviewed by the Special Investigation Branch and provided a statement, saying he had known Whillock at Dulag Luft and saw him later in Stalag Luft III.

Thomas added that Whillock informed him that while he was at Dulag Luft in the interrogation block, he had expressed pro-German sympathies, as he thought this might help him form an escape plan. However, he was taken to Berlin where he underwent espionage training on the understanding he would be parachuted back into England.

While in the German capital, Whillock told Thomas he was asked to make a radio broadcast, but refused to do this and was returned to Dulag Luft.

The story seemed odd: if he did undergo an espionage training course, why then ask him to make a radio broadcast prior to dropping him by parachute back into England? This would seem to be counter-productive for an agent's cover.

Other witness statements were soon obtained, including one from Warrant Officer Ronald J. Stuckley Service Number 922027. He had been an air gunner with No. 24 Squadron, South African Air Force stationed in the Middle East in 1943. On 20 March 1943, his Boston was shot down and he bailed out, being captured and sent to Dulag Luft.

At Dulag Luft, he volunteered for a gardening work party and met Sergeant Edward Whillock. The two men ended up billeted in the same hut where Whillock told him that he had been to Berlin and had a good time watching shows and going to cafes. While in Berlin, Whillock said he had worn civilian clothes. The Germans had wanted him to make radio propaganda broadcasts, but he told Stuckley these requests were declined.

Warrant Officer (former Sergeant) James Jennings Service Number 976466, also made a statement. He had been an air gunner with No. 7 Squadron at RAF Oakington, near Cambridge, in March 1943. His aircraft had been shot down by a night fighter during a raid on Munich and like the others, he had been captured and sent to Dulag Luft.

After his initial interrogation period with the solitary cell regime, Jennings was moved to a hut with about a dozen other prisoners in it. He worked in the kitchens and while doing some gardening work, he got to know Edward Whillock.

Whillock told him that he had been to Berlin and lived in a hotel with some other people. He was given German money, bread coupons and escape maps. Jennings thought Whillock was intimating that he had tried to fool the Germans and escape, but he had been brought back to Dulag Luft. Whillock also told him that the Germans had wanted him to make a radio broadcast, but he had refused before being returned to the camp.

Jennings recalled Whillock mentioning something about parachuting down over England, but he was not sure about it at the time he gave a statement to the SIB. Unbelievably, despite Whillock's claims, Jennings said he had no occasion to think he was collaborating with the Germans.

Gunner John Thomas Spence of the RHQ, 2nd Regiment, Royal Horse Artillery, also came into contact with Whillock after being captured in Greece in 1941. He too made a statement.

He was taken to Stalag 18A at Wolfsberg in Austria and went out on various POW work parties. On one of these work parties he got to know a Czechoslovakian woman and was sentenced, in September 1942, to three years imprisonment for having intercourse with the woman. He was returned to Stalag 18A and placed in confinement.

Two months later, Spence was taken to Berlin, placed in a private house at 49 Ahornallee, Charlottenburg and locked in his room. One evening he was visited by a man who spoke perfect English wearing Air Force trousers and a shirt. After shaking hands, he told Spence he was an RAF sergeant air gunner who had been shot down. He had been brought to Berlin with the Germans expecting his help, but he was planning to do as much sabotage as possible. He was also planning to get the Germans to send him back to England as an agent so he could double-cross them.

Spence only knew his Christian name, which was Ted, he was housed in an adjacent room and was between nineteen and twenty-two years of age. He had very dark wavy hair, he was growing a moustache and his cheeks were red with a darkish skin. He was about 5'08" tall and slim. (This description matched that of Edward 'Ted' Whillock.)

Spence saw Whillock again the next day in a civilian suit. The two men were taken out under escort to watch a football match around Christmas 1942. On another occasion, they were both taken to see the Palace and Cathedral in Potsdam, as well as a variety performance in a Berlin theatre.

In time, Spence was given a pass and allowed to go out on his own. One day he went out with Ted, without an escort, to meet an Irishman called Mullally. He was supposed to be training Spence for radio broadcasting.

On 14 June 1945, Whillock was interviewed by SIB and made a full statement under caution. After explaining how and where he had been shot down, he explained an initial visit to a Luftwaffe airfield near Chalons-sur-Marne in France, before ending up at Dulag Luft.

Whillock said he was placed in a cell on his own and the next day, a German Officer came into his cell. He said he was from the Red Cross and wanted him to fill in what he assumed was a fake Red Cross form. Whillock said he only gave his name, rank and number, but the officer had a folder with *35 Squadron* written across its cover. From the information contained within the file, the officer filled in the form for Whillock.

The next day, a German captain entered the cell and asked Whillock about the GEE box on the aircraft. Whillock told him he knew nothing about this as he was an air gunner. He was also asked about Pathfinder techniques and other matters which he could not answer.

This went on for about a week, with the officer attending the cell every day and asking the same questions which Whillock declined to answer.

After this period, Whillock said he told the officer he would like to work for the Germans and asked if it could be arranged for him to go back to England to do this work. The officer asked how Whillock could help in England and he told him that he could transmit messages back to Germany.

They talked about the 'under-paid working classes in England' and the officer asked Whillock why he was fighting if he felt that way. Whillock told him that he had been unemployed and only joined up to do something. He had been seventeen and three quarter years of age when he volunteered and eighteen when he joined the RAF. However, Whillock said his real plan was to get home and rejoin his squadron.

After this discussion and the offer to work for the Germans, Whillock said he was moved to the stone house quarters (where the permanent and special prisoners were held), but still locked up.

The German captain came and took him for walks, during which they would talk, before he was placed in the camp with Squadron Leader Elliott, Flight Lieutenant Thomas, Flying Officer Hardy and Sergeant John Slowey.

Whillock said he complained to a German Leutnant (possibly Eberhardt?), that he was fed up and wanted to go to a Stalag. The officer told him, '*We'll see*', and about ten days later he was put on a train for Lansdorf, but was immediately taken off before the train had moved and placed in a car with a German guard. He was then driven to the nearby Hohemark hospital and locked in a room on his own.

After a week, a Gestapo Captain came to see Whillock. Whillock again told him that he wanted to go back to England and transmit information to Germany. The Gestapo man left, but returned a number of times, taking him for walks in the woods and into Frankfurt. All the time, he was in RAF uniform and never signed a parole agreement.

In late October 1942, the Gestapo man took him by train to Berlin. He was taken by car to 46 Arhon Allee in Charlottenburg (note the slight differences to the address given by Gunner Spence). He was given a room and allowed to move around the house, but always locked up at night. Whillock kept his RAF uniform on, but he was told to remove his sergeant's rank chevrons and his air gunner brevet.

After about a week, another Gestapo captain, who Whillock thought was called Hartmann, arrived at the house and they talked about England.

Whillock also recalled Gunner Spence arriving and being called John Brenner or Brennan. He had made several voice tests for the radio before he started making radio broadcasts and moved to another house.

At Christmas (1942) Hartmann brought Whillock some civilian clothes – a grey suit, black shoes, a shirt and tie. Every Friday, the German Sergeant who managed the house gave Whillock 20 Reichsmarks. When he went out to the café for dinner, Whillock would pay with this money, but he also received Red Cross parcels and saved some of the cash.

Whillock was able to write home to his parents, his letters being addressed as originating from Dulag Luft, this was on the directions of Hartman.

Whillock also recalled going to a football match and attending the Palace in Potsdam with Spence. He also attended the cinema and a variety show, all this information corroborating Spence's own statement.

A German Major arrived and told Whillock he had to learn German, as the espionage teacher only spoke German. He told Whillock if he didn't learn the language he'd be returned to a Stalag.

In March 1943, Whillock was taken by train back to Dulag Luft where he was placed on work party with men like Jennings and Stuckley. In the clothing store Whillock met Flight Lieutenant Thomas, who asked where he had been. Whillock said he told him and asked for a compass so he could escape, but the next day he was moved on to Stalag Luft III at Sagan.

At Stalag Luft III, Whillock claimed to have told Sergeant 'Dixie' Dean what he had done and handed him or the camp's escape committee, 80 Reichsmarks and some meat coupons he had received while in Berlin. Whillock also claimed to have given his account to Warrant Officer Frederick Brotherton. Eventually, Whillock was liberated by British forces in 1945 and repatriated to the United Kingdom.

On 17 August 1945, Squadron Leader Thomas (RAF SIB) completed a full report concerning Whillock and his activities in Germany.

Thomas pointed out that there was no definite evidence that Whillock did anything to assist the Germans. Exactly what he did whilst collaborating with the Germans was unknown. In addition, the SIB had been unable to interview any of the Germans who handled Whillock in Berlin or at Dulag Luft.

Squadron Leader Thomas also highlighted that Whillock appeared to have never divulged to the Senior British Officer or anyone else at Dulag Luft what his intentions were when he was first at the camp in 1942.

Knowing the conduct of others who were later taken to Berlin and processed through the system (Hughes, Alcock, Freeman and others), it appears that Whillock collaborated and assisted to the necessary extent of establishing the confidence of the Germans that he could be useful to them.

Squadron Leader Thomas (SIB) finally added:

> *'His case, on the evidence, is not a bad one, but it shows that he did collaborate with the Germans and failed to carry out what he had been directed to do in the event of being taken prisoner, and in the circumstances, I suggest that he should be seriously considered for court martial procedure, as a court martial appears to be the only exemplary measure the Air Ministry can take regarding those who have improperly collaborated with the Germans and have been, at least, a potential danger to this country.'*

On 31 August 1945, Air Commodore Walmesley of the Judge Advocate General's (JAG) Office, stated that there was no evidence obtained to discredit the explanation of Whillock's own actions. In these circumstances, in the opinion of the Air Commodore, there was insufficient evidence to justify any proceedings against Whillock.

What happened next is unclear, but on 28 March 1946, Group Captain Wickham from the RAF SIB wrote to Major Patterson at the War Office stating that the JAG had replied in August 1945, that there appeared to be insufficient evidence to justify proceedings. In addition, the statutory three-year time limit for charges of assisting the enemy under the Air Force Act had now expired and no prosecution could take place for that offence (as in the case with Michael Joyce).

No further action was taken against Sergeant Edward Whillock and he disappeared into the mists of time. I have been unable to locate any further information about this man. This is exacerbated by the RAF data protection policy, which will not allow the RAF Air Historical Branch to disclose details of service records to anyone, unless they are next of kin.

* * *

Flight Lieutenant David W. Thomas was, as already mentioned, the adjutant to the Senior British Officer at Dulag Luft. He was different to the others as he was not actually aircrew but ground staff.

Although there was no concrete evidence against David Thomas in 1945, there was an air of suspicion which surrounded him, this was mainly due to his presence on the permanent staff, his links to Squadron Leader Harry 'Wings' Day, Squadron Leader Elliott and some of the other alleged collaborators named in this book.

In his statement to the British authorities after the war, Leutnant Gustav Bauer-Schlichtegroll spoke about Thomas. He said Thomas was the adjutant to Squadron Leader Elliott and regarded by the German staff as a stool-pigeon.

Leutnant Bauer-Schlichtegroll stated that Thomas had initially been handled by Hauptmann von Miller-Aicholtz. Miller-Aicholtz told Bauer-Schlichtegroll, that Thomas was a remarkable man who he had not been able to stop from talking on service matters. Thomas was apparently disgruntled over promotion and readily agreed to act as an informer on conversations within the camp.

Bauer-Schlichtegroll explained in his statement that it was the custom for interrogators to pass questions for the prisoners to one another. This allowed them to obtain information, especially if one of the prisoner handlers had a free-talking prisoner who could provide answers on the subject they were investigating.

Leutnant Bauer-Schlichtegroll said he knew Miller-Aicholtz had obtained information from Thomas on RAF service matters, and after Miller-Aicholtz had moved on, Ober Inspecktor Horst Barth took over the handling of Thomas. When Barth was too busy, Bauer-Schlichtegroll would handle Thomas. (Barth had only been at Dulag Luft a few months having arrived in January 1943.)

Gustav Bauer-Schlichtegroll said he found Thomas to be very approachable and on the face of it, very willing to collaborate, but he was not sure whether the RAF man was withholding some information, or even obtaining information for his own (British) authorities.

Thomas received no advantages and Bauer-Schlichtegroll said, both he and the other handlers were baffled about Thomas's motives for collaboration.

As an example of information provided by Thomas, Bauer-Schlichtegroll said he would approach him if a prisoner had given information that was different to the German records. Thomas would then go and get clarification. Sometimes Thomas would get a quick response, but sometimes Bauer-Schlichtegroll would have to wait two or three days to get a reply from him.

The Germans fastidiously kept reports and Bauer-Schlichtegroll explained that any report found showing information given by Wing Commander Shepherd was actually the intelligence provided by Thomas.

Thomas was said to have carried on as a stool-pigeon for about two years at the camp. When the transit camp moved to Frankfurt, Bauer-Schlichtegroll would visit Thomas. The last time he saw him was in November 1943, when Thomas was moved on to Sagan.

A German intelligence report, reference number VE/2240/43, and dated 19 October 1943, was exhibited by Bauer-Schlichtegroll. This, he claimed, was a report regarding a meeting he had with Thomas and the intelligence the officer gave him.

Leutnant Heinrich Eberhardt, in his witness statement, explained that Bauer-Schlichtegroll handled Flight Lieutenant Thomas at Dulag Luft. He added that he had nothing to do with Thomas as no one interfered with another handler's prisoners.

We have already seen in this book that David Thomas gave statemented evidence against Hughes and Whillock, so was he loyal or was he, as the German officers' state, a stool-pigeon and a traitor?

On 4 June 1945, David Thomas was interviewed and made a statement to Flight Lieutenant Nicholls (SIB). Thomas explained that he was serving in North Africa as a Fighter Wing Administration Officer when he was captured during a German advance in early 1942. He was transferred to Crete, Rome, Munich and finally Dulag Luft in March 1942.

Thomas claimed that as a ground trade officer, the Germans initially suspected him of being a spy. They therefore kept him in solitary confinement until a full report of his capture arrived from Africa. (Why they would think he was a spy if he was in RAF uniform is unclear.)

When he arrived at Dulag Luft, Thomas says Lieutenant Commander Casson warned him about Pilot Officer Benson Freeman, who was a fascist and very pro-Nazi.

Thomas became the officer in charge of the clothing store and met Sergeant Whillock there. Whillock had told him that he had expressed German sympathies, as this might help him in a bid to escape, but he had been sent to Berlin. Thomas recalled Whillock returning to the camp and telling him that he had been placed on an espionage course, after which he was to have been dropped by parachute into England. As a sign of good faith, the Germans had wanted him to make two radio propaganda broadcasts, but he had refused and they sent him back to Dulag Luft.

Thomas described seeing Raymond Hughes being taken away in a Feisler Storch aircraft. He learnt that Hughes had been interrogating new prisoners of war and asking them to fill in the false Red Cross forms.

Thomas claimed that POWs were paid five reichsmarks a week and pay sheets were sent across for countersigning. From these sheets, Thomas ascertained that in the Interrogation Centre was a Squadron Leader Carpenter, a Polish Flying Officer Zuromski, and an American Sergeant called Tricks. An Austrian soldier whose name he could not remember was working in the German offices and would give information in return for cigarettes. By this means, Thomas was told that Flying Officer Zuromski was going to broadcast anti-Russian propaganda to Poland from Berlin.

Thomas was also informed that Carpenter had signed a parole but did not assist the Germans. Thomas also claimed a Squadron Leader Mayer had told him that Carpenter had said the best thing to do was to sign the parole and have an easy time.

Not surprisingly, Thomas did not say anything about giving information to the German officers at Dulag Luft in his statement.

On 4 August 1945, an SIB report detailed the case against Flight Lieutenant David Thomas. It outlined the evidence of Bauer-Schlichtegroll and Eberhardt, as well as the fact Squadron Leader Elliott had stated in his interview that he could not believe Thomas would give information to the Germans.

Sergeant Parker, who assisted Thomas in the store at Dulag Luft, said he had no reason to suspect Flight Lieutenant Thomas of collaboration.

Thomas was to be a witness in the (then) forthcoming court martial of Sergeant Raymond Hughes and there was no likelihood of any new evidence corroborating what Bauer-Schlichtegroll and Eberhardt had alleged.

The report was forwarded to the Judge Advocate General's Office and it appears no action was taken against Flight Lieutenant Thomas, as the only direct evidence came from Leutnant Gustav Bauer-Schlichtegroll and was uncorroborated.

Whether any other Dulag Luft intelligence reports bearing the name 'Wing Commander Shepherd' as the source were ever found is unknown. Some papers do exist in the UK National Archives under reference AIR40/2267, but these are only a small fraction of the number that must have been generated and amassed during the war.

Again, what happened to David Thomas after the war, in unknown.

Chapter 16

Sergeant Frank TIPTON No. 975105

Sergeant Frank Tipton falls into a very different category to those already discussed within this book. Tipton was apparently an immature young man who, like the others, found himself in an invidious position. Unfortunately for him, the German intelligence team at Dulag Luft took advantage of him.

Tipton was a flight engineer attached to No. 51 Squadron at RAF Snaith (the same unit as Sergeant Jack Alcock). On 14 May 1943, he took-off with his crew to attack Bochum in Western Germany. Their aircraft was 'coned' by searchlights and hit several times by flak, which killed the aircraft's two gunners, and the machine fell from the sky out of control. The order was given to abandon the aircraft and Tipton successfully bailed out, but he was quickly captured and sent to Dulag Luft.

At the end of the war, there had been no information of any alleged wrongdoing by Sergeant Frank Tipton. However, that changed when Leutnant Gustav Bauer-Schlichtegroll was interrogated after his own capture in 1945.

Leutnant Bauer-Schlichtegroll told the SIB investigators that he knew Sergeant Tipton at Dulag Luft as a collaborator and he was referred to in German intelligence reports as Sergeant Brown. Although he did not handle Tipton himself, he heard what had been disclosed by the airman via Ober Inspektor Horst Barth. (At the time of Leutnant Bauer-Schlichtegroll's interrogation, Barth had not been traced by the Allied forces.)

On 5 July 1945, Captain Graham F. Hay, a member of the Royal Army Medical Corps, gave a statement to the Special Investigation Branch. In it, he stated that he was a prisoner of war and in March or April 1944, a Sergeant Clark of the RAF had reported that a man called Tipton seemed to be suffering from mental illness. Tipton had been a member of the camp band, but his ability to play his instrument had deteriorated, as had his own personal cleanliness due to his condition.

Captain Hay spoke with Frank Tipton and quickly decided that he was a case for a medical repatriation to the UK, referring him to the appropriate medical panel. Hay did not know the actual medical diagnosis, but he believed there was certainly a case of possible anxiety and even schizophrenia. Tipton attended a Medical Commission in May 1944 and it was decided to repatriate him on medical grounds.

A statement was taken from Warrant Officer Arthur Lloyd George Knight, Service Number 1454177, a flight engineer in the same squadron as Tipton. Knight and his crew had been shot down on 12 May 1943 during a raid on Duisburg. Knight ended up in Dulag Luft with his wireless operator Sergeant Goodchild.

After going through the now standard routine of being kept in a solitary cell and interrogated, Knight asked to go to the hospital as his nerves were in 'pretty bad shape'. Knight and Goodchild were both sent to the hospital, where they assisted in looking after other patients.

A few days later, about 20 May 1943, Sergeant Frank Tipton arrived in the hospital. Knight believed he was not ill or injured in any way, but he would pick lettuces and gooseberries from the hospital garden.

Knight recalled seeing Tipton in conversation and walking with Ober Inspektor Horst Barth in the hospital grounds. Sometimes Barth would telephone the hospital and ask for Tipton to go and see him in Dulag Luft. Tipton would then walk alone and without a guard to the Interrogation Centre to visit Horst Barth.

In addition, Knight said Tipton would be taken out by Captain Offermann and another German officer who was permanently at the Hohemark hospital. Offermann would say he wanted Tipton to do some electrical work at Dulag Luft, but the British airman would later admit to Knight that he had no electrical knowledge.

One day, Tipton went off to see Barth and returned about midnight with a brown civilian suit under his arm. Knight and Goodchild asked what the suit was for, and Tipton told them Barth had told him to get it pressed in the hospital laundry. The following day, having had the brown suit pressed, Tipton took it back to Dulag Luft. He returned in the early hours of the following morning, when he told Knight he had been in Frankfurt with Ober Inspektor Barth's secretary. They had been drinking and visiting cafes together. Knight said it was clear from his condition, that Tipton had been drinking alcohol in Frankfurt. The next morning, Tipton admitted that Barth's secretary had been pumping him with alcohol and questions, but he didn't tell them anything.

Knight said he had questioned Tipton about why he was associating with the Germans so much and what happened when he went to the Interrogation Centre. Tipton said he had confirmed a list of airmen operating with No. 51 Squadron for the Germans, been shown a photograph of the Snaith briefing room and answered questions about its lay-out. On another occasion, Tipton was asked about navigators' charts and why some had wider margins than others.

Sergeant Tipton was always questioning Goodchild the wireless operator about technique and these questions always followed a visit to or by the German staff.

On another occasion, Tipton said he was given the uniform of an RAF Flight Lieutenant and told to go into the cell of a Squadron Leader from a Typhoon squadron and get him to talk. Tipton said he had told the Typhoon pilot he was a phoney as soon as he entered the cell.

Knight said he had warned Tipton that he was laying himself open to a serious charge when he returned home to England, but he continued to go along with the German collaboration.

On one occasion, Tipton told Knight he had a good mind not to return home after the war, but when he saw him later at Stalag Luft VI, he had twice said he was going to commit suicide. Knight recalled Tipton being sent to the hospital at Stalag Luft VI. He told Knight that Inspektor Horst Barth had told him to make a nuisance of himself at the Stalag, so he would be put in the cooler and then recalled to Dulag Luft.

Sergeant Kenneth Goodchild, Service Number 1330530, also made a statement which corroborated that of Knight. He also added that he remembered Tipton once asking him questions about how the IFF system worked.

Squadron Leader Allen Henry Corkett, Service Number 41903, was quickly identified as the probable Typhoon pilot approached in the cell by Tipton. He made a statement stating that he was a Hawker Typhoon pilot with 197 Squadron at RAF Tangmere in 1943.

On 1 July 1943, he was shot down by flak and made a forced landing in France. After twenty-four hours liberty, he was captured by two German officers and ended up at Dulag Luft. He was kept in a solitary cell for about ten days and refused to answer any questions after two different German officers had entered his cell.

After about four days alone in his cell, Corkett recalled seeing through his cell window, a Sergeant within a khaki battledress with an observers brevet outside the building. He stopped and told Corkett not to tell the

Germans anything, before saying he would try and get him some bread that evening.

At about 6:30pm the same man reappeared and put a chunk of German bread through the bars of the cell window. The Sergeant was being followed by a guard, so he quickly told Corkett that he had been on heavy bombers before he moved away from the window. The Sergeant was described by the Squadron Leader as standing about 5'09" tall, medium build, dark hair with a dark moustache.

The statement appears to relate to Tipton, but there was no mention of a Flight Lieutenant's uniform as described in Knight's evidence.

Sergeant (later Warrant Officer) Ronald P.L. Mogg, Service Number 744979, gave a statement to the SIB on 25 May 1945. He recalled being at Stalag Luft VI and Tipton being brought to the camp SBO's attention because of his actions at Dulag Luft.

Sergeant Frank Tipton was interviewed by Mogg and the Senior British Officer. No evidence was obtained from him, but Tipton was warned about his future activities in the camp.

Perhaps the most damning piece of evidence was a German intelligence report from Dulag as we shall see later.

A statement was taken from Tipton at Stalag Luft VI and kept secure until the wars end, when it was handed to the SIB. The statement described how he was shot down and hid in a corn field all day until dusk the next evening. He believed his position was just west of Dortmund and he could not skirt around the town, so he took his RAF blouse off and walked straight through the town. Tipton claimed there were fires still burning from the raid and no one took any notice of him.

He did remember seeing an RAF man hanging from a piece of protruding debris. He thought he was an officer as his left arm was visible and there were no sergeant's chevrons on his sleeve. The man was also wearing his Mae West, but his hands were tied behind his back. (This appears to describe a lynching of a downed airman, although it is impossible to identify him or the location. Although the summary murder of downed airmen was not unknown at the time, most were meted out in 1944-45 and not in May 1943.)

Tipton said he walked for the remaining five days via Bochum, Wuppertal and Dusseldorf to a position near Aachen where he was caught by a policeman. The local Burgomaster questioned him through an interpreter, but the only thing he gave them was his name, rank and service number. He was then taken to a Luftwaffe airfield at

Monchengladbach. He was interrogated by a Luftwaffe officer, but still gave nothing away.

Eventually, Tipton was taken to Dulag Luft, but the cell was hot and the heating turned on, it was so hot, he had to lay on the stone floor with his nose to the crack under the door to get air.

Eventually, a German officer came to his cell with a fake Red Cross form which he refused to fill in. The German then filled it all in for him.

Tipton said that by this time, he felt bad and ill. He felt weak and lost all power of resistance, so when they questioned him again, he gave them part of his service record. He was asked if he would like to do a radio broadcast home, but he declined this offer. The Germans then asked him if he would like to send a message home and he agreed. This was just to tell everyone he was alive and alright.

In his next interrogation he was shown a list of 51 Squadron airmen, but it was out of date and he hardly recognised any of the names. He said he played along, telling them he knew about seventy per cent of the ones he did not know, while saying he didn't know the few names he did recognise.

Tipton said the Germans were quite pleased with him, but he was getting deeper and deeper and couldn't pull himself together. He was asked about Pathfinder techniques but didn't give them much satisfaction. He was given a 3 kilometre parole for walks and also allowed to work in the hospital.

Later, Hauptmann Barth (Horst Barth) arranged for him to go to work in Berlin for the propaganda department, but he changed his mind which annoyed Barth. One day, he was taken into Frankfurt in civilian clothes and given a lot of beer to drink. Later in the evening, his escort told him there was a fighter pilot who would not give his squadron or aircraft type. He agreed to speak to the pilot who he named as Squadron Leader Corkett.

Tipton said he went to the cell and gave the pilot his name and home address to cover himself. Tipton said he would take an oath that he never obtained any information from Corkett or encouraged him to give any.

Tipton said he had got away from Dulag Luft on the pretext of needing to get an official POW number. He told Hauptmann Barth that he would return in four to six months by seeing his new camp commandant, although he had no intention of doing this. He concluded his statement to the camp SBO and his Adjutant by saying everything seemed like a horrible nightmare to him and he was sure medical attention would have found him to be mentally unbalanced.

As a follow-up, the Special Investigation Branch took their own statement from Frank Tipton.

His explanation of how he was shot down and the RAF man hanging were very similar to his camp statement, but this time he said he had met a Polish man with some horses. He had given Tipton food and hid him in a barn. The Polish man also provided him with some civilian clothing. He carried on walking and set out for Wuppertal and Dusseldorf, before resting in a park. With no water to drink he was very thirsty and entered a shop, asking a German woman for water. He told her in broken language, that he was an Italian and she gave him some water and bread.

As he crossed the Rhine on a bridge, he was stopped by a sentry. Once again he tried to say he was an Italian and that he had comrades on the other side of the river and once again he was allowed to go on his way. Eventually, he was stopped by a policeman and finally detained. His statement continued in the same vein as his initial camp statement and he moved on to his incarceration in Dulag Luft.

He again detailed the German officer coming to his cell with the Red Cross form and filling in the form, but this time he named the man as Beir.

Tipton recalled Ober Inspektor Barth asking him questions about Pathfinder techniques and what *Musical Paramatta* was (actually target indicator flares dropped using the *Oboe* system on an obscured target).

Barth asked Tipton where he had obtained his civilian clothes and he explained he had taken them from a pile, by a bombed out building in Dortmund. Barth told him he could have been shot for looting and went on to ask him about his service career. Tipton told Barth he had worked at the Farnborough Experimental Station and the German asked if he knew about the Merlin 61 engine and jet aircraft. In reply, Tipton said he knew nothing about the Merlin, but there was a single jet aircraft with no wings there.

Tipton again stated that he thought he was not quite right mentally at that time and he had asked Barth what the chances were of getting a broadcasting job in Berlin. Barth said he would speak to the Camp Commandant about this and placed Tipton on a working party in the hospital grounds.

Captain Tobler, a German Technical Officer, visited Tipton and asked him about Spitfires and the Merlin 61 and 67 engines. He then moved on to jet aircraft, although Tipton felt Tobler didn't believe any of his account.

Further interrogations by Barth continued with walks and visits to the Interrogation Centre, often unescorted. He was asked about *Monica* (the tail warning radar) and *Wanganui.* He then moved on to *Trombone* and *Oboe,* although Tipton did not give any details and did not know anything.

Tipton again mentioned the Typhoon pilot Squadron Leader Corkett and that Barth wanted him to wear an officer's uniform and get the prisoner to talk. He said he met with Corkett but told him not to tell the Germans anything. On a second meeting he gave Corkett some bread and cigarettes.

Tipton said he was also given a Pilot Officer's tunic with a bomb-aimer's brevet. He was told to visit the cell of an American Lieutenant who would not talk to the Germans. The officer, he thought was called Ireland and had flown P-47 Thunderbolts. Tipton said he visited the officer and told him to tell the Germans everything, as it would be to his advantage, but the American thought he was a phoney and asked Tipton to salute.

Tipton then stated that he had told Barth he did not want to go back to England because he was not getting on with his wife and he had met another woman. Tipton said he had no guts or willpower at that time. Barth was telling him to do one thing and Sergeant Knight was telling him something different, he was very confused.

Tipton explained in detail being taken to Frankfurt and visiting cafes and drinking with one of Barth's assistants, a man called Schwartz. On another occasion Barth arranged for him to go to see a movie with a medical orderly.

Eventually, Tipton said he told Barth he wanted to go to a Stalag. Barth tried to stop him, but he went to Stalag Luft VI. Tipton had told Barth his aim was to get a POW number as this would look better for him (to the British authorities), then he would return to Dulag Luft.

A Luftwaffe Intelligence report dated 27 May 1943 reference VE/2909/43 and by Bth (believed to be Ober Inspektor Horst Barth), was perhaps the most damning piece of evidence against Tipton. The report stated that 'Sergeant Brown reports about his squadron' (Brown being Tipton and 51 Squadron at RAF Snaith).

The report described the briefing room in minute detail, before moving on to how the briefing was managed and orchestrated. It also described the Intelligence unit at Snaith, its structure and Pathfinder code words.

The report went into detail about navigators' briefings, bombing leaders' briefings and the signals briefing. It touched upon *Tinsel,* the codename of a means to jam German radios. (This was an audio microphone mounted inside a bomber engine nacelle. This noise was then transmitted on German night fighter radio frequencies.) He also spoke about *Mandrel,* which was a radar jamming device carried by bombers.

This on first appearances was one of the most detailed interrogation reports found at Dulag Luft after the war's conclusion.

A statement was taken from Squadron Leader Harold J.C. Seymour, Service Number 73787. He had been the senior Intelligence Officer at RAF Snaith from April 1943, a time when both Tipton and Sergeant Jack Alcock had been with No. 51 Squadron.

He was shown the Dulag Luft intelligence report and told the SIB staff that this was a good general outline of a pre-operations briefing and the layout of RAF Snaith. He also added that he could not remember the Pathfinder code names *Oboe* and *Trombone*, but the comment about *Wanganui* should have been *One Guinea* which was a code name.

(Despite the intelligence officer's statement, *Wanganui* was actually a Pathfinder Sky marking method like Parramatta, both methods being used to mark obscured targets for bombers.)

Seymour stated that he gave security lectures at Snaith, but he could not remember Sergeant Tipton (or Jack Alcock). Aircrews were told they must always empty their pockets of all property which may assist the enemy. In addition, they should only provide their name, rank and service number if captured. They were not allowed to give their parole to the enemy and if given work, they should make themselves as much of a nuisance as possible and endeavour to escape.

It was clear to the RAF Special Investigation Branch, that Sergeant Frank Tipton had collaborated with the enemy and lived a better life than other prisoners of war. In a report dated 27 June 1945, Squadron Leader Thomas of the Special Investigation Branch stated:

> *'He was repatriated to this country in 1944 on medical grounds and during an interview at this office on 26 June 1945, he did not appear normal, either mentally or physically.*
>
> *'The evidence regarding him does not present his case, at the moment, as a serious one, but before proceedings against him are considered, it is suggested that he should be medically examined and a report obtained respecting his health, medical and mental history.'*

On 24 July 1945, a medical report on Sergeant Tipton was sent to the RAF Special Investigation Branch.

It noted an over indulgence in the use of alcohol by Tipton and unsatisfactory conduct. There was no neuro-psychiatric disability detected by the doctors, the medical officers declared Tipton to be somewhat irresponsible and immature, with a lack of perseverance and a tendency to give up easily in the face of difficulty.

They noted that Tipton was keen to stay in the RAF on aircrew duties and to that end, the board recommended a return to operational flying.

Whether Sergeant Frank Tipton returned to operational flying is unclear from the records in the National Archives, but on 18 September 1945, the case against him assisting and collaborating with the enemy was discontinued.

Air Commodore Walmesley, in the Judge Advocate General's office, stated that he was of the opinion that there was medical evidence from which it was possible to infer that Tipton, at the time of the alleged assisting of the enemy; was suffering some mental derangement and no useful purpose would be served by pursuing this case any further.

Chapter 17

The Courts Martial and the Aftermath

The result of the MI5 and SIB enquiries into the men contained within this book was odd, especially when examined alongside the decision to indict people like William Joyce, John Amery and others. Only three of the men contained within this book were indicted and placed before a court martial, this was despite evidence of collusion by others. The men indicted were Pilot Officer Benson Freeman, Flight Sergeants Raymond Hughes and Jack Alcock.

It is very clear why these men were indicted, but why no action was taken against Squadron Leader George R. Carpenter and Flying Officer Julius Zuromski is not clear, especially as files on the men either do not exist, have been destroyed, or are not available for public scrutiny.

Others like Flying Officer Michael Joyce and Sergeant Frank Tipton were not placed before a court martial due to legal technicalities, but in the case of Joyce, they could have been charged with a more serious offence and one without a legal time limitation.

Flight Sergeant Raymond Hughes

Hughes was charged and indicted with a number of counts, some of them carrying the possibility of the death penalty. These included:

1. Giving the enemy information about RAF bombing methods.
2. Aiding the enemy by asking other prisoners questions for the enemy.
3. Making radio propaganda records for broadcast.
4. Broadcasting propaganda for the enemy from Berlin.
5. Lending money to British Free Corps personnel.

6. Advising the enemy on combating RAF bombing raids.
7. Being employed by the German Foreign Office.
8. Being employed by Berlin Radio etc…
9. Giving evidence on the Peenemunde air raid in August 1943.
10. Conduct prejudicial to the good discipline of the Royal Air Force.

The courts martial started at RAF Uxbridge on 22 August 1945. Hughes was defended by a civilian solicitor Mr T.U. Liddle, but he had served as a Flight Lieutenant during the war.

Opening statements were made by the defence and prosecution before the first witness was called – Squadron Leader William Percy Thomas of the RAF Special Investigation Branch. Mr Liddle immediately challenged the officer about whether Hughes was under arrest when he interviewed him. Thomas said Hughes had not been under arrest at the time and he was giving him the chance to explain himself before he arrested him. Liddle then asked if Thomas knew Hughes had been arrested previously in Brussels and interviewed by Army Intelligence. Thomas said he did not know this.

The newspapers did not go into all the details of the witnesses called, but *The Times* reported on 25 August 1945, that Haferkorn had given evidence and told the court that Hughes had been introduced to him and the defendant had written some radio scripts, but these were not suitable for production.

At the end of the day, legal arguments led to a number of the counts on the indictment being dropped. These included broadcasting on German radio, conduct prejudicial to the good discipline of the RAF, advising the enemy on how to combat RAF bombing raids and giving information about the Peenemunde raid. Later, Hughes was also acquitted of attempting to get fellow prisoners to fill in the fake Red Cross forms at Dulag Luft.

After a couple of days of prosecution evidence, Hughes entered the witness box. He stated that he had told fellow prisoners not to enter their civilian occupations, especially those who had been laboratory assistants or technicians before the war. The reason for this he explained, was that he had heard a rumour the Germans used such prisoners and made them work in their own establishments.

He also stated that he did not know the Red Cross forms were fake. He claimed that the Germans had probably called him Herr Becker, so local people didn't know he was actually English and this was nothing untoward.

Hughes told the court that he did not think he received any privileges at Dulag Luft and the civilian clothes he wore were not a privilege.

He then admitted meeting up with Squadron Leader Carpenter in Berlin and that they wore civilian clothing. When it was pointed out that they went to a hotel, Hughes said it was, '*More like a home for waifs and strays'*.

He was asked if he suspected Squadron Leader Carpenter of collaborating with the enemy, but he replied that he actually suspected him of working for the Allies.

It is unclear from the files whether George R. Carpenter actually attended the court and gave live evidence at the trial. The various newspapers (cuttings of which are in the archives files) certainly did not mention his participation. This prompts the question, where was he and why was he not called as a witness if that was the case? There is also no mention of Flying Officer Zuromski in the files.

On 26 August 1945, the trial came to an end and Hughes was found guilty of four charges which could end in his execution. They were:

1. Aiding the enemy by asking other prisoners questions for the enemy.
2. Making radio propaganda records for broadcast.
3. Giving money to British Free Corps personnel.
4. Being employed by the German Foreign Office and earning 350 RM a month & Radio Metropole earning 600 RM a month.

The findings and the sentence needed to be promulgated with the possibility of the death penalty a distinct possibility.

The media were quick to report that Hughes' fiancé had stated that she would stand by him and their marriage would go ahead as soon as possible, regardless of the sentence.

Eventually, the sentence was promulgated and Raymond Hughes was dishonourably discharged from the Royal Air Force and sentenced to five years imprisonment. An appeal for clemency followed and the sentence was reduced to just two years imprisonment.

Upon release he ended up in the West Country and died in Cheltenham in April 1999, aged seventy-five.

Why had a man so clearly involved, who assisted in the interrogation of British POWs, made radio propaganda reports, given money to and associated with the British Free Corps, not to forget being paid a wage by the Nazi regime, escaped with such a light sentence?

It appears, upon face value, that the main witnesses who could have given much more damning evidence were not called to give evidence, or they were not even interrogated fully in the first place. Carpenter and Zuromski do not appear from the records and the newspapers to have given evidence and as previously stated, the likes of William Joyce and Baillie-Stewart do not appear to have been questioned about the actions of these RAF men.

If we bear in mind the accusations by some, or the throwaway comments by others, that Carpenter was thought to be a British agent, could this have been true and he was hidden from the ordeals of court? It is unlikely he was an agent for the reasons previously outlined in this book, but there remains an air of suspicion.

Flight Sergeant Jack Alcock

Alcock was also tried at RAF Uxbridge in August 1945. The same officer who prosecuted Hughes, Squadron Leader Goff, led the prosecution.

Nine charges were laid against Jack Alcock. Four concerned him giving information and aiding the enemy during various meetings and there were four more alternative counts for each of these, being that his conduct was prejudicial to the good order and discipline of the RAF. This included gathering evidence via fake Red Cross forms and giving information about the Halifax bomber and the Monica radar warning system. The ninth count concerned him giving his parole not to escape.

Squadron Leader Goff pointed out in his opening address that the four main charges of giving information and aiding the enemy each carried the death penalty, while the four alternatives each had a maximum sentence of just two years imprisonment.

Goff gave a summary of the evidence before he called his first witness – Inspector George Nicholls of Carter Street Police Station in London. Nicholls had been a Flight Lieutenant and a member of the RAF SIB during and just after the war's conclusion before being de-mobbed and returning to the Metropolitan Police.

Nicholls described his arrest of Jack Alcock with Flight Sergeant Inglis at a hotel in Euston. He had asked Alcock what had happened to him after he had been shot down and Alcock had given an account with no outstanding incidents of note. Nicholls then recalled telling Alcock that he had information that he had collaborated with the Germans. This, he said, caused the defendant to break down and cry. Alcock was formally cautioned and he made a full statement giving a different explanation to his initial account.

Nicholls evidence was corroborated by Flight Sergeant Inglis, who was the next witness.

The defence counsel (Flight Lieutenant Cooke) immediately objected to the arresting officers' evidence, stating that Alcock should have been cautioned as soon as the SIB men approached him and this was unfair. It was also unfair, that he was basically told to, '*say everything, as the authorities would find out sooner or later*.' This shock basically meant that Jack Alcock was so distressed he was not fit to make a written statement at that time and did not give it freely. As such, Flight Lieutenant Cooke made a submission that it should be ruled as inadmissible and struck from the record.

After some consideration, the Judge Advocate ruled that Nicholls had not made any inducement to Alcock and the defendant was not complaining about the two SIB officers' conduct. He added there was no doubt that Sergeant Alcock had been cautioned and knew he was not bound to make a statement.

Whether he was fit to make a statement was another issue, but being upset did not mean he was unfit to make a statement. As a result, the court ruled that the statement made under caution by Alcock was admissible.

Sergeant Hicks, from the RAF SIB, gave evidence of charging Alcock and his reply when charged. Alcock allegedly replied to caution after charging, '*As I said in my statement when I came back to England, I made a fool of myself. I was tricked into it by the German Intelligence Staff. When I found out I had made a mistake I demanded to be sent to a prison camp.*'

Hicks also added that later, Alcock stated he was very worried about the matter and was sorry that it had happened; he added that as Squadron Leader Carpenter was doing the same as himself, he thought it was alright to give his parole. (Again, where was Carpenter? Any decent counsel or solicitor would surely have asked for his presence and evidence.)

The next day, the court called Leutnant Gustav Bauer Schlichtegroll to give evidence. He gave lengthy, detailed evidence of Alcock's actions at Dulag Luft. He was then cross-examined by Flight Lieutenant Cooke.

Straight away, Cooke challenged the German officer's memory of Jack Alcock, claiming that he could not have such a good memory having interrogated nearly 1,000 prisoners of war over two years at the camp. He also challenged the premise that the Red Cross forms were fake and created to obtain intelligence from prisoners. This line of questioning went on for some time, as Cooke tried to prove that the German witness had a clouded memory and the forms could in the eyes of Alcock have been genuine.

This line of questioning seemed to continue with Cooke asking if Schlichtegroll had offered an inducement of better quarters and food to Alcock. The German said he could not remember and when challenged about Alcock apparently saying he knew nothing about parole, the German said he could not remember it.

Cooke continued his cross-examination and asked Schlichtegroll if he remembered telling Alcock that Squadron Leader Carpenter had given his own parole, but again the German said he could not remember one way or other.

Cooke than asked if Schlichtegroll could remember any one thing of military significance provided by Jack Alcock, but the German could not.

Moving on to the fake Red Cross forms, Schlichtegroll said he believed Alcock was clumsy and was not very good at obtaining information for the forms. He also confirmed that Alcock never used any pressure to solicit answers from the other POWs.

The lengthy cross-examination continued and Schlichtegroll was asked how often he wore his Luftwaffe uniform – as clearly there was an issue of whether Alcock thought he was a Red Cross official and not a German. Once again, the recollections of the Luftwaffe man were clouded and confused.

The next witness was Squadron Leader Oak-Rhind. He gave evidence about the radar warning system Monica and the fact it was still secret in 1943, the time Alcock was alleged to have given details of its operation to the Luftwaffe.

He was followed into the witness box by Squadron Leader Seymour, the Intelligence Officer at RAF Snaith. He was questioned about intelligence and security briefings for aircrew at the airfield from which Alcock had flown in 1943. This included whether they were briefed about information security and how it was delivered to aircrew through lectures, pamphlets and posters in the crew rooms.

It appears that most of the prosecution and defence case concerned the arrest and Bauer Schlichtegroll's evidence about Jack Alcock. It appears, like Hughes, that Carpenter did not give evidence and there was no attempt (at least no recorded attempt) to call the Squadron Leader or any others to give evidence.

The end result was Alcock was found guilty, reduced in rank and discharged from the service in ignominy. He was sentenced to four years penal servitude, but this was reduced to two years imprisonment with hard labour upon appeal.

Pilot Officer Benson Freeman

After Hughes and Alcock had been tried, it was the turn of Benson Freeman to face justice. The *Daily Mirror*'s headline on 29 August 1945, proclaimed, '*RAF Officer to face death penalty charge of having joined the Waffen SS.*'

There were four charges he faced were:

1. Serving in the Waffen SS.
2. Conduct prejudicial to the good order of the Royal Air Force.
3. Voluntarily aiding the enemy by writing propaganda scripts.
4. Improperly residing as a prisoner of war in Berlin under the name of Royston and earning 200 Reichsmarks per week in employment.

The defence counsel for Freeman, Mr Derek Curtis-Bennett KC, asked the President of the court martial to consider restarting the trial and replacing the Court Officials and prosecution counsel. His reasons were that he believed it unfair, as they had already tried Hughes and Alcock in the same court room in previous weeks. It appears the case was adjourned but continued a few days later.

The trial eventually started in early September 1945, and after opening statements, the first witness to be called was an army Major who could only be identified as 'X'. He gave evidence about the formation and role of the SS and in particular the Waffen SS.

The defence counsel for Freeman, Mr Derek Curtis-Bennett KC, claimed that Major 'X' was an expert in hearsay only and had no direct knowledge of contact with the Waffen SS. He asked the court martial to consider ignoring this man's evidence.

The Judge Advocate General overruled defence counsel and allowed his evidence as expert opinion regarding the Waffen SS.

Benson Freeman's written statement after he was detained, was read to the court and this was followed by Wing Commander Harry 'Wings' Day entering the witness box. As the Senior British Officer at Dulag Luft, he said he had heard Freeman express British Fascist views and sympathies, but he also agreed that Freeman was always thinking of the British Empire.

The next witness was Flight Lieutenant (now Squadron Leader) Vincent 'Paddy' Byrne. He told the court he had been at Dulag Luft for eighteen months and said Freeman had always been anxious to talk politics. However, he did state that Freeman had prevented the Germans from discovering an escape tunnel. As far as Byrne was concerned, Freeman was pro-British, but he was a supporter of Mosley and fascism.

Further witnesses followed, including Intelligence Officer J.M. Davies who had interviewed Freeman. He said Freeman had told him that he had never done anything to the detriment of his country, but he never made a secret of his membership of the British Union of Fascists. He added that Freeman had admitted to him that he wrote to William Joyce and met him on two occasions. However, Freeman also said he disagreed with William Joyce's radio talks and as a result of this William Joyce hated him.

Davies told the court that Freeman had called the Waffen SS a sincere organisation and pro-English. He then offered to go with a nominated British official to contact the now underground members of the Waffen SS.

Freeman had also stated that enquiries should be made of Squadron Leader John Keast and Flight Lieutenant Vincent Byrne (who had just given evidence), stating that they were collaborators, as was the deceased Squadron Leader Roger Bushell.

After a break in proceedings, Mr Curtis-Bennett KC told the court that Freeman objected to the *Daily Mirror* headline on 29 August, which had proclaimed, *'RAF Officer to face death penalty charge of having joined the Waffen SS'*. He claimed such a headline before the case had even started was a contempt of court. He also claimed the *Mirror* newspapers image of Freeman in a service cap was a fake, as Freeman had never had his photograph taken while wearing a service cap.

After considering the issue, the court ruled that there was no contempt and Freeman was able to take a civil route for defamation etc himself if he chose to do so.

Like Hughes and Alcock, no other witnesses were listed as giving evidence in the media or the archives files. Whether this was the case, or they were subject to court orders banning publication of their names is unclear, but again the likes of Carpenter and others were not called as witnesses. The fact Major 'X' was mentioned, seems to eliminate the possibility of court orders prohibiting the identification of witnesses in this case.

The *Daily Herald* on 10 September 1945, reported that as the defence and prosecution counsel made their closing speeches, Freeman sat in the dock 'doodling' on a piece of paper.

The case against Benson Freeman was complete and he was found guilty on all four counts of the indictment. Counts one and three (joining the Waffen SS and aiding the enemy by writing propaganda scripts), carried the possibility of the death penalty which had yet to be promulgated.

Eventually, he was not sentenced to death, but given ten years imprisonment. He is said to have told his counsel Mr Curtis-Bennett KC, his sentence was rotten and '*The Germans would have had the honesty to shoot me.*'

Imprisoned in HMP Wormwood Scrubs, he continued his rhetoric, and in April 1947 he stated he was a political prisoner, '*Imprisoned in the State's criminal establishments, while my wife has been left to her own resources.*'

Benson Freeman dropped off the proverbial radar and nothing more was heard from him. He is believed to have been released in 1955, having served the full ten years, but he disappeared with his wife Muriel. Some think they went to live in Ireland and he may have died there, but no one knows for certain.

After he was found guilty and awaiting promulgation of his sentence, the RAF Special Investigation Branch team decided to make an approach to Freeman. They were still investigating a number of other collaborator suspects, including Flying Officer Julian Zuromski.

In file KV2/631 enclosure 215a at the UK National Archives, is a report dated 4 October 1945, marked TOP SECRET from Flying Officer F.R. Wickham (SIB) and countersigned by his Group Captain (name unclear); it was sent to the Officer Commanding SIB. It states:

> *'In furthering the enquiry in respect of Zuromski, alias Kowalsky, it was decided to interview P/O B.R.M. Freeman, who had not been questioned about this Polish officer, as to his knowledge and his activities in the Reichssportfeld.*
>
> *'As Freeman is at present in custody at Uxbridge waiting promulgation of sentence, I saw his solicitor, Mr Claude Hornby, in order that he could make arrangements to be present at the interview, if Freeman so desired. On 3 October 1945, Mr Hornby communicated with me the fact that Freeman could be seen anytime and did not require the presence of his solicitor.*

> *'The same day, I saw Freeman and showed him a number of photographs, including one of Zuromski, but he could not definitely pick him out, saying, "If he's a short man I think that will be him." Freeman would give no valuable information concerning this man, although he admits knowing him. He refers to him as the "Poor bloody Pole" and by his conversation, mostly an attempt to justify his (own) Russian views. I should imagine he is sympathetically inclined towards him and will not assist us.*
>
> *'Freeman then asked me a direct question as to what is being done about Carpenter, Major Stevens and Captain Best, and the army man Winter (William Colledge), who he alleges should be dealt with. I told him I knew nothing of these men but would welcome any information supporting what he had just told me. He then gave me verbal information about these men, which is listed below. He refused to make any written statement and the information obtained is sorted out from his general conversation and his lapses into an anti-Russia-Jewish thesis. Prior to my departure, Freeman asked if we had an anti-Russian Intelligence Section, as with his knowledge of Germany, Britain and the people who could give us information, he felt he could perform useful work in such a department. I told him he was in rather an awkward position to make such requests and although I could not answer the questions one way or another, I felt sure the authorities were well aware of his capabilities.*
>
> *'Squadron Leader Carpenter: He knows him as Carter and Boyd-Carpenter and from what he was told by Oberst Leutnant Boninghaus, that he was writing scripts for broadcasting. Boninghaus also told him that Carpenter gave away a lot of information to him when he was interrogating him after capture.'*

Freeman then provided a list of Germans who could talk about Carpenter, these included a civilian employee at the Reichssportfeld called Teulischen, Dr Hetzler, Dr Hohmann and two German female typists who he could only describe. The report continued:

> *'Freeman told me that Carpenter, with Hughes, was issued with tickets to purchase overcoats and they used to go to*

> *various stores and obtain overcoats by means of a trick. They were arrested by the German CID, locked up and tried before a German Court. Some "string-pulling" went on and eventually Carpenter was released and sent to a prisoner of war camp. This instance, although hearsay, may be the true reason for Carpenter's dismissal from Berlin and not the reason given by him, that he refused to work for the Germans.'*

Freeman then made allegations against Winter (William Colledge) and Major Best and Captain Stephens, who he claimed were the *'biggest rogues of the lot'*. He claimed the two men had not been traced and realised they would have something to answer for if the British authorities asked them the question, '*Why didn't the Germans shoot you?*'

William Colledge has featured in this book, but Best and Stephens were the two British agents captured in the Venlo incident in Holland, in November 1939. The two men were working for MI6 and attempting to work on an anti-Hitler plot with what they believed were German patriots. Unfortunately, it was a Gestapo SD operation, and they were both captured. They were interrogated in Berlin before being sent to Sachsenhausen concentration camp, Dachau and then Buchenwald. In April 1945, they were moved with a group of other high-profile prisoners but liberated by the US Army in Austria. The two men were eventually located and repatriated, no further details of an enquiry etc. are known.

It was clear with this report that the RAF SIB investigators were continuing their enquiries into Flying Officer Zuromski and possibly Squadron Leader Carpenter.

Squadron Leader George R. Carpenter

As we have seen, there were numerous allegations made against Squadron Leader George Carpenter, who was named by Freeman, Hughes and Alcock as a fellow collaborator. In addition, Harry 'Wings' Day had heard about him while in captivity and arranged for his barrack arrest and a court of inquiry, once Carpenter arrived at Stalag Luft III in 1944.

Carpenter does not appear to have been called to give live evidence at any of the three previous courts martial and there is no open file available at the UK National Archives regarding the investigation of this man – in fact there is no listing of a closed file. So where is this information and how and why did the Judge Advocate General and SIB reach a decision on 21 November 1945, to take no further action against Carpenter?

The case against Carpenter is probably the most confusing of all the airmen listed within this book. Initially, Sergeant Jackson claimed that while held in St Gilles Prison in Brussels, he was surprised that Carpenter seemed to know all about him and his crew.

When he arrived at Dulag Luft, Carpenter was allowed civilian clothes and housed in the special prisoners' stone house block, along with Hughes, Alcock, Trickes, Zuromski, Wilson and other important prisoners, such as the American Ambassador's son. Why was he held there if he was not collaborating? Was it because, as Carpenter himself stated, the Germans thought he was related to Winston Churchill?

Why was he taken to Berlin along with Zuromski? He claims he did not collaborate with radio propaganda and Professor Haferkorn confirmed he would not co-operate; in fact, he thought Carpenter was a British agent.

Why was he known to the Germans under the alias of Herr Carter? And why were his hotel bills of 200 Reichsmarks per month paid by Peter Adami?

Why does Roy Courlander claim Carpenter was housed in the Schlieffen-Ufer in Berlin for three days with other high-profile prisoners, yet George Carpenter made no mention of this location in his statement and debriefing post-war?

Why did Carpenter say he was held up in Berlin and not moved to a POW camp, because his papers had been burned in an air raid, while Francis Paul Maton claimed it was due to him being passed from the Luftwaffe to the Wehrmacht, which caused an administrative tangle?

Benson Freeman claimed Carpenter wrote propaganda scripts and this, he says, was confirmed to him by Leutnant Boninghaus. Boninghaus also allegedly claimed that Carpenter had given information when interrogated after his capture in 1943. Where is this evidence, or a statement if correct?

Francis Paul Maton claimed that Carpenter had been a friend of Goering pre-war and worked under Norman Baillie-Stewart, broadcasting on the South African radio propaganda channel. Was this ever checked by the British?

Hughes and Carpenter were very closely linked in Berlin and there is the question of whether they were engaged in acts of sabotage. If he was a British intelligence agent, it is possible Carpenter would engage in sabotage, but would he be happy to utilise Hughes, a man he clearly thought '*had his head in the clouds*' and was irresponsible? I think it is unlikely as this would have created a risk to Carpenter himself.

There is one other question in relation to Hughes and Carpenter – why did the Squadron Leader advise the air gunner to avoid a meeting with the camp SBO Group Captain Wilson? Was it because he believed Wilson was a collaborator or because Hughes and Carpenter were?

John Wilson says Carpenter told him over dinner that he had no contact with British Intelligence, but hoped he would make contact soon. William Colledge also says he had the impression Carpenter was working for British intelligence.

We also have Hughes speaking with the members of the SS Kurt Eggers propaganda unit and the British Free Corps and passing information on to Carpenter. What are we to make of this?

Finally, if he was working for British Intelligence, would Carpenter have put this at risk by becoming a fraudster and shoplifter? I very much doubt it. To keep your cover, you need to prove your value to the enemy or become an invisible man. Drawing attention to yourself is not productive and could be life threatening.

So, what can we make of Squadron Leader George Robert Carpenter and why was he not indicted like the others?

George Carpenter left the RAF after repatriation to the United Kingdom and returned to South Africa in 1947. Little is known about his later life and he is believed to have died in Durban, in February 1978, aged seventy-two years. His older brother Alfred had died in the country in 1963.

Many have speculated about this man since the war, some thinking he may have had far right views in South Africa, but the main far right sections did not embrace the British element of South African society and therefore Carpenter's involvement is unlikely.

Flying Officer Julian Zuromski

As previously stated, very little is known about this man after 1945, apart from his time with the Pakistan Air Force. He died in May 1999 and was buried in Surbiton, Surrey.

Group Captain Douglas Wilson

It is clear from the evidence that Wilson was probably not the most tactful and considerate of senior officers, at least that was the belief of Flight

Lieutenant Read in 1943. The fact Wilson was talked into a sortie which ended in his imprisonment must have angered the Australian officer, but does that explain what was later alleged?

Wilson, according to Raymond Hughes, had given Leutnant Boninghaus details of Pathfinder bombing techniques and it was claimed he was a Master of Ceremonies Pathfinder leader. We know this was incorrect, but had Boninghaus made this up for the benefit of Sergeant Hughes or had Wilson misled his interrogator? It is more likely a fabrication, as Boninghaus and other Luftwaffe interrogators, as we have seen, had an expansive set of files and records and could easily identify a squadron and therefore a Pathfinder pilot.

We know from both Hughes and Alcock, that Wilson was in the same special stone house quarters as them, as well as with Carpenter, Trickes and Zuromski. The question is why, was it just because of his senior rank?

Within a few weeks, Wilson went to Berlin, where we know he made one and probably two appearances on a propaganda radio programme, called Anzac Tattoo, in early September 1943. Was Wilson tricked into this or did he do it thinking it would do not harm? At least his family would know he was alive and well in captivity.

It is possible he had been playing along with the Germans, telling them about Pathfinder techniques etc, then going to Berlin. Whatever happened, he was quickly moved on to a POW camp, before ending up at Sagan where Carpenter warned Hughes to avoid a meeting with him.

After the war, the RAF Special Investigation Branch, having heard accounts from the likes of Hughes and Alock, requested Wilson complete a full debriefing. However, he gave scant detail of his time in German custody, with no mention of Dalag Luft or Sagan. He could easily have given information about the other alleged collaborators, but he chose not to do so.

Group Captain Wilson retired from the Royal Australian Air Force in March 1946 and died after an illness in 1950. Did the British and Australian authorities know more about him? Did they cease to take the matter further because it was a low-level issue and Wilson was ill and possibly dying? We may never know.

Wing Commander Harry 'Wings' Day

Harry 'Wings' Day was suspected from 1940 onwards of being a collaborator. MI9 must have been very confused in the early years of the war, with information being sent home via the coded message system by

Day, while prisoners at other camps were making allegations against him and his permanent staff at Dulag Luft.

Harry Day supported Peter Casenove at Stalag Luft III, preventing a possible catastrophic miscarriage of justice, while holding Robert G. Carpenter to account when he arrived in 1944.

In his early years at Dulag Luft, Day, a man from a somewhat more chivalrous pre-war air force school of thought, who hung on to the honour of the First World War, appears to have been content to communicate, meet with and even accept alcohol from First World War German pilot and Camp Commandant Theo Rumpel. The fact Rumpel was using this tactic to gain intelligence from the RAF prisoners, does not appear to have been considered by Day, as he believed his officers and men acted honourably.

Day clearly wanted to keep his fellow prisoners fit, healthy and out of danger, while not antagonising the enemy. Like many people, he knew they were better off in a Luftwaffe camp than in the hands of the dreaded Gestapo.

Wing Commander Day gave a number of his men positions at Dulag Luft, which included managing the clothing stores and Red Cross parcels, but a number of these men would go on to become collaborators.

Unlike many other officers and airmen mentioned in this book, Day gave evidence at the court martial of Pilot Officer Benson Freeman. Day also took part in a number of escapes, including the Great Escape, when he was lucky to survive, although he was sent to a series of concentration camps.

After being liberated and returning to the UK in 1945, Day was promoted to Group Captain and retired from the RAF in 1950. As a famous and influential airman, he was the subject of a 'This is your life' biography TV programme in 1961. He died in Malta in 1977, aged seventy-eight.

There is no doubt, Wings Day played a careful game, but his patriotism cannot be challenged.

Chapter 18

What Happened to the other Britons Named in this Book?

Throughout this book there have been two types of collaboration. The first was perpetrated by British prisoners of war, while the second group were those who sought sanctuary in Germany prior to the war and then assisted with its anti-British radio propaganda.

Prisoners of war like Freeman, Hughes and Alcock were collaborators for a number of differing reasons, but those who had started the English Station within the German Foreign Office were apparently deemed to be more treacherous by the British authorities. This can be evidenced by examining the MI5 files in the National Archives on the likes of William Joyce, John Amery, Norman Baillie-Stewart and others. While there is a fair amount of cross-referencing to the other men within this group, there is very little comment on the POW collaborators.

In many ways, there appears to have been an apparent fixation by the authorities to deal with Joyce and Amery, men who were very well-known to a vengeful post-war British public.

The British people had sat and listened on a nightly basis to Joyce and his *Germany Calling* radio broadcasts, as well as 'Lancer' Baillie-Stewart. It is clear from the files that the investigators knew all about those involved, including the POW collaborators, but there appears to have been little effort to expand upon the activities of the prisoner collaborators.

There was no apparent questioning of Joyce, Amery, Baillie-Stewert, or the other main pre-war traitors concerning the POW collaborators, many of whom were in Berlin and linked to the propaganda system. If there had been further questioning, maybe further evidence and prosecutions, even capital cases, would have followed against some of the POWs.

Consequently, William Joyce and John Amery would hang, while others received what now appears to have been reduced prison sentences or no punishment at all.

Pearl Vardon

Pearl Vardon evacuated Berlin in late 1944 and ended up in Wilhelmshaven. She was detained by the British Army when she enquired about obtaining a set of new identity papers. She was interrogated and later tried at the Old Bailey in February 1946, where she pleaded guilty to assisting the enemy and was imprisoned for nine months. She later married a German national and lived in Germany, dying in Bavaria in 2011, aged ninety-six years of age.

Norman Baillie-Stewart (alias Lancer)

Baillie-Stewart was arrested in 1945, at Altausee, wearing traditional German dress, including lederhosen. He was returned to England and after interrogation, a decision was taken by the Attorney-General not to charge him, as it was believed they could not successfully prosecute him for High Treason. This was because he held German citizenship. Instead, he was charged with committing an act likely to assist the enemy and sentenced to five years imprisonment.

After release from prison, he moved to Dublin, Ireland (like Benson) and married, having two children. He died of a heart attack in 1966.

Edwin S. Bowlby

Captured at the end of the war and interrogated, Bowlby was not prosecuted as he was an Irish citizen.

Private William Colledge (alias Winter)

Colledge was captured and put on trial for treason, he was sentenced to penal servitude for life.

William H. Griffiths

Griffiths was put on trial and sentenced to seven years penal servitude.

Gerald Percy Sandys Hewitt (alias Smith)

Having already been detained in later 1944, Hewitt was sentenced to twelve years penal servitude at the Old Bailey for offences under the Defence Regulations in March 1945. He pleaded guilty to the charges, but was released after just five years, telling the media he was prosecuted for demonstrating the Russian danger. He is believed to have died in London in 1969.

Reginald Humphries (alias Father Donovan or Jeffries)

He was sentenced to five years penal servitude at the Old Bailey for offences under the Defence Regulations.

Lieutenant (RNVR) Roy Walter Purdy (alias Pointer)

Purdy was arrested at the war's conclusion and after interrogation, charged and put on trial at the Old Bailey. As a Nazi propaganda broadcaster and later a stool-pigeon at Colditz Castle, he was charged with High Treason. He was sentenced to death, but reprieved and his sentence commuted to a life term. This it was claimed, was because he was a follower rather than a leader in treason. He was released from prison in December 1954 and married, living in Essex. It is claimed he worked as a supervisor at the Ford factory for many years before dying in 1982.

Vivian Stranders

Stranders was a long-time collaborator and broadcast on the German radio service. He was detained after the war, but not charged as he had taken German citizenship in 1933. He returned to Germany and lived out his days in his adopted nation, dying in 1959.

Arthur Chappel (alias Lang)

Chappel was tried and given fifteen years imprisonment, although this was later reduced to ten years. No other details post-release are known.

Charles Patrick Gilbert (alias Kenneth James)

Gilbert was another Channel Islander who betrayed his homeland. He was given nine months imprisonment for assisting the enemy.

Lance Corporal Ronald Spillman

Spillman, after assisting the German propaganda system, was tried and sentenced to seven years penal servitude.

Corporal Francis Paul Maton

Although heavily engaged with other elements of collaboration, Maton is covered in this section as he worked with the Waffen SS propaganda unit SS-Kurt Eggers. He was detained in 1944 in Belgium, he was interrogated and made a full statement. He was court martialled in 1945 and given ten years imprisonment for voluntarily assisting the enemy.

Lance Corporal Roy Courlander

Like Maton, he assisted the Nazis by joining the SS-Kurt Eggers propaganda unit. He was detained in 1944 with Maton and interrogated by British Intelligence. He was linked to the British Free Corps and tried as a New Zealander by his own military authorities. He was sentenced to fifteen years imprisonment for voluntarily aiding the enemy.

Transported back to Auckland, New Zealand, he served his imprisonment, but in 1950 he appealed against his sentence and this was reduced to nine years.

After release, he worked for a time before moving to Lethbridge Park, near Sydney, Australia. He died in 1979, aged sixty-four years of age.

The other British Free Corps members named in this book

Private Arthur James Cryderman (alias Tilbury)

Despite being acknowledged as a member of the British Free Corps, the Judge Advocate General's Office decided to take no action against Cryderman.

Sergeant M. Robert Reginald Heighes (alias Reid)

Sentenced to two years imprisonment after court martial.

Private Edwin Barnard Martin (alias Bartlett)

A Canadian Army court martial sentenced him to twenty-five years imprisonment for being an informer and a member of the British Free Corps. He died in Ontario in 1987, aged sixty-eight.

Sergeant George Frank MacLardy (alias Wood)

A member of the Free Corps, he also worked at the Reichssportfeld radio stations and with the SS-Kurt Eggers propaganda unit. Sentenced at court martial to life imprisonment, it was later reduced to fifteen years upon appeal. He served just seven years, before being released in 1953, when he emigrated to Germany.

He married a local woman, had two children and lived and worked in Mainz, where he died in 1981, aged sixty-six years of age.

Sergeant John Eric Wilson (alias Montgomery)

Wilson was an integral part of the British Free Corps and court martialled in 1946. He was sentenced to ten years imprisonment.

Seaman Alfred Vivian Minchin (alias Milton)

Minchin was tried at the Old Bailey for offences in breach of the Defence Regulations, he was sentenced to seven years penal servitude.

Thomas Haller Cooper (alias Bottcher) – civilian

Haller Cooper was tried at the Old Bailey in January 1946, for High Treason and sentenced to death by hanging. He appealed, but this failed and his execution date was set for 28 February 1946. A week before his execution, his sentence was commuted to one of life imprisonment.

He was released in 1953 and is believed to have emigrated to Japan where he taught English. Although not confirmed, he is believed to have later returned to the UK and died in 1987.

Eric Reginald Pleasants (alias Dorran) – civilian

Pleasants escaped from the Waffen SS and was captured by the advancing Russians in 1946 after hiding in Berlin. He was sentenced to eight years imprisonment by the Russians. He was released in 1954 and returned to the United Kingdom, where the authorities chose not to pursue his case, as they thought he had been punished enough.

He died in Norwich in 1988, aged eighty-four years of age.

Private Thomas Blake Kipling (alias Meredith)

No action was taken against Kipling by the Judge Advocate General.

Fusilier John Leigh (alias?)

No action was taken against Leigh by the Judge Advocate General.

Fusilier Frank Stringer (alias Willy Le Page)

Stringer served with the SS Jagdveband Mitte – an SS special operations unit. He was sentenced to serve fifteen years imprisonment by a court martial.

Chapter 19

What Happened to the Germans?

The second Commandant of Dulag Luft – Major Theodor Rumpel – was not charged with anything by the Allies post-war. When he left Oberursel, he was promoted and commanded a Luftwaffe headquarters at Gorlitz.

Other officers at Dulag Luft, including his replacement Oberst Leutnant Erich Killinger, were less fortunate.

Once the prisoners of war had been repatriated and debriefed, it was clear there was not only a regime of collaboration, but various allegations of mistreatment by the Luftwaffe of the detainees.

Evidence was gathered from a number of RAF airmen by the Special Investigations Branch over a period of months. This led to a list of six witnesses, who provided affidavits as evidence against a number of officers at Dulag Luft.

Most of the evidence concerned the overheating of interrogation block cells, poor, or a lack of medical treatment, summary beatings, prolonged solitary confinement and threats of being handed to the Gestapo.

Five officers were indicted and placed before a Military Tribunal at Wuppertal in Western Germany, from 26 November to 3 December 1945. The men indicted were:

- Oberst Leutnant Erich Killinger (Camp Commandant)
- Major Heinz Junge (Adjutant)
- Major Otto Boehringer
- Leutnant Gustav Bauer-Schlichtegroll
- Leutnant Heinrich Eberhardt

The charge read as follows:

Committing a war crime –
At or near Oberursel, Germany, between 1 November 1941 and 15 April 1945, when members of staff of the Luftwaffe

> *Interrogation Centre known as Dulag Luft, in violation of the laws and usages of wars were together concerned as parties to the ill-treatment of British prisoners of war.*
>
> *Contrary to Reg. 4 of the Regulations for the Trial of War Criminals.*

Thirteen specific incidents were cited, where prisoners were locked in overheated solitary confinement cells. Killinger took full responsibility during the trial, although he pointed out that he never gave an order to overheat the cells. He explained that the overheating was undertaken while he was away, but he gave an order that it was not to be repeated when he returned, although he admitted that no member of staff was reprimanded or punished for the overheating.

At first, the prosecution sought to allege that prisoners were kept in solitary confinement with threats of beatings and being shot by the Gestapo, the intention being that any prisoner who did not answer questions would be considered a saboteur.

The defence were keen to highlight that on 6 September 1944, a Gestapo report at Frankfurt-am-Main, alleged that Killinger and his deputy Heinz Junge were undermining the morale of the Wehrmacht, by being too lenient with the prisoners of war. A Luftwaffe induced court martial took place on 7 December 1944, but the German Air Ministry acquitted Killinger and his fellow officers on all counts. Even the Nazi regime had to abide with its own judicial processes and the SD/SS were unable to place them on trial again!

The defence also called Air Commodore Ronald Ivelaw-Chapman. He was the highest ranking RAF officer to pass through the camp after he was shot down in May 1944. He was wounded and later captured by the Gestapo who mistreated him. Eventually, he was passed on to Dulag Luft, but he stated that Killinger and the other defendants were very concerned about his physical condition, taking him to hospital for lengthy medical treatment.

In the end, the prosecution withdrew the allegations of beatings and the Gestapo threats, leaving the main charge of overheating of prisoners' cells.

At the end of proceedings, three of the five German officers at Wuppertal were found guilty of the charges.

Erich Killinger was sentenced to five years imprisonment, as was Heinz Junge. Heinrich Eberhardt was sentenced to three years imprisonment, while Boehringer and Bauer-Schlichtegroll were acquitted and released.

Erich Killinger was released from Werl prison after serving three years of his five year sentence.

Evidence now exists, that Heinrich Himmler wanted to take control of Dulag Luft. He tried unsuccessfully on a yearly basis between 1941 and 1944 to take command of the Interrogation Centre, but the Luftwaffe's successful intelligence system prevailed. In many respects, if Himmler's SS and Gestapo had assumed authority of Dulag Luft, the allegations of war crimes would have been very much worse and the amount of intelligence obtained regarding the RAF much lower.

According to a United States War Department Military Intelligence report in November 1945, the interrogation of prisoners at Dulag Luft was correct as far as 'physical violence' was concerned. It did note however, that occasionally, a prisoner may have been struck by an angry interrogator, but this was never beyond a slap across the face. The interrogators used intelligence and subtlety to obtain information. As well-educated men, using an excellent intelligence set-up, backed up with detailed records, they employed intelligent debate and discussion to achieve their aims. This on occasion led to the recruitment of collaborators.

Other Dulag Luft officers named in this book such as Horst Barth, Tobler and Offerman, appear to have disappeared into the mists of time and a more peaceful post-war Germany.

One officer who appears in a number of reports contained within this was Theodor Rumpel's adjutant Hauptmann Fiergutt, often mispronounced and written as Viergood. He was known to the prisoners as *Fiery-guts* due to his propensity to become nastier the more alcohol he consumed. What happened to him post-war is unknown at this time.

The German officials at the Foreign Office Propaganda system in Berlin were not dealt with so severely.

Professor Reinhard Haferkorn, after interrogation by the British authorities, was released. He worked as an interpreter in Oldenburg and then as a teacher.

In 1953, he went to work as Legation Counsellor for the Diplomatic Training in foreign languages at the Foreign Office in Bonn. From 1961 he was an Honorary Professor at Heidelburg University. He died in 1983.

Dr Erich Hetzler and Dr Fritz Hesse were detained and interrogated at the end of the war by the British authorities. However, they were more interested in the main British traitors such as John Amery and William Joyce, plus there was an issue of the peace overtures which Hesse had assisted with in 1945. Certainly, the politics and main non-POW traitors, appear to have taken precedence over the RAF collaborators. Because of this, both Hesse and Hetzler were not indicted and lived private lives in Germany until their deaths.

Hauptsturmführer Hans Werner Roepke of the Waffen SS, who took command of the British Free Corps in September 1943 until November 1944, fought with the SS Viking Division and spoke good English. He left after disagreements and an ineffectual Free Corps and was assigned to the SS *Jagdverbande* operations unit. He is believed to have survived the war, living until his death in Germany.

SS-Standartenführer Gunter d'Alquen was the head of the SS-Kurt Eggers propaganda section. In 1955 he was sentenced to a high level fine by a Nuremburg denazification trial and lost his service pension, as well as all civil rights for a period of three years. He died in 1998.

The other SS-Kurt Eggers man mentioned in this book was SS-Sturmbannführer Anton Kriegbaum. As we have seen, he died in a car crash at the end of the war in May 1945, aged thirty-three years of age.

Postscript

It is now nearly eighty years since the end of the Second World War. As we have seen there were over a dozen men who were alleged at one time or another to be Nazi collaborators while held in prison camps and in particular Dulag Luft.

The reasons for their collaboration range from having far right views, to seeking better conditions for themselves, or having an alleged mental illness. In one case, it appears he may have been a German agent who took the opportunity to abscond and then fabricate his account, leading to the award of a Military Medal and a King's commission.

Three RAF men were imprisoned, but in the opinion of many, several others should have also served time. In fact, there is an argument one or two should, or could, have paid the ultimate sacrifice with the assistance of Albert Pierrepoint at Wandsworth prison.

It is clear the British authorities could have pursued more vigorous investigations, but they apparently failed to gather evidence from the main traitors which may have assisted in prosecuting the RAF collaborators. In addition, there is the issue of Squadron Leader George R. Carpenter and Flying Officer Julius Zuromski.

There is no doubt that 99.99 per cent of British and Commonwealth airmen who found themselves in the hands of the enemy during the Second World War, were patriotic and loyal, but a few certainly 'let the side down'.

Sources Used in this Book

UK National Archives: The files listed below contain public sector information licensed under the Open Government Licence v3.0:

KV2/631 (P/O Benson Freeman)
KV2/262 (F/Sgt Raymond Hughes)
KV2/259-261 (Walter Roy Purdy)
KV2/826 (Reinhard H. Haferkorn)
KV2/428 (Eduard R.A. Dietze)
KV2/915 (Dr Fritz Hesse)
KV2/1288 (Vivian Stranders)
KV2/2861 (Dr Erich Hetzler)
KV2/245-250 (William Joyce)
KV2/185-6 (Norman Baillie-Stewart)
KV2/258 (Reginald Humphries)
KV2/442 (Arthur Chapple)
WO416/3/335 (Sgt Jack Alcock)
WO416/406/515 (F/O Julian Zuromski)
WO/208/3331/769 (Zuromski SIB file)
AIR79/1589/176409 (Sqn Ldr George R. Carpenter)
WO416/58/18 (Sqn Ldr George R. Carpenter)
WO416/111/24 (Sqn Ldr Eric D. Elliott)
AIR40/2305 (Sqn Ldr Eric D. Elliott)
WO416/331/483 (Sgt J.G. Slowey)
WO344/101/2 (Sqn Ldr E.D. Elliott)
AIR40/2296 (Sgt F. Tipton).
AIR40/2295 (Sgt E. Whillock).
AIR2/13438 (Sgt/F/O M. Joyce).
KV2/426 (Gerald Percy Hewitt)
AIR40/2466 (Dulag Luft Camp history)

AIR40/2267 (Dulag Luft collaborators)
WO208/4642 & WO311/1327 (Ill treatment of POWs at Dulag Luft)
WO235/41A, B & C (Trial of Oberst Killinger & officers from Dulag Luft)
WO224/67
WO208/3330-3338 Liberation reports from prisoners of war.
AIR27/293 (ORB No. 24 Squadron).

Australian National Archives

A705, 166/43/232 (Group Captain Douglas Wilson)

Bibliography

Wings Day, by Sydney Smith, Pan Books, 1970.

The Interrogator, Hanns Joachim Scharff – master interrogator of the Luftwaffe, by Raymond F. Toliver; Schiffer Military History books, 1997.

Letting the side down, by Sean Murphy, Sutton Publishing, 2007.

War Crime Trials Vol XI Dulag Luft, (Killinger & others) HMSO, 1947.

One of Churchill's own, by John Greenwood, Pen & Sword books, 2016.

RAF Fighter Command losses of WW2, Norman Franks, Midland Publishing Ltd., 1997.

The Great Escaper, by Simon Pearson, published by Hodder in 2013.

From Dogfight to Diplomacy, by Donal MacDonall, Pen & Sword books, 2005.

Footprints on the sands of time, by Oliver Clutton-Brock, published by Grub Street books, 2003.

The Lonely Path to Freedom, by Derek Thrower, Robert Hale Publishing, 1980.

After the Battle Magazine (No. 106), Dulag Luft, published 1999.

Night Fighter Ace, by Tony Spooner, published by Sutton Publishing, 1997/2003.

Flying into the Flames of Hell: Flying with Bomber Command in World War II, by Martin Bowman, Pen & Sword Aviation 2006.

Prisoner of War 'my secret journal', by Sqn Ldr B. Arct, published by Webb & Bowler, 1988.

Others

wallyswar.wordpress.com

Kenfentonswar.com

Index